TEACHER

MARK EDMUNDSON

RANDOM HOUSE / NEW YORK

TEACHER

THE ONE WHO MADE

THE DIFFERENCE

All rights reserved under International and Pan-American
Copyright Conventions. Published in the United States by
Random House, Inc., New York, and simultaneously in Canada
by Random House of Canada Limited, Toronto.

RANDOM HOUSE and colophon are registered
trademarks of Random House, Inc.

Library of Congress Cataloging-in-Publication Data
Edmundson, Mark.
Teacher / Mark Edmundson.—1st ed.
p.   cm.
ISBN 0-375-50407-9 (alk. paper)
1. Lears, Frank.   2. High school teachers—United States—
Biography.   I. Title.
373.11'0092—dc21   LA2317.M49 E36 2002   2001048981

Random House website address: www.atrandom.com

Printed in the United States of America on acid-free paper

2   4   6   8   9   7   5   3

First Edition

Book design by Jo Anne Metsch

TO MY MOTHER AND BROTHER
AND TO THE MEMORY OF MY FATHER

Contents

TEACHER

A PHILOSOPHER COMES
TO TOWN

I see Franklin Lears now, through the long prism of time past, shambling into the Medford High School building on the day before classes begin. He climbs the sadly worn steps, enters the building, and begins walking down what's come to be called the New Corridor, a passage that connects the two wings of the high school that are still intact. A fire has destroyed the school's central classrooms and offices, so this hallway, the one down which Lears is walking, cuts its way through a nest of burned timber and blackened, crumbled brick. He walks with back bent, dressed in a tropical suit, two sizes baggy, lugging a briefcase loaded down with a small library of books that, though he will probably have no occasion to read them in the next few hours, provide a sort of companionship for him. Except for his copious buzzing thoughts, except for the books, Lears is now, as he almost always is, alone.

But he is also, as I see him, in a state of high expectancy. He has stored his energies all through the summer and he is ready to begin. Students arrive tomorrow. Lears has drawn up the plan for what will be the gemstone of his course offerings for the 1969–1970 school year: his class in philosophy, designed for a select group of seniors. Together with these bright if perhaps slightly underprepared youngsters (Medford—pronounced Me'ford by the majority of its inhabitants—Massachusetts is a working-class city, not renowned for its cultural life; it's not Concord, home of Emerson, home of Thoreau; it's surely not Cambridge), he will ponder the eternal questions: beauty, truth, free will, fate, reality, and appearance.

The class will start out reading *The Story of Philosophy*, by Will Durant, then go on to Plato's *Dialogues*, some Aristotle, Spinoza (a particular favorite of Lears'), maybe a little bit of Kant, then maybe on to Bertrand Russell's effort to clear everything up with an injection of clean, scientific logic. Lears has just graduated from Harvard; all of his intellectual aspirations are intact.

Strolling through the building the day before classes started, Lears saw desks and blackboards, large windows that slid up and open with a cheery metallic gurgle, supply closets stocked full of papers and books and all the other paraphernalia of education. He smelled the dusty smell of chalk, taken fresh from its carton and broken apart so that it won't make the screaming sound that shoots students up from their desks in a genuine agitation that morphs quickly into Looney Tunes excess.

Encountering these things, Lears no doubt believed that he was in a real school, a place where people quested by their lights after the truth, its elaborations and its antitheses.

But Medford High, at least until Frank Lears came and did what he did, was not a school at all. It was a place where you learned to do—or were punished for failing in—a variety of exercises. The content of these exercises mattered not at all. What mattered was form—repetition and form. You filled in the blanks, conjugated, declined, diagrammed, defined, outlined, summarized, recapitulated, positioned, graphed. The subject was of no consequence: English, geometry, biology, history—all were the same. The process treated your mind as though it were a body capable of learning a number of simple choreographies, then repeating, repeating.

Our bodies themselves were well monitored. When the bell rang we were expected to rise and file into the corridor, stay in line, speak quietly if at all, and enter the next class, where we were ordered to sit down, sit quietly, feet beneath the desk; we were, all day long, presided over by teachers, a significant fraction of whom were going—at greater or lesser velocities, ending sometimes with a bang, sometimes with subdued, heart-emptying sobs—out of their minds. The place was a shabby Gothic cathedral consecrated to Order, and maybe it was not without its mercies. If you'd done what you should have at Medford High, the transition into a factory, into an office, into the marines would be something you'd barely notice; it would be painless, sheer grease.

But Medford High School students did not, at all times, do what they were supposed to. We knew little of the world, little, in general, of ourselves. But we did sense that we'd been tossed into a decrepit penal colony, and we fought back with whatever resources came to hand. When the teachers and administrators, the turnkeys and wardens, were vulnerable, we went at them with a fury. Those close to going off the deep end got a hearty push from us. It was a battleground that Franklin Lears was walking onto—us against them, and us against ourselves, against, that is, our own interest in learning something, on the off chance that Medford High had anything of value to teach.

It obviously took Lears a while to figure out what sort of rabbit hole he had fallen into and in what kind of Wonderland he'd be spending time. But eventually he pieced things together. And during the course of that year he became a great teacher, though of a singular kind. Free in himself, he tried to make us, his students, free as well. In my case, at least, he had some success, though the freedom wasn't without costs.

He brought us the spirit of Socrates—the homely Athenian, who never accepted anything on faith, questioned all matters under the sun, took no crap, ever, and knew how to laugh. He turned us into Socratic questioners, strangers in our own lives, who stopped gulping down general opinion (*doxa*, Socrates called it) or, nearly as bad, rejected all received ideas without pondering them. He taught us what thinking was, which is to say that—in the beginning, at least, when his ways were just taking hold—he made us miserable.

Lears was also a spirit of the sixties, though not of the predictable sort. The sixties turned up in some places, appeared to some people, decked in beads, bare-chested, with a swallowtail coat and an American flag top-hat, clanging finger cymbals and chanting the body electric, dispensing the sacrament of marijuana in tiny, bone-white J's, "Truckin'" or "Sugar Magnolia" pouring in from nowhere and everywhere. To us, in the Medford High philosophy class 1969–1970, the sixties came in the guise of a diminutive guy who wore what looked to be his grandpa's suits and shoes so formidable and square that they would certainly outlive us all.

When I encountered Franklin Lears, I was a high school thug. I was a football player, a brawler, who detested all things intellectual. The first time I saw this meager guy with his thick, swinging briefcase, I wanted to spit on the floor. He was absurd, a joke. If you had told me that in eight months I would have decided to live my life in a way that was akin to his, I would have told you that you were crazy; I would have spit, probably, at you. But that is exactly what took place: I went on to become an incessant reader, a writer, a university professor.

The French thinker Simone Weil said that evil, when you encounter it in life, is often infinitely wearisome—dull, obsessive, plodding, repetitious. But good is much different. When you meet up with goodness in day-to-day experience, it's so novel and fresh that it's often difficult to recognize for what it is. Frank Lears was a remarkably good man, though it took me some time to see it. Lears' goodness was of a peculiar sort. He was always doing something for himself as well as for you. In the process of working his best deeds, he didn't mind affronting what you might call his spiritual enemies. Lears' goodness, like that of almost all great teachers, always had an edge to it.

Great teacher, good man: Frank Lears would surely blanch at this kind of grandiloquent talk. I see his eyebrows rising now, and his usually mournful face going into a benevolent, mildly exasperated grin.

I thought a great deal about Franklin Lears during the year or so after I left Medford High School. I was a student at the University of Massachusetts then, and deep into philosophy myself, along with rock music and high times and stopping the war. But slowly Lears' direct influence—as well as the influence of rock and other such things—began to wear away. He was replaced in my imagination by other, ostensibly more accomplished, figures. It was only after thirty years, when I was well into the middle of life, that I began thinking about Lears again.

I had become a teacher myself by then, not in a high school (though from 1977 to 1980 I did a stint teaching at a hippie boarding school that self-destructed in a screaming psychedelic blast; Woodstock School, it was called), but at a university, Thomas Jefferson's University of Virginia. I'd been to graduate school, to Yale no less, and had gone on to a dozen years of successful teaching. At least my course evaluations, my enrollments, and student comments indicated that I was a success. But gradually I became sure that things were going wrong. My students went on at fluent length in their evaluations, saying how enjoyable my courses had been, what an amiable and entertaining guide I was to the material at hand—Blake or Shakespeare or Whitman. But their papers, written with more technical skill than anything I could have mustered at nineteen or twenty, were empty; they had a void, anonymous feeling about them. No one seemed to be home. Their class comments were often two- or three-word interjections, unpromising seeds that I, always obliging, tried to raise into expansive blossoms before their classmates' eyes. Virtually no one, from what I could tell, was changed by taking my classes.

But I had been changed by Frank Lears, no doubt about it. I had been in classes with some of the most renowned humanists of the day, and surely they had all had their impact. But I had only one teacher who really effected a major transformation, and that was Lears, a man of twenty-two or twenty-three, who had little prior experience as a teacher and who left teaching after a year, no doubt feeling less than ecstatic about what he found there.

So I needed to do all I could to think back over three decades and make contact with a long-forgotten island of my experience. I had been brutally, miserably unhappy in high school. But isn't almost everyone? And those who are not—high school's kings and queens and duchesses and dukes—often find all the rest of life a sad, outstretching desert, for rarely does their ascendancy last beyond graduation day. So in one sense it was no joy to go back. But I persisted, because here, if anywhere, might be the key to my quandary. How could you make of the reading of books—not holy books, not books dictated by the Lord God of Hosts or discovered, as the Mormon prophet Joseph Smith claimed his book to be, with the aid of a sojourning angel, but secular books—something that might turn a life around? And, more broadly, how do you approach students, how do you talk to them in a classroom and outside, so that your teaching actually has an impact?

The process of remembering is no easy one, of course. And that is often true not because there are too few memories (try focusing every day for a half-hour or so on some phase of your life that strikes you as dead and departed, and you'll see) but because there are too many, and because they are not always of the anticipated sort. For even if I only thought of education, of what I'd learned that last year in high school, I had to admit that among my more prominent influences were a gang of football players and coaches. And I had to think of my father, now long dead, for a father is every young man's primary teacher, like it or not. Franklin Lears and Mace Johnson, my football coach, both in their singular ways wrested me away from my father and all he meant to me. It was a freeing and a remarkably sad process, for I left my father, who greatly needed me, almost alone in the world. Over time, in other words, as I thought more and more about it, the story became more complicated, the morals less certain.

In writing a book like this, it is necessary to face one of the least appealing figures to have traversed the earth's crust—that is, one's high school self. Professors enter their trade for a number of reasons, but almost always they do so at least in part because they are drawn to authority; they seek standing, respect—even if they are at the same time suspicious of these things. To return to one's high school self is to leave any pretense to perfection far behind, or at least it is for me. In graduate school, I had professors so august that it seemed that there probably never was a time when they had not read *The Faerie Queene*—perhaps they entered life with that, and most of the other classics, already under their belts. The image of myself that appears in these pages is nothing close to so magisterial. But it seemed worth dispensing with professorial pride and going back to depict an earlier, more refractory self. In doing so, I hope I might make some contact with others whose condition now is akin to what mine was before I met Frank Lears.

I kept on with my remembering and writing, uncomfortable as they sometimes were, and, to cut to the final frame, the process worked, or at least I believe it did. Remembering Frank Lears and the life in Medford that Lears made me so much want to leave behind, I came to understand what I wanted to do now, in the present, as a teacher. And though when I tell my students on the first day what we'll be up to and how they'll never say that they "enjoyed" this course, some of them head promptly for the exits, I learned how to do what I hoped for. Lears helped me change my ways and be something like the sort of teacher he was. He put me on the right course in life—not once, but twice—though neither time was it a simple and painless shift. Grateful as I am, I want to try to get some of Lears' story into words to see if others might be able to make use of it as well.

Most students will not encounter a Frank Lears or anyone like him. They will never be exposed to a transforming teacher. Is it possible to be moved by such a person secondhand, to be inspired by someone who did his work thirty years ago? I hope so, and that hope is another reason I have written this book.

But I wonder if when a teacher like Lears comes along, he is generally recognizable for what he is. Surely it took *us* a long time to see it—and that was in 1969, a time that was ripe for novelty, when one expected constant renewal, or at least ceaseless change.

In America today we treasure a long-standing myth of the great teacher: call it the Mr. Chips–Robin Williams myth, if you like. The teacher of this myth is infinitely kind, infinitely benevolent; he loves his students first and last, almost more than he loves himself. He memorizes their names on the first day. He tells amusing, self-deflating stories that make everyone feel at ease. He is a source of benevolent, socially sanctioned advice: be kind, be good, be true. If he challenges anything, it is orthodoxies that are already dead in the world at large and have reared their heads in one last corner. Most of all he adores—and is adored by—his students.

It would be churlish to demean this sort of teacher, for his kind does turn up in life sometimes, as well as in books and movies. And his kindness is often a balm to students, particularly the bullied and the misunderstood. There are few of us, especially in adolescence, who can't benefit from a dose of pure benevolence.

But one of my motives for writing this book is to remind readers that great teachers—and perhaps the great teachers who matter the most—do not always come in this all-benevolent mode. The two greatest teachers we know in the West, Socrates and Jesus, were not without kindness, to be sure, but both had a sharp edge. Jesus asked people to do the impossible. He wanted them to give up all of their possessions and follow him, to change their lives utterly around. Socrates asked one badgering question after another about why his contemporaries behaved as they did. In the end, society could not tolerate either of these men, and did away with them.

Our mythologies make us forget that the great teacher is not always just a bringer of sweetness and light. Socrates often did not like what he saw when he looked into the lives of his students. In fact, he was demoralized by it. He fought against their worst side, kindly, with their souls' interest at heart, all the while admitting that he too was fallible. Lears, like Socrates, can remind us that a great teacher is not necessarily a friend, much less a "facilitator." He can be a spiritual antagonist and goad as much as an ally. As Emerson suggests, the best thing that another can provide us with is often not so much tuition as it is strong provocation. Of such provocation Frank Lears gave us plenty.

So I have written this book to make Lears and his kind a little more visible when they do manifest themselves in the world. And I have written it, too, to give teachers who see their job as a combination of care *and* provocation a measure of encouragement at a time when many forces are trying to make them members of the service economy—people who provide *skills,* marketable knowledge, negotiable habits, but not inspiration, not the wherewithal to change a life around.

The act of remembering a period thirty years back in time is not, ostensibly, easy. But senior year in high school is an especially vivid moment for nearly everyone. I can say with some confidence that I have a gift—which is also something like a curse—for recollection. Which doesn't mean that I've done anything like a perfect job carving this tribute and confession. For a variety of reasons, we often can't help seeing former teachers in a semi-mythical light; and high school itself, like every rite of passage, can be a rich source of mythmaking. Surely not everything here stands as others would recall it. (The material in quotation marks, for instance, is true to the substance of the exchanges as I remember them, but of course it can't be right sentence for sentence, word for word.) With that in mind, I've changed names, and here and there an identifying characteristic, to protect the privacy of the characters. On a few occasions, I have merged two or more figures into one. My main objective has been to tell the story as I saw and felt it, as it all has occurred to me, even when the events recounted (not to mention the author recounting them) don't come off being as admirable or as elevated as one might wish. This is a memoir; as such it is my truth, the way it was for me.

As to Lears, he is now—at least in the provinces of my imagination—near the end of his day. His first look at Medford High School completed, he has driven off through the fierce Boston traffic—"a savage servility slides by on grease," Robert Lowell says of it. Lears is home in Cambridge now, where his books stand like troops, pacifist forces, row on row. Tie off, suit jacket thrown over a chair, he is sitting down to a consideration of life's ways and means with Emerson or Thoreau or some other heir of Socrates. Reading, reading long into the night, he is enlisting allies for the enterprise that will begin tomorrow at Medford High. Given what we, his students, have in store for him, Lears will need all the help he can get. This is the last day before the Fall.

Chapter One

FIRST DAY

What have we here?

None of us had ever encountered anyone like Franklin Lears, at least not up close. On the first day of class, we saw a short, slight man, with olive skin—we thought he might be Mexican—wearing a skinny tie and a moth-eaten legacy suit with a large paper clip fastened to the left lapel. On his feet were Ivy League gunboat shoes, lace-ups designed in homage to the *Monitor* and the *Merrimack*. He had hunched shoulders, a droopy black mustache, and Valentino-type eyes: deep brown, sensuous, and penitential. Even when he strove for some dynamism, as he did on the first day, explaining his plans for the course, he still had a melancholy Castilian presence, the air of an instinctively comprehending reader of *Don Quixote*. Like the Don, Lears could somehow look dolorous and hopeful at the same time.

He walked into the room where we were assembled, fifteen or so of us, in our evenly serried desks, and stared out at us, his philosphers-to-be, the baleful look tinged with optimism, like a rainbow playing along the edge of a quiet pool. He slouched in his suit, two sizes too big, Chaplin on a dismal day. Then he gazed long and hard at his feet, as though expecting some sympathy from the gunboats. He began to talk.

Lears told us this was a philosophy course and that philosophy meant the love of wisdom, and that that was interesting and worth knowing but it was no end in itself, for it led you on to other questions: What was wisdom? How did you get it? Was there anyone who had it? He asked us if we knew anyone who might be wise. Of course no one answered, though he left open a silent vacuum, inviting and a touch unnerving, for us to push our newborn thoughts into. (It was the first of many, many such vacuums.) And how would you love it—wisdom, that is—once you'd found it? The way you loved your family, your friends? And what if wisdom meant giving up or turning away from other things you loved?

He spoke very softly, with an impeccable, refined intonation that nonetheless carried the words to the back precincts of the classroom, where I sat gazing at this strange creature who had crossed our path, as self-assured, it seemed, and as vulnerable as a cat. I was studying this man—almost all of us were—for the critical signs. We wanted to know what we had on our hands. What manner of man was this? What, given the ongoing war of us-against-them, would we be able to get away with?

So far the signs looked good, fabulous in fact. The fellow was small, soft-spoken, polite, and, by the hypermacho standards of Me'ford, on the effeminate side. We might have struck gold. And yet it was too early to be sure. Miss Minty, who taught math, was tiny, with a pixie haircut, and nervous, sparrowlike movements. She danced in front of us wearing her white lab coat, covering the board with equations and coating everything in sight with snowy chalk dust. She too had looked to be an easy target. But by the end of day one, it was clear that she ran the show. She could screech, ridicule, dole out punishments. And she also seemed to come fit-ted with a Medford High teacher's primary asset. "I have," she often said, "eyes in the back of my head."

Lears stepped away and put on the board a quotation from Nietzsche. The script was neater than anything that we would see from him again, yet still—in terms of the Palmer penmanship method we'd all been raised on in grammar school, waiting at the end of each month with collective breath held for our rating from Mr. Palmer, or one of his minions, a gold seal or star, a blue seal, or the school-disgracing black star—Lears' writing was deplorable. It looked like a great variety of insects had been set loose to scramble on the blackboard and then froze simultaneously in mid-wriggle.

Tom Capallano, the quarterback on the football team, our one bona fide star and a pure high school alpha male, turned in the direction of me and Rick Cirone, split end and cornerback, and said, "See, I told you Nitschke was smart." Capallano, usually known as Cap, was talking about the ferocious linebacker Ray Nitschke of the Green Bay Packers, and he was—I'm pretty sure—making a joke. Still, we had barely heard of Nietzsche, if we'd heard of him at all, and certainly no one in the class had read a word of his up until this moment. As for myself, I had never read all the way through a book that was written for adults and that was not concerned with football.

So what was I doing in a philosophy class? What was I, someone who cared exclusively about shooting pool and hanging out with my friends in the parking lot of Brigham's ice cream shop and, above all else, playing football, doing listening to someone discourse about the love of wisdom? I owed it to my guidance counselor, Mrs. Olmstead, who was trying, by her lights, to save me.

*   *   *

NOT LONG ago, she and I had had a talk about my future. Mrs. Olmstead was a short woman with tightly coiled blond hair. Everything with her was just so. She had large breasts that looked like a shelf for storage of some kind and a slightly elfish face, with narrow eyes, tight, pursed lips, and cheeks that seemed like they'd been applied with an ice cream scoop and then heavily rouged. Her perfume conjured up the tones of the Mantovani string section, sentimental, lush, and all-conquering.

The office where we met had no windows and fluorescent lights so strong that when you first walked in, you felt like a small-scale blast might have recently gone off. They made a constant nosy hum. On her shelf were few books but many dolls, peasant dolls from all over the world.

We talked about my prospects, which were not bright. I ranked 270th or so in a class of about seven hundred. I was well into the top half, she said, smiling, but alas I hadn't quite made it into the higher third.

But it seems I wanted to go to college? Strange enough! I had, she noted, high Board scores, but that might only be a disadvantage. Because, you see, there were new surveys out about college performance, and what the surveys showed was that students with high Boards and low grades sometimes did very, very well in college. But they often did very badly, too. And there was one other factor. It seemed that these students were more likely than any of the others to get themselves in trouble with the administrators, to start political demonstrations and smoke pot and engage in free-form mischief of all sorts. The kids with their feet up on the provosts' desks, puffing the big cigars, Groucho-style, after a successful takeover of the building? They were likely members of the high-Board-score, scrape-by-grades crew.

As to the high Board scores, I had a confession that I could have made but managed to hold back. It was that before taking my seat for a full day's testing in the dismal high school cafeteria, I'd heard—we'd all heard—that dragging a nickel (I think it had to be a buffalo nickel) across the answer sheet would put the test-correction machines in an obliging mood and would result in a perfect score. But mightn't that information have been wrong? (Medford scuttlebutt often was.) Mightn't the rubbed nickel send the test-combine awry and give you a flat zero? I equivocated. I dragged the nickel, with the stoical Indian staring out disapprovingly at me, across about half the answer sheet, then stopped. So whether it was the buffalo and the brave who had racked up the respectable scores or whether it was me was something of an open question.

Mrs. Olmstead and I talked about Massachusetts Bay Community College and Salem State College for Teachers—these being the schools to which my credentials opened the doors. They were, I knew—everyone knew—high schools with ashtrays, where I'd have the chance to take all the courses I'd loathed at Medford High one more time, with teachers perhaps a shade less loony and a shade less despondent. It would be a phase in the eternal recurrence of the same thing, where I could continue to live at home and suffer interminably prolonged adolescence.

At least Mrs. Olmstead hadn't come on strong with a pitch for Miss Fannie's School of Cooking—associated, I believed, with Fannie Farmer chocolates—as the place to finish off what Medford High had begun. She'd done that to my friend Chuck Fiorello, whose mother and father had just died and who seemed to have even fewer prospects in the world than I did. But Fiorello wasn't cowed. Fiorello affirmed his willingness to work in a gas station forever rather than apply to Miss Fannie's. And Fiorello could wax eloquent on the view that working in a gas station—and he'd worked in plenty—was earthly hell. His position was that all the jails in the Commonwealth should be emptied and the prisoners assigned to combination gas dispensaries and auto repair shops—strong punishment; potent deterrent, too.

But beneath the bemusement, or my attempt at it, I was furious. Mass Bay! Salem State! That wasn't the sort of thing I had in mind for myself at all. No, somehow I aspired to something better, though I couldn't have said exactly what. I'd done nothing to distinguish myself, nothing to earn a half-decent future; still, I felt some right to one.

Mrs. Olmstead and I discussed my working for the city of Medford; perhaps I'd start by collecting trash (another loop in the precincts of hell), then graduate in time to a desk job.

"Does your father know anyone?" Mrs. Olmstead asked. This was then a Massachusetts mantra, and I suspect it still is. Do you know somebody? Does he know anybody? Posed in certain circumstances, in a certain tone of voice, this meant, Does somebody owe you or your family favors? Are you connected? Because it was simply assumed around Boston, by working-class types, that *everything* was done on the basis of connections. It was a residue from the old rebellion, when the poor Irish (from whom I was descended) had laid siege to the city of Boston and its environs, kicked the WASPs out—or at least propelled them upstairs, into the law firms and medical schools and universities—and then taken control of the joint. My grandmother, Irish, would put her fingers to her ears if anything irreverent was said about the beloved James Michael Curley, who, local lore had it, once learned of his victory in a Boston mayoral election from a prison cell.

Was I connected? When I was growing up in Malden—an equally rowdy city, where I lived until I was thirteen—my father had, on at least one occasion, taken me and all his traffic tickets in tow and gone down to the police station, where he'd laid a few dollars on the desk sergeant and walked unceremoniously out. (Once, said sergeant had turned up at our house. Why, I can't tell you.) Could that sort of connection count?

Year to year, a small trickle of free Patriots tickets, free tickets to the Bruins and the Ice Capades and other extravaganzas, made its way through our apartment. My father did some favors and—I assumed—got some done for him. At election time, his car, usually an ancient, badly rusting Cadillac, bore a sign endorsing the mayor of a neighboring town, who won all the time. (When my father pulled one of these baroque campaign barges onto the campus of Bennington College, where I was to become the classmate of Yasmin Aga Khan, daughter of Rita Hayworth and the Ali Khan, and others nearly of her ilk, and parked the thing on the lawn in front of my ultramodernist dorm, so it looked like some ancient beast that had surfaced from deep in the waves after foraging on the decay of Atlantis, someone inquired if it was a piece of conceptual art.) But my father was anything but what many of the local dads qualified as—a switch point for favors, cash, tickets, spare parts, stolen goods, knockoff appliances, and the like. Some houses I knew had nearly turned into railroad yards because of all the gray commerce streaming in and out of them. Our stuff came from stores; we owned nothing that "fell off the back of a truck."

Torby Macdonald, Jack Kennedy's roommate at Harvard and a former Malden High football star, had lived close to us in Malden, on the other side of an invisible fence, behind which the property values were impressively swollen. He greeted us in the street, calling me by my father's name and my father by some name that perhaps belonged to a long-lost cousin. He wasn't going to be a likely savior, either.

Nope, I told Mrs. Olmstead. Probably I didn't know anybody. I wasn't in line for that most prized of post–Medford High positions, a laborer's job on a construction site, starting at the piously intoned union wage of ten bucks an hour—one word it came as, tenbucksanhour. I was destined to begin at the bottom, on the off chance that I could get a start at all.

I looked down from the bookshelves and entered into prolonged study of my shoes, some snappy black Fusco numbers, with lacings on the side—all dressed, I was, for a quick game of dice in the back alley, in case anyone wanted to take the time to teach me to play and relieve me of my three-dollar allowance.

Mrs. Olmstead, always ready to show off her ed-school erudition—and actually, by her lights, to do the humane thing, too—looked up from a beaming study of my record and said in her syrupy voice, the Mantovani perfume providing atmosphere for her vision of the rest of my life, "Why do you think you don't really achieve in school?" She meant that I obviously had some ability but that unlike John Cosgrove and Bobby Seaman, intelligent boys who tested where I did and who were suffering through high school because they believed that good things existed on the far side, I had simply decided to drown at Medford High, to never do my homework, to rarely pay attention, to do a kind of zombie walk through all my classes. I was drowning willingly, too, it seemed—not even kicking or waving for the sake of appearances.

I gave a standard Medford answer: "I dunno."

Undaunted, she asked again.

I changed gears. "I'm lazy, I guess." But was I really lazy? Football, odd as it may sound, demands intense mental energy, and I put every waking thought into the game—how I might improve, how I could stand out, dominate, win. As to reading and writing, the things that I was supposedly good at, they seemed to me an unremitting bore. The English teachers at Medford High saddled us with books like *Ivanhoe* and *The Good Earth* and *Silas Marner*—dull, virtuous books that had no more bearing on the Medford life I saw around me than the platitudes the priest at my church, St. Raphael's, dispensed from his podium. I thought all books were this way—that in effect they'd been coauthored by the Medford High faculty. I wanted no part of them.

Lazy. This was the answer Mrs. Olmstead had hoped for. I could hear the inaudible bell ring. For it turned out that The Psychologists were now of a collective mind that there was no such thing as simple laziness. Being an underachiever, a term beginning to come into circulation then, was the result of depression or anxiety or anger or something like that. I looked at this possibility like a trout regarding a gorgeous lure that had been set on the pond just for him, all red and blue and spinning gold. If I bit, I had a lifelong excuse. As the brats say in *West Side Story*: "My sister wears a mustache, my brother wears a dress! Goodness gracious that's why I'm a mess." But I didn't bite.

"Nope, I'm just lazy, that's all there is to it."

"There's nothing bothering you?"

"Nope." (Everything was.)

Mrs. Olmstead smiled, and sent her cheeks up in perfect symmetry. She gave me a sweetly exasperated okay nod, which meant that it was time for me to exit. My future, such as it was, was in my own inept hands.

As I was heading for the door, Mrs. Olmstead suddenly remembered something she'd meant to say, something that was obviously quite important to her. She began talking about a new teacher who was coming to the school, "someone we're very proud to have." He was scheduled to teach philosophy. Was I perhaps interested? I didn't know what philosophy was. But somehow I associated it with airy speculation, empty nothing. It seemed an agreeable enough way to waste time.

Last year, I had declined the chance to be in the Advanced Placement history class, even after Mrs. Olmstead had told me that some students would kill for the privilege. You had to read books over the summer.

To get out of the office, I conceded, provisionally, on the philosophy question. I'd check my credits myself. If there were enough, I figured that I could ditch the philosophy and get a study period. Football exhausted me. Study hall was a fine place to sleep.

SO THERE I was—it had turned out that I did need the credits—in a well-lit top-floor room, pondering the Nietzsche quotation and feeling dumb as a rock, a sentiment with which I, at seventeen, had no little prior experience. But what really had my attention was the strange fellow up front and the possibilities he might offer for the major Medford High School indoor sport—teacher torment.

Lears pointed in the direction of the quote—read it if you can—and asked us to write a few pages interpreting it, as "a limbering-up exercise." As I recall, but my memory is uncertain here, the Nietzsche passage was this one: "Genuine philosophers, being *of necessity* people of tomorrow and the day after tomorrow, have always found themselves, and *had* to find themselves, in contradiction to their today: their enemy was ever the ideal of today."

A limbering-up exercise! A few mental stretches and twists, the cerebral equivalent, maybe, of the Alabama Quick-Cals, robotoid calisthenics, jerky, stiff choreography with which we began every football practice. The fact that we might not be able to understand a word of the quotation seems not to have occurred to Lears. This was an excellent sign. It indicated that he was utterly out of touch.

Lears seemed to be set on overlooking the standard day-one protocols of the only sort of teacher who could glean respect at Medford High, the disciplinarian. This was the time to take roll call, as they did in the army, in the factory, and in jail; to assign seating; to look out into the class; and to discern, with the aid of a submaster's report or two, who the troublemakers were likely to be, then to get them separated. One needed to decide on the fateful question: troublemakers up front, where you could keep an eye on them, or in back, where their carryings-on might not suck in the whole class?

It was the day to gesture toward the clock on the wall, which was painted the yellow of prolonged depression, a yellow that no sunlight—and the classroom was benevolently, brightly lit—could lift to a pleasing shade, and toward the sign that sometimes appeared under it (Lears, perhaps, had taken his down), which said TIME WILL PASS; WILL YOU?

Clock-watching at Medford High was a complex activity. The clocks worked in mysterious ways. Rather than proceeding forward silently and regularly, as clockwork is supposed to do, these clocks were prone to stand still, like gate guardians who had fallen into a deep doze and left the aspirants outside, waiting in the cold. Then finally, when it seemed time to call for repairs or scream out against the injustices of the universe, the minute hand leapt forward, three or four or five minutes in a shot. The irregularity of these movements made our clock-watching a more absorbing, more anxiety-edged pastime than it was most anywhere else in the world.

It was time, too, this first day, to lay down the law and to sing a song in a dead key about quizzes and tests and lateness and pink slips and blue ones. It was time to get emphatic about bathroom visits, hall passes, sitting tight in your seat, raising hands as a prefix to all utterances. It was the day to inform the students that rewards would pass only to those who could do their homework, do their duty, mind their own small business.

Franklin Lears did none of this. He let the fifteen of us sit where we wanted (which meant boys all together in the back, girls tending to the front). And then, as though assuming we might be gathered for some shared intellectual endeavor, he asked us hard questions about someone not involved in football or local politics or Stag's poolroom (poo'room, as it was pronounced).

It began to dawn on us that this might well be a teacher who didn't know his business. We felt the air expand with possibilities. We set right to it. We started, in the universal high school parlance, to fuck around.

It was the natural instinct of the Medford High School student, particularly if male, to push any teacher as far as possible. The English teacher, Miss Cullen, had been brought to tears by our stealing her glasses, our purloining her rank book, our locking her in the supply closet. All this had been achieved under the leadership of Ted Cunningham (who wore Miss Cullen's glasses on the tip of his nose for the space of a class period) but with the general bear-baiting connivance of all the rest of us.

Miss Cullen was probably in her late forties, though she looked sixty-five. Her hair was gray, undyed, uncombed, unkempt. She was forgetful and easily distracted. She talked to herself. She often murmured stagy asides that she took to be witty and were not. Her clothes were ineptly ironed; they were not always clean. Her stockings had runs in them. She was, to us, like someone's alcoholic grandma who was staying in an attic room, with a lock on the outside of the door and maybe some iron on the windows, too. And for these high crimes we had reduced her, on more than one occasion, to tears.

Fucking around was a sign of high spirits and vitality, we believed, though too much of it could get you sent to the office of one of the submasters, Fran Todesco, or the universally feared Charlie "Jingles" McDermott: Jingles because he had the habit of jamming a hand in his pocket and making loud music with his keys and his change before meting out something cruel and unusual. You needed to stay just below the teacher's mental radar, fly at a level where you didn't quite register as a major irritant. You needed, in order to maintain the dignity of yourself and the race of your fellow students, to do what damage you could to the teacher's evolving program, but do it without getting identified as a standout miscreant, crucifixion material in the making.

Donald W. O'Day, also known as the Doober, Dubby, Dubbsabond, what have you, was a prince of fucking around, professional-caliber. And we had not been in Frank Lears' class for long when Dubby interpreted the salient signals and took a chance. Dubby began modestly enough. While Lears talked in his sweet, melancholy voice and stroked his Proust-on-the-town mustache, the Doober began to manufacture spitballs. He did this dutifully, perfunctorily, with just a slight air of irritation, as though this were something he was obliged to undertake, somewhat against his will. There was a minor boredom in all his movements, as if he were working at the behest of a higher power.

And in a sense, he was. For as Dubby tore, rolled, chewed, swirled, extracted, and enacted one quality-control inspection after another, all over Medford High, all over America, kids were playing a similar game: screwing around, preparing trouble, getting ready to annoy the authorities. All were enmeshed in the longtime and by now perhaps genetically coded animosity between proletariat kids and their teachers.

Dubby began lining his desk with a poised, military row of saliva-gelled spheres, Lilliputian armaments for the war with gentility's Gulliver. He may or may not have wanted to do this—as I say, it was part of a transpersonal program, something that was larger in dimension, silly though it may have been, than our mere selves.

Dubby O'Day was, I had to admit, my closest friend in the class. He was tall and pipe-cleaner thin, with an onion-shaped head, bulging a bit in the middle, and a long, Alice-in-Wonderland periscope-up sort of neck. But he was also, in a certain way, handsome; mothers picked him out, with an unerringly confident mothers' aesthetic, as a "good-looking boy." Boys so selected were, it is almost needless to say, of virtually no interest to girls their own age. The mothers chose these boys because their soft looks and compliant faces made them seem like viable alternatives to the mothers' craggier, more wayward husbands, some of whom had themselves looked like mothers' darlings before they were married.

The Doober had blond, almost sun-colored hair, a kindly grinning Irish face, which could quickly, under the right circumstances, assume a morose Hibernian frown, red cheeks, and blue eyes, sky blue, and a trickle of zits—they seemed a little like blood rivulets—running down each side of his chin.

The Doober was a fatalist. He swore over and over again—and theatrically, having, as he did, played Hamlet in a ninth grade production (I was the ghost, a part Shakespeare himself played, it's said)—that everyone could write him off as a nothing, a failure, useless, a walking cipher, soon to be heard of (and probably to live) no more. Our friend Art Mondello, who helped me give Dubby a haircut that disfigured him for two months, claimed that the Doober was destined to be a fireman whose status in the firehouse would run about equal to the station house's pet dalmatian—provided Dubby refrained from befouling the floor.

Like Huck Finn, Dubby was determined to go to hell, the place the righteously indignant had set aside for his type, in hopes that when they were box-seated in heaven they could entertain themselves, as Tertullian, the Church father, said all good orthodox people would have the right to do, by looking down at the torments below. But Dubby only aspired to be bad; he was actually sweet-natured, wounded, put upon by a frantically loving mother, and—here we reach the inner squares of the Doober's private hell—preternaturally bad at math.

In grade twelve, the authorities claimed, he was functioning at the math level of a ninth grader. In days past, Dubby, like George Orwell at his British public school, would have been caned into a rudimentary knowledge of the subject at hand: For some reason—it puzzles Orwell, but he can't figure out what it is—he has to admit that the prospect of a good hiding does wonders for the capacity to conjugate Latin verbs. Under the current school dispensation, with its multiple titles and entitlements, Dubby could have himself declared the victim of a numerological deficiency encoded in his biological string and demand to be served, sultanlike, with tutors, emotional advisers, test exemptions, and prime seating. As it was 1969, Dubby was designated as plain dumb and left to fend for himself.

And the news had just broken over Dubby's good-natured head that he was once again to be the mathematical ward of Mr. Leo Repucci. Mr. Repucci was a teacher who had, from early in life, one might imagine (he now was about fifty), gone over to caricature. He was a small, bent man, with the expression of a puzzled burlesque-show attendee—worn, tired, quietly greedy, not unfamiliar with disappointment in its many guises, a sort of washed-out Jiminy Cricket type, if you were ill disposed. And Dubby was, extremely.

But one quality of Leo's stood out beyond the rest. He was prone to harsh mockery, to the humiliation of his students. And he did it all in the only voice he had, that of Elmer Fudd or his slightly calmer, slightly less sententious (but just slightly) younger brother. As in: "Weww, Donawd, here for anoder term? What do you think your chances are dis time to pass geometwy? I am vewy dubious, speaking for myself." This was pronounced in a half-keening singsong tune. What Leo probably took to be a genteel discretion informed his speech. Donald fought back by developing—he was an actor of parts; he'd played Hamlet—a Leo ("Weo") accent to top Leo's.

One of Leo's tasks, probably self-appointed, was to patrol the boys' bathroom beside his class, scolding the boys for smoking, for taking too long on the toilet, for chattering at the urinals. One day, the story went, a furtive smoker caught what he took to be the Doober's rendition of Leo's punishing voice, telling him to get rid of his cigarette and to join the happy throng in the class-room, pondering the value of x. The smoker wasn't having any. He cat-whooped out from the toilet: "Screw you, Donny."

"I'm sewious."

"Eat me, Donny." Members of the male, aggressively hetero-sexual population of Medford High were perpetually issuing homo-sexual invitations to one another.

"It is not Donawd. No. It is Mr. Wepucci. And it is big twobble foh you." And of course it was, or should have been, big trouble.

The problem was that teachers like Leo were in an impossible position. To get the reprobates punished in a fitting way, they had to take them before one of the fiery submasters, Fran Todesco or Jingles McDermott. Detention would be handed down. But in the process, a story about the misdemeanor would have to be told; the story would make Leo look ridiculous. And then the tale would slither around the teachers' lounge all the next day. So Leo would take revenge by flunking his tormentor, flunking the Doober, and then next year he'd be back in the fourth row, last seat (this was in fact Donny's third run with Mr. R), and the drama would begin again, with predictable last act.

So far, it looked as though this Frank Lears character might have come with the same meager throw weight that Leo did. He seemed to be absurdly mild, easy to mock, a rank pushover, someone against whom we might score a collective victory to assuage us for the defeats we'd suffered from the truly fierce and respected teachers, the disciplinarians, like Mace Johnson and the hockey coach, Paul Tuppermann, who was perpetually having us copy questions out of the history book while he . . . what? Drew up hockey plays at his desk? Are there plays in hockey?

Yes, it looked as though this Lears guy was someone on the order of Repucci or of Manny DeNofrio, who wore a set of false teeth that looked like they'd come from a joke shop, white-of-the-eyes white, far-protruding, and synthetic in appearance, as though if someone wound a key tightly in them they would leap from his mouth and traverse the floor, making a rackety sound. On the paperweight that he used to hold down his math tests, someone had written in cruel red pencil, legible all the way to the back of the room, the words *Joe Choppers.*

There was Mr. Sweeney, who one day became intoxicated with an image from Hawthorne of someone spitting up blood and began to pantomime the event, signifying the blood with his shaking, compulsively manicured fingers: Again and again, he repeated the action of the blood bubbling up through his windpipe and out his mouth, as though he were being afflicted by a hilarious case of consumption. Then he toppled forward in hysterical laughter, staggered, had to sit down, and could not continue the class. There was sad Miss Cullen, the English teacher who served extended time in the supply closet and who one day, humiliated by John Cosgrove, the class smart kid, on some factual quibble or another, simply called out in Cassandra-like grief, "John! I went to college! I am right!"

Dubby had provisionally filed Lears in the bin with these weak-
lings and on the other side of the world from enforcers like Mace
Johnson and Paul Tuppermann, and Ed "Dirty Ed" Bush. It was
said that Jimmy Brown, the greatest football player ever to live, was
once asked by Johnny Carson who the nastiest player was that he
had faced. He skipped over the likes of Sam Huff, the Giants' middle linebacker, and cited Dirty Ed Bush, of Northeastern University, my gym teacher. Ed was an enormous polar bear of a man,
pale, with a white crew cut, and black GI glasses. He was so ferocious that you half believed he would kill randomly and then de-
vour his fallen enemy on the site.

Dubby worked assiduously, lining his desk with the miniature
cannonballs, about to fire the opening shots of the war. Now it was
time to cast the cannon. Easily done. Dubby put the point of his
Bic pen into his mouth, bit down hard around the tip, pulled once,
then again with his Wonderland neck, extracted the metal nib and
the tiny thin-plastic sheath and spat the whole business out onto
his desk. In front of him lay a standard school weapon, a spitball
blowgun. By now, Dubby had about divided the audience with
Lears, who was talking on about the tactics we might use to interpret the Nietzsche passage.

Who would the Doober fire at? This question meant a good deal
to me. Dubby was no alpha male, maybe not even a beta. But because of his acute—albeit non–number processing—intelligence,
he readily sensed the pecking order that was in place at Medford
High. If Dubby shot a spitball in your direction, you were a small-
time player.

It was clear enough who Dubby would not shoot. He wouldn't
shoot the star quarterback, Cap, or our wide receiver, Rick Cirone.
Cap had a thick beard; he needed a second shave by four o'clock.
Not tall, about five-feet-nine, he was heroically muscular, with a

low brow and a thick, slightly protruding jaw. He was simple and direct in his feelings, an almost courtly guy, whom I never saw commit a mean act. He was egalitarian, generous to just about everyone, a little pious, but with a small streak of whimsy. What Cap was preeminently, though, was a splendid athlete, who could run and bound and dodge in ways that made the local sportswriters search the whole bestiary for comparisons. He had a beautiful, rarely dispensed smile.

Rick and he had grown up together, and though they both had Sicilian good looks, they were much different boys. Rick's astrological sign was Taurus, the bull, and he was a strong Taurian, down-to-earth, realistic, a lover of strong tastes and smells, fiercely drawn to girls. He was dead practical, knew how much money he had in his pocket. But Rick was also a musician, played drums and guitar, and revered not so much the Beatles and the Stones as Jeff Beck, a guitarist with a lightning hand. Rick was circumspect but also witty, a splendid mimic, much liked, caustic, unexpected. At football, he spun off imitations of the great running backs, hopping over tackling dummies like the Packers' Paul Hornung, spinning down the field with Gale Sayers' stride. (He insisted on wearing a white plastic one-bar face guard, like the one Sayers had worn; it was flimsy and put his face in constant danger of rearrangement.) He could sing in various pop-parodic voices. Rick was an alpha type, seemed to know it (most of the time), and laughed about it internally. He talked about playing guitar with a kick-back country-rock band and living in a flurry of girls. Cap dreamed about going pro.

Rick is drumming the desk, moving his feet, living in his self-made music as Cap, it appears, tunes out Lears and lives in the sound of the crowd on Saturday. No way the Dub would hit either of them.

Nor would he dare to hit Nora Balakian, by male consensus surely the most comely girl in the room. (And what is high school but a sort of debased Classical world, where beauty and physical might matter more than all else?) She is dark, contemplative, poised, with black hair and gray-flecked eyes. She's intent on Lears but so far hasn't said a word.

As to me, no, I wasn't a likely target. Dubby was my friend, and besides, the demon in me who occasionally exploded on the football field, creating general havoc, might always spring to life. All of Dubby's friends periodically threatened him with physical harm, if only to give him the chance for some artful, Buster Keaton–style cringing.

I didn't think Dubby would aim at Tommy Buller. Buller was stumpy as a boss troll, thick-necked, scowling, with no social consequence whatever, a kid with a pack of younger, admiring friends at home, maybe, and aspirations to open his own auto-body shop. He had acne so livid it looked like someone had rubbed steel wool over his face that morning, with Buller's encouragement. He wore Sears, Roebuck stain-holding shirts that reeked of the night shift. He was so angry that it seemed like a fierce dog, a Rottweiler maybe, was always there beside him. You wanted to pull the fire extinguisher off the wall and turn it in his direction so as to put the nasty fire that was Buller out. Tommy was too mean to trifle with.

Then there was Sandra Steinman, the school's only hippie. Sandra, like Tommy Buller, was not a player in high school society. But Buller didn't know where the game was, didn't know that a game existed. Sandra did, and disliked it all—intensely.

On this, the first day of school, she'd opted out with her wardrobe. Sandra, who had always dressed "normally" in past years, came to class that day in loose, sloppy blue jeans and a man's dress shirt, long and untucked. She had wire-rimmed glasses pushed close to her face. And, abomination on abomination, she was wearing work boots: men's work boots. Sandra was well-to-do. Imagine—we hardly could—that wearing work clothes would be someone's idea of style. But it was more than mild class rancor that beset me, and the other boys too, for we all gasped in some derision when first Sandra came clomp-clomping in with the big-ditch mud slappers. Sandra was pretty, or would have been without the self-mutilations. She had ringletty blond hair and a sweet, slightly mischievous face, the face of a lower-order angel, maybe, who's perpetually annoying the higher castes, the thrones and dominions, as they're called; her twin brother, John, was endlessly popular with the girls. But here were the work boots, first day of school, and what they said was that she wasn't even going to try to be attractive to the local boys. It was as though the swan had gotten annoyed with all the attention and decided to turn back into an ugly duckling. She seemed to be telling all the boys, who wanted to imagine fine times with such a pretty, poised girl, exactly what she thought of them.

What would Sandra do if she got popped with one of Dubby's pellets? It seemed that Sandra was, in her own mind, about five years older than the rest of us and lived on the newly discovered planet of peace and love. Her response would be too unpredictable. No way Dubby would shoot at her.

Come to think of it, the work clothes probably scared us for another reason, too. They reminded us, I suspect, of what we would ourselves be putting on to head out to the factory, head off for the ditch, down to the road crew. We wanted one year more of glad rags and great good times before moving into what we did not want just now to imagine, thanks anyway for the invitation. This year was our time on the stage. High school at the time worked this way (and I suspect it still does): For three years, from ninth grade through eleventh, the students seem to be an undifferentiated mass, roiling and stumbling along through their lives. But then at the onset of senior year something happens. Identities crystallize. Kids become themselves in stark, hyperintense ways. By midyear, all the stock figures have gelled. Up until then it is a grand audition, with people pushing hard in an almost Darwinian heat to do what they need to in order to coalesce as the highest embodiment of their type.

Senior year in high school, it seemed to many of us, was the last chance to flower, the last chance to become who you are, with some verve. That was the vocation of the senior—to come into one's own, but within set categories: jock, brain, cheerleader, heartthrob, junior entrepreneur, femme fatale, class clown. There is something archetypal about the world of high school, something allegoric. The kids have formalized roles. The teachers have nicknames that fix their place in the meager cosmos. Even the building is full of highly charged locales—the place where this or that clique hangs out, the corridor where the fight took place, the detention room where Big Fran, the submaster, had to call the police. There is something eternally burning about this world; it lives in the mind ten, twenty, thirty years after the fact, as though it had been concocted and instilled by a small-time Dante, who had himself once been injured by it and wanted it preserved eternally as a reminder.

High school is, one fears, where ultimate identity is conferred. For it is here that, for the last time in life probably, people will pull back and tell you, or at least demonstrate in no mistakable terms, what they truly think about you. Once high school is over, the conventions of civility begin to take over. Mocking someone to his face is, by and large, out in adult life, unless you join the army or become a corporate demigod. But the fear is that high school was the last time the world was willing to offer you an up-front, unbiased readout of who and what you were. And that if the readout was negative—and it probably was—you've stayed fixed and everyone knows as much but is simply too polite to let on.

Most people suffer abominably from this dispensation, where everything is in the open, like in the last act of an Ibsen or an O'Neill play, when the truth comes out, with no quarter given. But some actually thrive in this cosmos. The way a few of my contemporaries took to high school might have made you believe in reincarnation. They knew precisely what to expect. They had mental clocks that chimed in their heads to forewarn them of mixers and socials and parties and official functions the necessary two months in advance. On the reincarnation theory, Suze Rodino must have been passing through high school for the fourth or fifth time, and she was getting better at it with every go. She was luminously pretty, dark-complected, with inky-black hair, and always had her schoolwork done and never missed a sorority social night and had a boyfriend (whom she'd marry) and a college picked out (the University of Connecticut) and a profession (physical therapy), and at Christmastime, once, sewed jingling bells to her slip so that when she walked or skipped (yeah, she did skip) down the halls, ringling holiday sounds came with her. She was unremittingly benevolent to all (and I mean *all*; the most noxious social outcast got a smile and a spray of kind words from Suze) good-hearted, curious, uncloyingly sweet, and always up. No, Suze had done it before; she was near high school satori. Had Dubby thought to mistreat Suze Rodino—she wasn't, as it happened, in this class—an invisible ring of social approval would have risen around her, guarding her high-note happiness, and, like a force field, sent the offending particle to the ground.

Against this high school world, Lears was already taking his first small step, though it was a step we could not perceive. The quote from Nietzsche had a point. It was simply that in order to be a thinker, in order even to study philosophy, you had to be willing to fall out of joint with your times. "Genuine philosophers, being *of necessity* people of tomorrow, and the day after tomorrow, have always found themselves, and *had* to find themselves, in contradiction to their today; their enemy was ever the ideal of today." To be at war with today and the ideal of today? That, of course, was exactly what we did not want. Everyone in the class, Sandra Steinman and Tommy Buller perhaps excepted, had bought all the rules that high school laid down, and we wanted to conform to them as well as we could. We wanted to look like experts, the way Suze did, to look like people who were passing through the gauntlet for the twentieth time and knew every step. This fellow Nietzsche and his diminutive friend Lears were telling us that by showing any interest in philosophy, we'd signaled a willingness to put ourselves a step or two at odds with the dance. And where would that leave us? Well, with the future in our hands: We'd live in the day after tomorrow, no? But by then the philosopher has taken another step forward, and again no one likes him terribly much.

It is the Socratic type that Nietzsche is talking about and praising in the passage about being untimely. For Socrates does not fit in. He annoys people. The Delphic oracle, fount of all wisdom for the Athenians (though often wisdom of a cruelly enigmatic sort), informed the world that Socrates was the wisest man alive. This puzzles him no end. So off he goes to talk with all the people the Athenians take to be wise. He chats with politicians, craftsmen, and poets. And what comes out of the discussions, according to Socrates, is that these people know nothing whatever that's worth knowing. They can't tell you what justice is, why one should tell the truth rather than lie, what kind of government is best. So

Socrates draws a simple conclusion. He decides that what makes him wise is his awareness of how ignorant he is. At least he, Socrates, knows that he knows nothing. This process makes the people he has questioned—the poets, tradesmen, and politicians—very angry. They become angry enough, in fact, to try him on trumped-up charges: They indict him for pretending to know what goes on in the heavens and beneath the earth, for teaching people to make the weaker argument appear the stronger, for corrupting the young. Then they sentence him to death.

THE DOOBER is shifting into third gear. His ritual is to wait for the small, pale fellow up front to look away, then take aim, shoot, and duck behind the back of the guy in front of him, like a desperado dodging behind a cactus. Ping—duck. Ping—duck. He nicks John Vincents, who wears his soccer cleats to class. But Vincents is so good-natured and fond of the Doober—they've known each other for about a decade—that he doesn't care. Then he tags Donald Bellmer again and again, Bellmer, with his Dumbo ears and big feet and hands. Bellmer was tall and pale and so shy and indrawn that he almost seemed like a ventriloquist's doll who was waiting for the master to come along, prop him on his knee, and let the show begin. He hit blond, open-mouthed Carolyn Cummer, and then he looked at her apologetically, like a low-rung courtier who'd sullied the empress.

Almost everyone is watching Dubby now. He's in the position of the prospector who's perhaps struck a vein of gold. Out ahead of us, he has taken the necessary daring step and quickly revealed what looks to be the way things will go with this new guy.

Tired of shooting, the Dub gets into another line. He stomps his feet a little, offers a few animal noises, maybe a lip-fart or two. And

Lears lets it all go. He pays the Doober no mind, though he seems to see Donny working away. Probably he's too afraid to confront him. Probably he doesn't know what to do.

We begin to loosen up. We drum the desks; we yack as loudly as we care to with our neighbors. We pull out newspapers. A few lay their heads down and begin a nap. Some kind of discussion does seem to be going on—yes, Sandra is dropping in a word here and there. And this Lears character, ignoring our antics, is talking back, taking her seriously. He thinks he's in an actual school. Occasionally, he stops and looks at all of us, contemplating the group en masse.

And what did he see as he looked out at us? Lears, you have to keep in mind, was here on leave from Pepperland. He came from the world where men wore beads and earrings and carried little purses and displayed muttonchop sideburns and walrus mustaches and decked themselves in army-surplus gear. They sported pink-tinted granny glasses, headbands, multiple rings, bell-bottoms, Mexican sandals. The idea, often, was to reach to both extremes. The real stylists would mix macho touches—boots, spurs, a Confederate cavalry cap, say—with female odds and ends—silver amulets and love beads and a sweet little braid or two.

The women wore minis (there were rules against these at Medford High) and long bread-baker skirts, and hair like bed curtains, hanging evenly down, and no bras (no bras!) and absurdly bright peasant blouses. Lears' contemporaries were at the time busy forming a ragtag peasant parody army, high as magpies on weed, mushrooms, and acid, pushing the pigs against the wall (and being shoved there in turn), getting it on, and reinventing (or trying to reinvent) America wholesale. Lears' legacy suit, with the lapel paper clip and the gunboat shoes, was a costume; he was goofing on the whole idea of straightness. He was fresh from the revolution, out of that great tragicomedy that's since been dubbed the sixties, but at the time simply looked like a standard-issue re-creation of the world from top to bottom that was going to continue forever.

What Lears saw was Dubby stupidly lurking behind the prop that was Rick's back and the rest of us following his antics like chimps seeking their lowest level of common amusement, straining to achieve our ultimate goal, which was to turn everyday life into a species of our favorite diversion, television. Yes, if you could turn school into TV, that would be fine indeed, well worth the labor of getting up, doing the ablutions, and boarding the bus.

What he saw when we sat still and tried to listen was also in some measure the world created by TV. For we looked like nothing so much as people who aspired to be in family sitcoms, aspired, that is, to a certain wholesomeness, fed as we were on American cheese and Wonder Bread, with Fluffer-Nutter sandwiches and sloppy joes on the weekends. The girls wore jumpers and pleated skirts and had their hair militantly lacquered, into imposing helmets. What our school alone used in hair spray would have been enough to burn a considerable hole in the ozone. He saw the boys all looking pretty much alike, with our modest bangs, courtesy of the Beatles, and our crewneck sweaters that made us look just a little clerical, and our penny loafers and socks that matched those crewnecks, or were supposed to. (A bit schizoid in the sartorial department, I wore this sort of stuff sometimes, and other times wore semi-greaser getups.) Perhaps Lears also sensed the reservoirs of anxiety and rank horniness and confusion, along with maybe a little bit of potentially usable desperation. Overall, he saw what must have looked like the most god-awfully unhip concatenation of people yet assembled in one small room in the West in the fall of 1969. We had no idea what time it was. People's Park and the Panthers' insurrections and the March on Washington had all taken place over our heads, like those scenes of heaven in Wagner-inspired paintings where the gods feast and cavort on high and the mortals toil stupidly below. He must have been ready to walk out, slapping the gunboats on the linoleum, and go back to Cambridge and get his commission reinstated in the anti-army of hip, get his proper togs back and rejoin the revolution.

He was in one of his legacy suits, a green twill number, hanging and disheveled, I think, of which I would one day, not quite knowing what I was up to, buy an imitation in a New Haven thrift shop. He had on a skinny tie, tamed-snake black, with a modest stripe down the middle, and the inscrutable paper clip. Lears was dressed in a certain kind of drag, but nobody in the room got it (except maybe Sandra); nobody moved with the joke.

As for us, we continued with our antics, raising the volume progressively. To look at it all from a distance, of course, is more than a little appalling. We were seventeen, a point in life where other people, at other places and times, are beginning to do their life's work, are writing bad early poems, scribbling music, concocting business schemes, or picking up the rudiments of a trade. And the world around us was more than alive. Our nation was busy bombing a peasant population into Buddhist rage and Buddhist renunciation of that rage. And here we were, with all the promise and absurdity that are inseparable from being seventeen, regressing as quickly as we could. We were regressing, maybe, as a sign of rage at how often—stand in line, don't talk, no short skirts—we were rewarded for regression. All right, I'll play along; I'll go where the conveyor belt seems bound to send me, and I'll go capering and grinning, too.

Now Mace Johnson or Paul Tuppermann or Dirty Ed Bush would have whipped around like a G-man, in a quick Eliot Ness pivot, sensing the apostasy at his back, and sought the "ringleader." Any one of them would have ripped Dubby from his seat—especially Dubby—and pulled him like a human mule, limbs flying, up the row toward the front, stretching, maybe tearing the collar of his new madras shirt, so new that the little band of cloth fixed between the shoulder blades, known as the fruit loop, was still intact.

Franklin Lears simply looked at us en masse and with an expression of mild bemusement. He didn't seem at all discomfited by our antics. He didn't seem ready to rush out the door in anguish at the way we'd messed up his first day of school. Perhaps he understood that the ability to be humiliated and take it in stride is crucial to a certain kind of teaching, the kind that will convey two virtues, which rarely come together—a modesty so intense that it borders on self-mockery, along with a conviction, absolute and unflappable, that one has to see it one's own way, speak one's truth, that having experimented in the chaotic laboratory of life, one must, for better or worse, publish the results to the world.

Socrates, after all, got brained with a plate of urine, thrown by his wife, Xanthippe, who was angry at him for neglecting domestic affairs. When people teased him about it in later life, Socrates simply said that with Xanthippe, you could be sure that after the thunder—after her shrewish harangues—would inevitably come the rain. During his early years as a philosopher, Socrates decided to define man as a featherless biped. He got a plucked chicken thrown at him for his pains. The sage took pleasure in these things, saw them as conducive to a modesty that was the obverse side of the mental fearlessness he also cultivated. As Falstaff, an Elizabethan Socrates, says, "I am not only witty in myself, but the cause that wit is in other men."

Lears simply kept talking to Sandra and calmly ignored the rest of us. As time went on, we would get to him. How could we not? But on this, the first day, he held his ground. He continued with a demonstration of what real teaching might be like—though we were too dim to see as much. For what we saw was rank weakness; another teacher had arrived who did not know his trade. The Doober, our guide, had shown us the way. This class was going to be fabulous. We could do anything we wanted. Good times were about to roll.

Chapter Two

MUSTANGS

If Franklin Lears' so-called philosophy class was going to be a circus, all to the good. I detested school; a little diversion would help me get through the day. What I cared about—and with an intensity that bordered on religious devotion—was football. The football field was where my real life was going to unfold. For I had grand hopes for this, my senior year. When I think back on the game and what it meant to me—and what it meant for Lears to pull me from it, as he eventually would—one day in particular stands out.

This was our last day of double sessions, two-a-day practices. (It might, in fact, have been the day that Frank Lears got his first look inside Medford High, faculty orientation day.) On the field, it was brutally hot. Eighty degrees is bliss on a leafy New England street; on a high school practice field, where the ground is so hard that you and the ballcarrier bounce like a couple of india-rubber dolls when you make a tackle and the dust billows perpetually in an ongoing simoom, it's something else again. I felt like I was being boiled alive in the cauldron of my helmet.

This was the only day all year that we did grass drills. As far as I know, the last pro football coach who could regularly get his team to do grass drills, or up-downs, as they're also called, was Vince Lombardi, the man of whom the defensive tackle Willie Davis said, "Coach treats us all like equals, treats us like dogs." Lombardi was a legend even during his life.

Mace Johnson was here today. He was my history teacher, our last year's backfield coach, now in charge of his own team on the other side of Boston, and he was legendary to us. Johnson had come to revisit his old squad, whom he'd keep track of through the year almost as closely as he did his new team. Though physically absent through the season, he often seemed more with us than the new coaches who had come on to take his place.

Most anything Mace Johnson asked we would have done, and what he asked for on this particular day was grass drills. It was time, as he said in his staff sergeant's drawl, to "get 'em up."

He is there, standing in front of us, in blue coach's jersey and shorts, with his close-clipped hair and his whistle dangling. Johnson was six-feet-two, about 190 pounds, all prime-grade Marine Corps muscle. He was handsome, with a face that looked like it had been cut from a block of marble. The cheeks were long and smooth, the forehead high and similarly unlined. Johnson had close-set eyes, soft blue, and a nose unremarkable and perfectly proportioned to the rest of his face. There was a simplicity and purity in Johnson's appearance, as though he were a knight who knew that he served the best of kings and that his causes were just. There was no room on the face or behind it for self-dissatisfaction, ambiguities, mysteries, doubts.

Johnson had the whistle between his teeth and he was striding up and down the rows in which the team was arrayed and running in place, his great thigh muscles rippling and relaxing with each step. When Johnson blew the whistle, we stopped our running, kicked our legs out behind us, and threw ourselves at the ground as though we were going to hit luscious feather beds. It was, he proclaimed, only the beginning of the second quarter—we'd just begun the drill—and we would have to push much harder if we expected ever to win a football game, if we ever expected to survive a football game alive and standing.

Someone passing by would have seen the arresting sight of sixty bodies, dressed a little like astronauts, a little like gladiators, heads and shoulders expanded, waists waspish, tightly feminine, all of us suspended for a moment in the air, as though by magic, on invisible carpets. Then down to the ground we went, onto the dusty near-concrete surface. There was the thud and the bounce, then up again onto our feet, and running, running in place, as Mace Johnson orated. It was eleven o'clock in the morning. The sun roared in the sky. We sweated and strained and watched Johnson, and hated him and adored him with about equal verve.

Doing grass drills at the end of what has already been a vicious practice, pushing toward what you know will be your far edge, you enter a hallucinatory state; you see the world as a gross illusion, the way grinning, half-mad convicts are supposed to. Nothing out there—not the chanting players pounding on their thigh pads or the bawling coaches or the stands that line one side of the practice field—is entirely real, and so your pain is part illusion too. But it's got to be dealt with, so you drop down inside yourself, stumbling and uncertain, and what you come upon is pooled rage, good octane, high-combustion stuff. I didn't have great physical skill or remarkable strength, but I had enough hot rancor to push myself through this drill and plenty more like it.

As we sweat, Mace Johnson's rhetoric is climbing higher, into the provinces of Christopher Marlowe and Herman Melville, masters of swelling poetic style. Johnson is launched. Up and down in front of our military rows he strides, hollering out to us that it's getting later in the game and that the team that guts it out is the one that will win; he tells us that we've been pussyfooting all day, we've been pussyfooting through our hit-and-shed drills, dogging it during wind sprints; that we've lived our lives in obscene luxury and that now it's time to wake up and become men. He tells us that in not too much time, many of us will be soldiers; some—the best of us—may be marines. He never mentions the Viet Cong by name, but it is after all 1969 and somewhere on the far side of the Hormel Stadium practice field, the Cong and the NVA are waiting, and they are doing something more drastically preparative than grass drills.

He bellows out one of his favorite injunctions: "You're gonna be lean, mean, agile, mobile, and hostile." Then a scream: "I mean hostile!"

Running in place next to me, wearing his helmet with the signature white-plastic face mask, Rick Cirone, my fellow philosophy student, rounds off Johnson's litany: "How 'bout infantile?" Rick can clown well enough, but he can also play. Neither of these things can be said with confidence of me.

Up-downs are like a collective madness; you get high, the whole group does, and you hear yourself say things, hear yourself call out injunctions to yourself and the other players, scream the baseline phrase "Get 'em up!" and bellow the line that will be with us for the first month of the season: "Beat Somerville!" "Beat Somerville!" "Somerville!" "Somerville!" "Somerville!" Somerville is our local rival, the team that broke the Medford Mustangs' winning streak last season in a game where player after Medford player was carried off the field, bloody and weeping. The chants shift. "Kill Somerville!" we scream. Neither Johnson nor any of the other coaches says a word to stem the blood lust.

Mace Johnson himself is off the Tamerlane-like tone and is now hitting a quasi-philosophical note that I've heard him touch before. "These are the best years of your lives, boys!" he cries at us, in a knowing, almost statesmanlike voice. "Best years of your lives!"

And as he says it, my heart gums up with fear. Could this possibly be true? Is there a chance that from here it runs downhill? For I cannot imagine anything worse than high school—at least anything inside the chain-link park-fence bounds of American life— that is more tedious, mean, anxiety-ridden, and sad. If this is the best, then I think I will do away with myself before I have to taste what's left simmering in the pot.

"Third quarter!" Johnson hollers. And I and all my compeers in pain scream out in antiphonal response, for this is religion, American religion: "Third quarter!" Kill Somerville (and the invisible Cong)! No mercy, not for anyone, least of all us, in the best years of our lives.

Mace Johnson was a man of mantras, talismanic phrases that sewed life together at its seams. "Atta boy!" was the leading commendation, applied to any display of guts. "First off the deck!" was another, meaning that once you'd gone down, you had to spring up first, faster than your opponent, and go block someone else; then you were two men rather than just one forked thing scrambling on the field.

Johnson's pet verbal formula, the one that, from his perspective, I imagine, elevated him to higher grounds of urbane eloquence, went this way: "There are three things in life that I cannot abide: small dogs, women who smoke in public, and [fill in the third spot with whatever abomination has just assaulted his eyes] quarterbacks who won't stand in and take a hit"; "linebackers who don't stick their heads into a tackle"; "runners who cannot understand that a good back *never* loses a yard." I'm sure Johnson was serious about the small mutts. He was the sort of man who would own a mastiff or a Doberman, and that dog would be *trained*. But did he really abhor women smoking in public? Did the new Virginia Slims—cigarettes of, by, and for the female—cause him bouts of anxiety as women hoisted to their lips derogatorily reduced versions of the royal scepter and manly wand? I can't really say.

Mace Johnson had little capacity for the ambiguous or the equivocal, much less for being in uncertainties, mysteries, doubt, without irritable reaching after fact or reason. (Keats called this negative capability and I had, up until Frank Lears, who eventually displayed it in remarkable measure, never met anyone with a turn for it.) It was Johnson's emphatic downrightness, his willingness to promulgate and live by a code that was nearly chivalric, that drew us to him. Here was a blue-collar bastion of Camelot, created by the coach; here was a place where you could be measured by a discerning eye and given a seat—or denied one—at the Round Table. You're not a man, it's been said, until the other men acknowledge you as one. In Mace Johnson, overemphatic, loud, monovocal, we had identified someone with the right of investiture.

It was a touch absurd, this male business—we saw it even then. We'd pass each other in the halls and call out "Atta boy!" or "Get 'em up!" and fall out laughing. But the whole enterprise was elevating, too; it pushed you to places you would never have reached on your own.

Football is a Homeric world, and like the assault on Troy, it attracts hitters, orators, and orator-hitters. In every coach there is the urge of Nestor or Odysseus to rally the troops with high-sounding hymns to fathers and manliness. Girls watch and chant madly from the sidelines, spinning and prancing, urging on the combat.

It's important that Achilles, the apogee of heroic culture in *The*

Iliad, the apogee of all male warrior culture up to the present, really, isn't just the great doer of deeds, the man, that is, who kills so many Trojans one day that he gluts a river with blood until the river god is revolted and tries to drown him. Achilles is also a great orator. His powers of expression are nearly incomparable. But you don't go to Achilles for an elevating discussion. He makes speeches, lays down the word, and in his orations he unfolds the heroic code. The code revolves around one issue—honor—and its preservation, enhancement, and demolition. Achilles always knows what he must do—what god he must respect; when he must sacrifice; whom he must kill and despoil. And when Achilles speaks, everyone goes silent and listens. If you don't, you'll be blood on the sand. The most maladroit peewee football coach urging his kids to hold the line is tied, however pathetically, to this rap-and-wreck tradition.

Socrates, who comes on later in history, is not prone to speeches. He'll give them if he's pushed, but he'd prefer to pose questions, endless questions. With them, he hopes to get his interlocutor to know something about himself. And, too, Socrates aspires to be improved by the exchange. Unlike Achilles, who assumes he knows everything worth knowing (including the fact that he'll die very young), Socrates says he knows nothing. For this, the oracle at Delphi commends him, calls him the wisest man in Athens. As soon as Achilles opened his mouth, Socrates would have begun badgering him with questions.

Though they are not entirely unlike, these two, Achilles and Socrates, they are much opposed. There was only one Socrates; we'll never see his like again. But his spirit is always abroad in the world, and when it meets up with the spirit of heroic manliness, Achilles' spirit—and this will happen before my eyes, soon—then one has to give way. And it will not always be the homely figure with the ready laugh who steps aside.

MACE JOHNSON, the spirit of football, the spirit of manliness, call it what you like, had anointed me at the end of last football season—though such investitures can always be revoked. Here is how it happened.

I came to football with precious little aptitude. My first year on the varsity, junior year, I was six feet tall, radically uncoordinated, tallowy in body, and bat-blind without my glasses. I missed getting cut from the team by a hair. On the fateful day of the last cut, the linebacker coach, Brian Rourke, pulled me aside and informed me that I was utterly without ability and that the only reason, the only reason in the world, I wasn't going to be cut was that I "hustled like a bastard" on the field and was an example to the "lazy shits" with which the team, that year, was rife.

Rourke came on like a Thoroughbred: He'd been the captain of the Malden Catholic team and had then gone to Harvard, where he was a star football player. The next year we heard he skipped away to Harvard Business School, and today, for all I know, he owns great expanses of cement and steel and whole choirs of computers and is worshiped by phalanxes of cell phone–yammering princelings of global commerce. At the time, what came through was that he was deplorably handsome, a movie star in the flesh, and absurdly tough. He spat tobacco juice down on us while we pushed the blocking sled along, him riding atop it like Darius of Persia. He was a triumph of prole genetics, was Rourke; I was a mutt, just managing to bark along after the team as it strode through the stadium.

Rourke was not a subtle motivator; he wasn't, I'd wager, trying to inspire me with a brash challenge. No, he was simply calling roll, letting me know where the scales of justice were poised. He was in charge of order and degree, like Odysseus in Shakespeare's play, and he was going to let me know where I stood in that great chain of being on which he held such an exalted place. He was good at everything; I, at nothing. Rourke, I surmised, believed that you either were born top-flight or should do the world a favor and cut from the nearest bridge.

I went at football with a novitiate's devotion. The coaches told us that before practice we were to do a set of exercises with an absurd device called an Exer-Genie, an isometric contraption that must have cost a good five dollars on the open market. The drill was excruciating, and though almost everyone else ignored the machines, I did double the amount. I never dogged it on the field. I filled every minute there, in accord with the Kipling poem that someone had posted on our bulletin board, with sixty seconds' worth of distance run. In fact, I worshiped that poem, "If," with its muscular, colonialist faith (and I was being groomed as a lower-echelon colonialist, wasn't I? For beyond the stadium walls there was Vietnam, and all the other American adventures abroad that were to come). I threw myself into every drill like a fiend hopping into the fire, hoping to ascend another degree of flaming rectitude.

I never did the one thing that would have made all the difference. I never contrived to go out and get myself some contact lenses or some sports glasses. No, I simply stowed my everyday glasses in my locker—they wouldn't fit under the helmet—and went out to practice. So I stayed nearly stone-blind. But other than that, I was close to transformed over time. From a disoriented, buttery boy in mid-August I had become, by late November, a pretty solid, pretty reckless head banger. Rourke, my devilment, had taught me a technique for flipping my forearm and sending the blocker coming at me spinning, and I practiced this one motion more than a dancer does her pas de deux. I can do it fluently still. (Come at me; come on!) Step with the left, flip with the right; step right, flip left, with no trace of wasted motion, as though your fore-arms are the moving bumpers on a pinball machine. If you can move your forearm fast enough, you can make a sound like a bass drum in a cathedral inside your opponent's helmet. Other players saw what I could do and began to duck me when we lined up to scrimmage.

One day, Mace Johnson presiding, Rourke attendant priest, we lined up for tackling drills. Two large blue tackling dummies, smelling of sweat and sawdust, are placed five yards apart. In the middle is an offensive lineman; back behind him, a ballcarrier. Nose-up to the blocking lineman, crouched in his stance, football's Zen meditative position, is a defender, with forearms poised if he's a linebacker or an end, down, in three points, if he's a tackle.

I step into the defensive slot, get my forearms—seal flippers, they look like in their thick, laundry-scented pads—into place. In front of me, blocking, is Tommy Sullivan, a nice, nice kid, my year, a junior, who plays a lot in the games, at linebacker and at guard. ("You ain't never never gonna play," says Rourke aloud, of me, while the team is watching my filmed self blitz the quarterback at the behest of J. T. Tedesco, senior, thus leaving my slot open over the middle and getting us burned for a touchdown pass in a scrimmage with Salem.) Tom is a freckle-faced kid with a great shock of Woody Woodpecker–red hair.

Behind him is Frank Ball—built, in Medford parlance, like a brick shithouse. Ball is actually a cowardly lion, a Baby Huey. He is a rich kid (by Medford standards); his father owns a used-car dealership. He is also a handsome one—in the off season, he wears a carefully tended mustache.

I can tolerate Frank Ball; Tom, I like a lot. But right now I am filled with a rage that simply pours through me like fast-rushing water; I can hear it move. For on the human map, and on the

Homeric map of football, I am simply an unequivocal nothing, a flunky in school, of less than no account socially, with no money, no connections; I've got zip and zip-minus listed in every account book that matters. I can no longer bear the shame of being simply myself. I am raging so much internally that I'm surprised my body doesn't lift off the ground and rise, corkscrewing into the air.

But though I may be a nothing on the football field, at least so far, I am coming to feel very much at home here. In particular, I love my uniform. In the beginning, when I first started to play, I didn't understand how anyone could sustain all this gear for hour after hour. I was alternately frantic, like someone locked in a dark closet, and despondent, like a horse that has never felt a saddle until one very rough and heavy one is applied. But now things are different. I feel that when I pull on my helmet, I am completely transformed; the great cage, three bars horizontal, one down the middle—designed, come to think of it, much in line with the helmets that they wore at Troy—confers a new identity. I'm wearing a mask. It's a Jekyll-and-Hyde thing. Now the animal can get into play.

I love the feel of the shoulder pads and the thigh and knee protectors and the smell of the harsh shirt—like rotting leather, really, but appealing to me. Suddenly, within the armor, I—who am usually a human incoherence, ready to fly off in every adolescent direction—pull almost completely together. I am now all of a piece, unified, self-contained. And I am also blissfully, beautifully, isolated: No one can get in; no one can get at me. A lovely place to hide.

But mainly it's the sense of power that I love; every piece of armor ensures some protection, but most of them are weapons as well. The shoulder pads are bludgeons; the helmet is a battering rock.

We always go on the second "hut," our offensive line. Knowing this, the defender has an advantage. Tom and I move at about the same time. He leads with his helmet, getting a good push out of his stance. I know what is coming. Never cock your forearm—he'll be on you before you get it thrown. It's like a short punch, a jab, but I know how to sink every fiber into it. I do. Sully simply flies to the ground in a thrown-rag-doll heap. He rolls over and groans a little, more in humiliation than pain.

This leaves Frank Ball unprotected. He appears, for all his size, terrified. Which adds, if possible, urgency to my rage. I feel at that moment like a wolf bearing down on some large, injured thing that is not dangerous at all, despite its tusks and girth. I spear him just above the waist with my helmet, and all the air goes out of him. There's not even time to wrap him with my arms. He's on the ground—gone—just like that. He grunts twice, on the first hit and then as he smashes down.

"Frank, get outta here," says Rourke. Ball is a disgrace to alpha maledom. He has all the biological sine qua nons, but he won't activate them. Rourke presumably wants him chloroformed. Then he spits. "Sull, you all right?"

You are always all right, whatever has happened to you on a football field. If you have your limbs scattered at random across the grass, like the Scarecrow in the Oz movie, you are nonetheless all right. Sully shakes his head in assent. Rourke asks how he could have let Edmundson do that to him. This sends me into a million furies.

Sully lines up again. No runner now. He comes fast off the line, jumping the count by a fraction. No problem, because I'm jumping it by a little more. This time I rap him with both forearms and send his helmet up on his head; his chin strap goes over his mouth, his cage lifts up; he reels back. Then, foolishly, he bends at the waist and takes a step forward. He wants to make one more stab. This time my right forearm knocks his helmet off his head and into the dust. His nose is bleeding wildly. Now I can really destroy him, bash his brains right in (you let Edmundson do that?), and it is—I say to my shame—all I can do not to throw a stone fist at his down-tumbling innocent head. It's all I can do not to jump on him and throttle him when he hits the ground as a warrior out of *The Iliad*, a thug like Diomedes, would do, though I would have no fine rhetoric to accompany the assault.

Sully rises, dusts himself off, and walks ignominiously away. Then other linemen, with no inducement from the coaches that I could see, line up in front of me and take their turns. Some I blasted, a few I fought to something like a draw, but none of them came close to blowing me out. Rourke stood there and spat tobacco and whistled his soft, ironic whistle and took off his baseball hat and rubbed his curly hair, like rich black lamb's wool. Mace Johnson was more demonstrative. Every time I won a round, he'd whoop or throw his coach's cap onto the ground. He was the back-field coach, not my boss, as Rourke was, but he was in a form of identificatory ecstasy that's hard to reach day to day.

For Johnson and I were actually of a similar species. Though he was hugely strong and fast, like Ajax to Rourke's Odysseus, Johnson wasn't terribly well coordinated. I'd seen him play baseball for the Pantops Bullets, a local semi-pro team, and his contributions mainly consisted of hustle, "huss" and "extra huss" as he put it. He stole bases often and roared down the path like an out-of-control train. Once, the story went, an umpire had called him out on a close play. Johnson rose, looked at the opposing second baseman, and said, "Son, *you know* I'm safe." The man, who was probably a year younger than Johnson, took the coach's flaming stare for a moment, then nodded. The umpire reversed the call. But such scenes made up the major glories of Mace Johnson's baseball career. Unlike Rourke, who was the star short stop, Johnson wasn't bred right for big-time glory. He recognized me that day as one in the confraternity of the striving breed, and he was well pleased. He gave me his nod.

How did I feel that day? In Homer there are moments when, it's said, a god descends and makes himself manifest to a mortal, proferring him some much needed help. But we moderns have learned to read it differently: We see the mortal as temporarily embodying the prowess of this or that deity. Suddenly the thinker glows with Athena's power of mind. Occasionally, for the gods are whimsical, they pick someone low in the pecking order of life to favor with a visit, and so some randomly skipping cosmic force did for me that day.

After the day of trial by combat, I had a new identity on the football team; I was reborn, though modestly enough. No one cut in front of me anymore in the line where we waited for the trainer, Pete McKusick, to tape us up. On the practice field I was no longer "Hey, Emunson" or "Hey, sixty" (my number that year) but Marco. The rogue seniors, the linemen with all the talent who had come back flabby, to be ignominiously benched, took me up. I became their surrogate weapon against the less gifted, sometimes brownnosing upstarts who'd taken their jobs. "Hit 'em wid da flipper, Marco," Frankie Donatello would holler in his mock North End accent (which was really a heightening of an authentic North End accent). Donatello weighed well over three bills and was the only one who could move the seven-man sled solo.

In the last game of my junior year, the game against Malden, I saw some genuine playing time. I went in at offensive guard, beside Steve O'Malley, who was our all-league tackle, by far the best football player on the team. On my first play, our quarterback

called a simple blast—halfback follows the blocking back—
through the hole between Steve and me. We trot to the line. Steve,
who has been playing both ways, offense and defense, for more
than three quarters now, is streaked with dirt, grass, and blood and
he is, to say the least, in a state. He is drunk with what the epic
poets like to call battle joy. As we crouch preliminary to taking our
stances, he stares at the linebacker and tackle across from us, grins
a broken-toothed grin, and screams, "Right here! The play's going
right here!"

He points to the hole where, in a moment, Phil Campesio will
come firing through, followed by Tony Eagan with the ball. I am up
against a first stringer in a real game that, give or take, is still at
issue, and O'Malley is telling them the plays! He turns in my direction and looks sheer death at me. As we come off the ball, I hear
a horrible noise, like a truck collision. It is O'Malley, pushing his
helmet under the defensive tackle's chin and making his face mask
and pads ring like iron. I'm on the linebacker. He throws me
down—he does have some advantage in this one—but I go to all
fours and crab-block him out of the play. Campesio goes through
untouched, headed for a very unlucky defensive back, and the ballcarrier follows—a pickup of a dozen yards. On God's verdant earth
there may have been people happier than I was then, but I could
not imagine who they were.

It is not a Christian game, football. It is not about following a list
of prohibitions, a decalogue. The game is about achievement, not
renunciation; you make the most of every chance, create chances
where you can. And honor is always won at the expense of others.
Before Achilles leaves for war, his father tells him, quite simply,
that he must strive to outdo everyone else in *any* activity he under-
takes. This way of life, the way of honor, is built on your own vision
of self and what you believe you owe it, and, second, on what oth-

ers on par with you think. By exercising his prowess, the warrior gains an enhanced fullness—his justly won pride expands, and expands him.

I can picture Steve O'Malley standing alone along the sidelines during one of his rare breathers. His arms are padded from top to bottom, and by mid-game the tape and bandages have begun to unravel and are smeared with the dreck of the field. From his left hand dangles his helmet, with its massive cage; it's embossed on either side with a red skull and crossbones, his rewards for ferocious play. His nose seems to have been repeatedly broken; at seventeen, he looks like a veteran of a dozen barroom brawls. His presence is so powerful that standing there, slouched insouciantly on the sidelines, rammed with the confidence that anything in the world that comes after him will not depart in one piece, he presents, at least to my sixteen-year-old self, a glowing and rather beautiful image. The circumference for about ten yards around him is his own space, alight with his dangerous aura. No one—not even the coaches—readily steps into it.

If you had asked, up until the afternoon of the great trial by combat, what was to become of me when I left high school, I would have shrugged and said I didn't know. ("I dunno.") But I had my fears on the matter, and they were dire enough. I pictured myself—and this is perhaps why the guidance counselor's lines hit a nerve—actually working for the city. In my thick glasses and green fatigues, I turned up daily to pick up trash from the roadsides or to empty barrels. I made a joke or two from time to time, but mostly I tried to avoid subtle humiliations, steer clear of major disgraces. After work I went home to TV, the Red Sox or the Patriots, a quart bottle of beer, my special chair, where I sat fat and lumpy and loaded, hating the hours. Maybe this was a dun basement apartment of my own; maybe it was in my parents' house. But it was death in life, as the poet Coleridge called a similar condition, brought on by opium withdrawal and failed imagination, and the thought of it kept me up at night.

But after that day, a day spent banging heads and being a grim blind-as-a-bat warrior under Mace Johnson's eye, the worst kinds of imaginings I had about the future receded a little. I thought that maybe there was hope for me, that rather than standing on the edge of things, I might enter into the game, such as it was, and not always go down. Life ahead may have looked harsh, but in some part of myself I was ready for that now. I had something in me as bad as most things out there, and that, oddly, was a comfort. I was not going to die stillborn. Though what sort of life I would have was still hard to describe. It was that feeling of hunger unslaked and with no object, but a hunger that now assumed a right to food, that made me good and ripped, if only internally, at the kind guidance counselor when she told me that Salem State was about as far as I was likely to go in the world. Before that day, when I'd tried by my lights to murder Tommy Sullivan, I would have bought it all and decided that State was surely the best I could do.

FOURTH QUARTER, final minutes. At this point hell, or your best high school conception of it, swallows you whole. The pain of leaping up and smacking the ground yet again brings you near to tears. You push and grind and pump, and suddenly there's the feeling of the captive dancing in chains, sensing that he'll never be free unless he so tortures his body that the right pain-conquering chemicals kick in and take over and the world disappears.

And now the coaches talk more forcefully, more fluently, risen as they are on the wings of our pain; they go on with epic panache about how, compared to what we'll face someday, this is nothing. Compared to the burdens we'll have to bear, this is just small potatoes. Not long ago, the United States Marines have gone nose to nose with the Viet Cong during the Tet offensive. A war is being waged, prisoners taken and prisoners shot. And we are the raw material that is now being processed for that war. We're being readied for a great jump into the dark. These are the best years of our lives. After this, the conflagration.

I once heard a pontificating expert deliver a derisive line about the American troops who went to fight in Vietnam. He said that their main preparation for the debacle was nothing more than high school football. High school football! And what poor chumps must they have been who went into the jungle with only that? High school football players, inept and maladroit and not ready for anything so bad as those heroic VC. Well, yes, I see what he meant. But a lot of those football players fought like Spartans, first for victory, then, years and resolution to win passing, for their lives and the lives of their friends. The war was the most appalling thing I ever encountered; it threw me out of love with America nearly for good. But I'd never say a dismissive word about the Americans who fought in it. I got ready with those kids for the same game. My ineptitude was theirs. (The fourth quarter, I can see, is almost over: The coaches are coming off their contact high, registering their impatience a little.)

For I was, even at best, going nowhere very special, and to have thrown myself into something and to have emptied myself to the bottom for it—well, football taught us that was not something to be sneered at. Or so I might have said then had I the words, as we began to walk, in tired World War II Sergeant Rock strides, off the practice field, across the running track, and into the Hormel Stadium locker room. There's a dignity in getting as bone-weary as we were then—a feeling akin to triumph, though it is not easy to explain.

But when I think about it, I remember many of the men my father's age, in their fifties, who came to his funeral. They were big; many were drink-ruined, with great hands and weary, weary expressions, as though they'd spent their lives rolling the boulder up an endless hill. They had done their work, laid concrete, driven the bus, dug the ditch, and now they were truly and honestly tired, tired and ready for the end. Uncomfortable, genuinely sorry, not knowing what to say, in their too-tight, once- or twice-worn Sears, Roebuck suits, they still exuded vast dignity. Working guys, from the beginning of life to the near end, they were pure proles, all class.

It was from this world—from their world and that of Mace Johnson and of football, and most of all from the world of my father—that Franklin Lears would wrest me away.

Chapter   Three

BLIND GIRL

Paul Revere rode through Medford, Massachusetts, on his famous midnight ride (on the eighteenth of April, in 'seventy-five),
immortalized in verse by my ancestor Henry Wadsworth Longfellow, onetime professor of modern languages at Harvard, who,
could he have visited Medford in the fall of 1969, might have been
surprised at how far his descendant had fallen. Revere, seeing the
two beacons burning in the Old North Church in Boston and so
knowing that the British were coming by sea, took off to spread
"his cry of alarm to every Middlesex village and farm," flying
through Medford ("it was twelve by the village clock, / When he
crossed the bridge into Medford town") on his way to Concord,
where the Revolutionary War would begin.

Medford wasn't entirely without distinctions beyond Revere's
ride. The great historian Francis Parkman spent summers there as
a boy, hiking, swimming, and canoeing in what was eventually to
become the Middlesex Fels Reservation. (My friends and I spent
many hours there drinking beer and dodging the MDC police. De-

pending on whom you asked, MDC meant Metropolitan District Commission or More Dumb Cops.) The great aviator Amelia Earhart lived in Medford for a while; when she came back from her transatlantic flight, the town held a parade, for which 20,000 turned out. Four were arrested for pickpocketing. It's said, too, that Medford was the site of the nation's first traffic light. More certain is the fact that Fannie Farmer wrote her cookbook while living in Medford and that "Jingle Bells," the Christmas song, was written there.

In the past, Medford had days of relative prosperity. During the eighteenth and nineteenth centuries it was a port town; ships were built there, and sailed in to dock on the Mystic River, which traverses Medford Square. (The city had relatively easy access to the local trading hub, Boston, eight miles away.) The most salient commodity in the town's commercial life then was Medford Old Rum, touted as "the best rum made in the States." The days of Medford Rum were the days of what historians refer to as "triangular trade": New Englanders, sometimes the descendants of the Puritans, traveled to the coast of Africa, where they exchanged simple manufactured goods for slaves. Then the slaves traversed the horrid Middle Passage to the West Indies, where they were in turn traded for the molasses that, in America, in Medford, was distilled into rum. Various citizens of Medford, some of them perhaps stern abolitionists—slavery was abolished in Medford in 1787—profited from this trade no end.

By 1969, Medford was a sad, somnolent working-class city of about 60,000. It was full of triple-decker houses, dreary, weed-grown parks, and an unremarkable square, which to me was principally defined by Brigham's ice cream parlor, Stag's pool hall, and Papa Gino's pizza joint. The majority of the population was Italian; there was an Irish constituency, along with a few Jews and, in West

Medford, where I lived, a black neighborhood. Though only a few miles from Boston and Cambridge, Medford was substantially another world. Many residents of Berkeley and Madison would have known more about the cultural life of Cambridge and Harvard than we, a twenty-minute drive away, did.

All these things Franklin Lears understood about Medford before he arrived. He had probably taken a driving tour or two through the town. He had no doubt read up on the city in one book or another, sitting at his ease in the great reading room at Harvard's Widener Library. But still, he would not really have gotten the flavor of the place, the high school in particular. You could stack up postcard visions and yellowing prose accounts forever and not convey the sense of what Medford, at least as I tasted it then, was all about.

One simple story tells more about the place than any exterior mapping could reveal. This is the Doober's story, not mine, and Dubby could at times be a little wayward with the truth. Life wouldn't always arch itself in quite the graceful parabolas that Dubby's imagination required. Sometimes life needed help. But he told this story so graphically, with such conviction, that I had to believe him. True or not, let it stand as a metaphor for all that was true for me about Medford High School, circa 1969.

THE DOOBER'S incident occurred in the New Corridor, where I had gone to see Mrs. Olmstead to learn that my prospects on planet Earth were less than modest and the place that, for whatever it may be worth, most often appears in my dreams when they go back to high school. Dubby was on the far end of this corridor, the bright passageway through the old, burned-out sector of the school. Up at the other end, he spotted a girl who was known to everyone not by anything so civilized as her name but simply as the Blind Girl.

She was, from all appearances, stone-blind, navigating the halls and classrooms of Medford High with a cane and, on occasion, a Seeing Eye dog. She'd been in my Latin class (first row, first seat) and she was quite a good student, though the voice in which she offered her translations seemed to come from beyond the grave, a softly wailing cry. The teacher coddled her in that class, and after a while she coddled me, too. The girl and I had something of a bond.

It was an advanced Latin class, featuring a year-long troop through Virgil's *Aeneid,* master poem of imperial triumph. I was, not uncharacteristically, one of the worst students there. I never brought the book home, never studied the stuff. When it was my turn to translate, I'd simply take a running whack at the text, making liberal use of English cognates and soundalikes and also of an overall sense of what was likely to happen next in the story. This I had acquired from my reading, somewhere around the age of eight, the Classic Comic Book versions of *The Iliad* and *The Odyssey,* the poems on which *The Aeneid* is based. Actually, that's putting it kindly: Virgil cribs outrageously from both. Thus there was some justice, as you'll see, to what was going on in the class. I generally got a B or a C in the translation sweepstakes. But overall I didn't acquit myself too badly, in part because I knew all the mythological references, based on an agreeably semi-pornographic illustrated book of Greek myths, which I'd also read when I was eight—my classical phase, you might call it. From time to time I would put the poor Latinist who taught us out of her misery by revealing, for about the ninth time, who Jupiter and Juno were.

But on this particular day the Latin matron, with her broom-straight backbone, detected something that made her frozen blood warm a little. It was maybe a rustling and a thrustling of papers under someone's desk, a muffled, clandestine sound of some kind. But then maybe she had been preparing for this Latin class shoot-out for a while.

She flung herself toward the miscreant's desk and at the same time shouted to all of us to keep quiet and not to move. We were to keep our hands in plain sight, on our desks. Cowboy TV junkie that I was, it sounded like a stickup to me. I raised both hands in the air. With her bony hand, she snatched something from off the desk, or perhaps from between the legs, of poor Betty Anders. It was a book, a paperback book. Was it possible that Betty was reading something in class, the way that she had read *Peyton Place* beneath her desk in ninth grade and been caught by Miss Tuttle? Miss Tuttle had crowed in rage at the "filth." (We were then studying *Hamlet*, that fount of purity; when it came to the business about "country matters," the territories between Ophelia's thighs, and other such things, we simply skipped past.)

The book Betty was perusing turned out to be not a porn classic but an English translation of Virgil—a trot, as they were called. As she snatched the offending volume, our Latin teacher, tall and white-haired and straight as a chessboard bishop, called out that all of us should now surrender our cheat sheets.

Around the room she trolled, looking for erring souls. And she made quite a haul. From between the knees and behind the propped-up books and under the notebooks of nearly every student in the class she pulled a translation of the famous poem. Some were books; others, on the desks of the more industrious, were translations copied out in careful longhand. Almost everyone in that small class was apprehended as a scapegrace. Among the few righteous ones were the Blind Girl and me—me not because I was so silver-sheened honest but because I simply didn't give a sufficient damn to figure out that this was the way to thrive and that, sitting in a middle row, in a very back seat, two seats deeper than my nearest neighbor on either side, I had never noticed the malfeasance. As to the Blind Girl, she was clearly innocent. Anyway, I felt a certain kinship with the Blind Girl. So what Dubby told me rang a somber bell; eventually it evoked the feeling of mortal kinship, the still sad music of humanity, as I'd later hear it called.

Anyway, here is the Doober's tale. On one end of the New Corridor, the pine-paneled and brightly lit passageway where I'd ducked into the guidance counselor's office, there is Dubby. He is late, per usual, for a dose of geometry (or *geometwy*, depending on your meanness quotient) from the teacher he's taken to calling the Waskally Wabbit—that is, Mr. Repucci.

Enter from the other side of the corridor the Blind Girl. According to Dubby—a footnote here—the Blind Girl was not born blind. One day she simply popped on the bathroom light and took a full look in the mirror and was struck by what appeared and, lo, could see nothing. Is this too mean to write? Too cruel? It is simply the common coin of high school, the last place where Darwinian laws apply without amendment. Think back to the worst thing you ever did or said in those precincts before moralizing too fervently.

The Blind Girl looked like the figure in Edvard Munch's much-reproduced painting *The Scream*. Her eyes were hollowed caves; her cheeks were indented. It was as though she'd fed on the winds. Her mouth stood open in a look of sorry expectancy: The worst might arrive at any minute. She had a ravaging case of acne. As she walked, she moaned quietly to herself, sometimes in ghostly melodies. She was a haunted being passing you by, a pained soul come back, Ancient Mariner–like, to tell you how it was with her and could readily be with you. But high school being what it was, no one much noticed or cared.

The Doober sees the Blind Girl, with her red-bottomed cane tapping her way down the New Corridor, where it is so bright that one almost feels it is stage-lit. But Dubby himself is in medieval darkness, waiting in the wings, for the areas that adjoin the corridor on either end are windowless. They're full of classrooms with thick, dungeonlike doors, which are now—Dubby is late for class—slapped shut.

Suddenly, behind the Blind Girl's subdued tap-tap, there rises up another pattern of sound, something aggressive and strong, summoning up the image of a well-engineered train, maybe, smacking its way down the track, very metallic, very sure. And soon there is a shape coming up fast behind the Blind Girl, who moves at an unvaryingly deliberate pace, making mystical-seeming half-circles over the floor with her cane.

He's gorgeous: Sicilian hair, blacker than Presley's dyed do ever was, slicked back in a phenomenally beautiful duck's ass, which he strokes compulsively. He wears skintight pants that ride about two inches above his black knifepoint shoes. He's decked in a jack shirt, a button-up that doesn't tuck in, with two buttons low down over the belt to hold it in place. It's trimmed with velvet, or velvet substitute, and purchased at (or boosted from) Medford's preeminent men's shop, Frank's, a place where I myself can afford nothing but the socks when they are on sale (three pairs for $2.50), though I often go to look in wonder at the shark-wear splendors on display.

Paulie Costello, for that is who Dubby sees, has the composed face of a Renaissance sculpture, calm, indifferent, masterly, without any sense of burden or strain. He walks, generally, as if he were on his way to a liaison with a Venetian countess, to whom he need bring no offering of flowers or verse, nothing but his own immaculate and stunning form.

Though Paulie is only a sophomore, he is a significant figure at

Stag's pool hall. He plays at table one, the best lit freshly velveted table close up to the cash register. There, he participates in a seemingly never ending game of "action" with Hank the Hat, skinny, ball-pounding, in tiny porkpie hat and spaghetti-strap T-shirt, and with a leopard tattooed on his thin but sinewy left arm—where the leopard's claws meet Hank's flesh are flecks of inky blood. There too is likely to be Steve "Porky" Parrotta, bull-like, looking like a longshoreman, with a crusty, forty-year-old's face, though he's only seventeen, whose uncle was a prizefighter, whose grandpa was a pool hustler, and whose father is in meat-packing and is so prosperous that he can give his boy a full-size pool table down in his basement.

Stag's was a male sanctum. One night Louis "Little Rudy" Valentino came running up Main Street, breathless with astound-ing news. Rudy had all the inflections of a street thug—*dis, dat, dese, dose*—but his voice was so sweet that if you were only listen-ing, not looking at him (he was thick-featured and wary), you swore you were encountering an angel who had somehow been shuffled early and unjustly into a boys' reformatory, where he learned his rough cadences.

"Mahhk! Mahhk!" Rudy was coming on at a run.

"Mahhk, you're not gonna believe this. There's girls in the pool-room [poo'room]."

The news was traveling out in every direction, like vibrations from the midst of a spider's web, and before long, guys from all over, from Brigham's and Papa Gino's and from down by the bridge, where they'd been emptying bottles of Bud, were flying downstairs into the sanctum. Stag, a fifty-year-old man with dense, white, well-tended hair, sat completely composed behind the desk, where he stored the balls and where the stud players kept their personal cues in a rack, as though all were fine and the world was not, effectively, cracking in the middle.

Stag had something of an urbane-thug style. One day, when I decided to forgo using a bridge and to climb up onto one of Stag's tables to sink a quick eight ball—it was an easy shot once you were in position, a tit shot, as they were called at Stag's; I can still hear the voice of poolroom denizen Oscar Venell screaming at top volume about an eight-ball shot that would have bolixed Minnesota Fats, "C'mon, get it over with, Mark. It's tit. Just a piece of tit"—and Stag saw me draped over his property, in danger of toppling it, or at least warping the precious slate, he purred into his microphone, "Mr. Edmundson, are you shitting me there on table six?"

Playing in proximity to Stag on table two were a couple of girls, seventeen years old, maybe eighteen. Neither played particularly well; neither had ever been seen in Medford before. By the time they were partway through their game—a pointer it was, as I recall: The first one to sink twenty-five balls wins—there were easily sixty guys surrounding them. And, odd as this sounds, we were quiet as a gang of church mice. We watched, and waited for someone to lead the way with a piece of rank invective. But no one did. The girls looked only at each other, playing as if we were not there. They finished their game, paid up, and walked out. For the rest of the evening, the poolroom was quiet; it was as though a religious shrine had been subtly desecrated. Something had perished, however temporarily—we weren't sure what—and we quietly played our games and mourned.

PAULIE, THE poolroom prince, came up to the Blind Girl, Dubby said, from behind, with his hands extended in front of him. There would be contact, no doubt about it, but Paulie, a Me'ford poo'-room Brahmin, was about to finger an untouchable, so the less actual touching the better. She had cooties—the high school and elementary school term for the age-old religious notion of the un-clean, the polluted.

According to Dubby, the Blind Girl was in a state of agitation. What could it be, she must have wondered, all metal and strut, that was pursuing her down the hall? She was clearly terrified. For his own part, the Doober froze where he stood, in the dark.

So she begins to move faster, accelerating, her eyes blinking. But Paulie is too quick. He comes up on her like a sleek pirate ship bearing down on a heavy frigate. When he gets directly behind her, he pauses to savor the moment, then he grasps her around the waist with both hands and he spins her around. Up in the air her cane flies. Her mouth opens further but emits no sound; her feet begin scrambling over each other. Fighting, fighting, she tries to hold on to her balance.

She's nearly sent to the floor, but with the greatest effort—huffing and puffing and pulling and grasping out and a lucky catch at the glowing pine wall—she manages to hang on and stay up-right. By the time this whole stumbling movement is over and she is safe, Paulie is halfway down the corridor. According to Dubby, he is whistling. He is, Dubby says, whistling a song by the Buck-inghams, a lucky-day no-flies-on-me number, with a line that runs, "My baby is made outta love / Like one of them bunnies outta the Playboy Club."

Dubby steps into the corridor and *now* Paulie sees him. Paulie sees Dubby—it is crucial to point this out, and Dubby swears it—*for the first time.* Paulie had obviously imagined he was alone in the corridor with the Blind Girl. Paulie of the Michelangelic counte-nance clearly had not done this to show off to the Doober or to anyone else. He was not an insecure boy set on making a name for himself. He wasn't out to add to his reputation for outrageous be-havior, Dubby was sure. On the contrary, this spinaround had been done strictly for his own amusement, his personal diversion. He did it on a whim. Paulie was fucking around in earnest and he was doing it with an eye toward entertaining no one but himself.

When he saw Dubby—who was probably a better pool player than Paulie, but without style, wearing, as he did, cockeyed glasses and sometimes a crazy beach cap when he played—he simply nodded and inquired whether the Doober would be in attendance that afternoon at Stag's, as though it were some sort of salon. Maybe Paulie was going out of his way a little from guilt, since Dubby did not, in general, merit a word. But Dubby thought not. As Dubby recounted it to me, the whole action had been, for Paulie, simple, natural, and about as morally freighted as spitting your gum out when it turned gray.

How did I react to the story when Dubby laid it out, pausing over every nasty detail? Some unpleasant candor is necessary here, I'm afraid. On first hearing the tale, I was shocked by it, no doubt about that. I felt that Paulie's caper was horrible; he'd crossed a line. But to be dead honest, I also took some satisfaction from the tale. I felt vaguely proud to be ensconced in a place, Medford High, that was conducive to something like this. It was the same sort of pride, perhaps, that certain felons feel when they're in one of the worst lockups in the federal system and are contemplating one or another atrocity that's gone down there.

Frank Lears had not yet arrived at our school at the time of the incident, and Dubby, as far as I know, never told him the story. Probably the newly arriving Lears would have thought of the event simply as an aberration, not the key to Medford High protocols that I knew it to be. He would have sighed and swung his hand and looked sorrowfully at the *Monitor* and the *Merrimack*. But it would have been a mistake not to find instruction here rather than in whatever reading he might have done about Medford and environs. Much is published, as his idol Thoreau said, but little printed.

FOR THE next couple of months, Franklin Lears was, to us, his enlightened philosophy students, something like the Blind Girl: We tried to spin him around.

It came naturally. He was, after all, a weird little dude. He did peculiar things. For instance, when we came into class at the end of the first week, on Friday, we found that he had reconfigured the room. The chairs were now arranged in an oval, a rather ragged one at that. We entered uncertainly, with double our usual reluctance, loitering and yacking and moving unsteadily forward, as if we were being herded in by an invisible and singularly inept shepherd, whom we obeyed out of noble boredom. What we saw was truly a puzzle.

Now of course matters are much different. Any classroom discussion that *does not* begin with everyone in a circle, Iroquois-style, is antediluvian. But at the time, this was unheard of, a true innovation: The possibility of moving the desks from out of their military rows had never crossed my mind.

The weirdest thing was that Lears was himself sitting down in one of the pathetic little chairs, just like ours, with the straight back and the writing arm attached. They resembled devices for some sort of Puritan punishment, these chairs. You looked for holes to stick your thumbs through. It was as though the students were being humiliated by being put into the tiny seats they had occupied when they were ten or eleven years old. Small as he was, even Lears looked absurdly large for his.

But there he was, sitting in an undistinguished place in the oval, not, as one might expect, close to the provision station and authority source of his desk. He was floating out at sea, in his sad-sack suit, with his head tipped down, studying the Durant book.

We all sat down. The Doober—never at a loss—got a routine going. He pulled his glasses from his pocket, squashed them haphazardly onto his face, slapped open his book, whipped a pen (unchewed) from out of his pocket, and began to parody a devoted scholar at work, began, if you were at all discerning about it, to parody Lears. Dubby went at the Durant book with his pen. He was writing in the text. He'd noticed that Lears had written things in his book. Why not the Dub? But if what Lears did when he wrote was to leave illuminating marginalia on the white edges, Dubby had a different end in mind. He began coloring in the o's in his book. There are a lot of o's on a page; in a book, there are numberless numbers. Dubby had a good deal of work to do.

The process was, for Dubby, relatively subtle. What was going to make it funny would be his sheer persistence. Dubby, as I readily understood it, planned to be doing this every day, with only an occasional break for, maybe, a glance up someone's skirt or a sneer for pillish Jean Delmire, and for the rest of the year. This was going to be the content of a course in philosophy, the love of wisdom, for one Donald O'Day—sent, as we all are, weeping into the world, searching for succor or the right road—the regimented, ceaseless coloring in of o's in a textbook.

With the class reconfigured and the Doob at work, Frank Lears initiated a discussion about Plato. His method was to bring up one idea after another from Plato's work, or from Durant's digest of it, then ask us what we made of it. That day, as I recall, he talked to us about Plato's doctrine of the tripartite soul. He said he wanted to remind us of this rather beautiful vision from Plato, who had imagined the soul as a thing prone to the most horrible servitude. For the soul, Plato and Lears told us, was easily overmastered by passion; it then became like a chariot where the horses took over and pulled the poor rider wherever they wished him to go—often into error, humiliation, and grief.

But the good news was that the soul could escape this fate. Reason could assert itself against the passions. It could take its rightful supremacy and direct the appetites to moderation and urge the passions for violence and glory into their proper channels. By calming down, by living moderately, we could be saved from the only true enemy anyone has in this world, which is none other than oneself. For, as Plato insists, you can never do harm to a just man. It was on this point that Lears ended. You could never hurt someone whose soul was truly in order, because the only genuine and lasting pain there is in life is to suffer an ill-governed, turbulent soul.

And so, according to Plato, it is always better to receive harm than to do it. Because hurting someone means giving in to your passions, to anger or the urge for revenge, to the desire for glory (Plato is writing here against Homer and his war-thirsty heroes). And as to being harmed, well, if the soul is truly balanced, that simply won't happen in any long-term way. The well-tempered soul knows how to deal with the loss of money and estates, the death of a friend, the prospect of dying. The just soul, knocked off center, recovers and rebalances itself.

It was likely that no one had read the book, and that if anyone had, he or she had probably understood barely a word. In fact Lears' digest of Plato was at least partly opaque to just about all of us.

And the way he delivered it! He spoke in this queer, overrefined voice, a lilting, sweet tone that no self-respecting male would ever assume unless he were mimicking a woman or a fag. All this refinement, all this highly articulate business—sculpted sentences, architectonic verbal constructions, replete with words so remote and difficult that he might, at times, have been talking in another language: It was maddening. We phased back what little amperage we were putting out. A circle-wide brownout began. We folded ourselves into our standard schoolroom states, waking sleep, death-in-life.

But despite the almost mannered eloquence, it's clear that this idea matters to Lears. As he talks, he's entering further and further into Plato's thinking, maybe without fully knowing it. This business about not doing harm, about preferring to be harmed even, moves him. He's not near tears about it or anything. It's simply clear from his voice that he's touched.

Tommy Buller apparently senses this, and wakes up. Buller, in his own brass heart, was the troll king—a being who dwelled at all times deep in the earth and who, in the farthest reaches of sediment and sludge and rock, found his truth. He wrinkled up his prematurely aged face and rubbed his callused hands together and pulled at his ear, then cleared his throat, a sound in which you heard great digging implements laboring away far underground.

"Wellllll." Buller yawned the first word. Buller's opening words tended to be yawns, irritated yawns, as though you'd just woken him up from some highly nutritive, long-lasting dragon-sleep. He had the presence of someone who worked nights and who used the daylight hours to try to grab the requisite zzzz's. "The thing is, that's a stupid idea. I mean, if somebody burns your house and kills your family, then they can't hurt you because your soul is in the right order? That's dumb. But I'm not surprised. This Plato is an idiot, basically."

Had Buller somehow discerned Lears' investment in the idea? Is that part of what made him so rabid? I suspect so. A teacher, from the moment he appears in a classroom, has to understand that he brings more than his own character with him. He is himself and more than himself. For in the student's mind, the teacher summons up, as if by some quotidian magic, the image of every figure who has ever presented himself as an authority. Frank Lears was not only Frank Lears but, to each one of us, also the whole concatenation of mentors and bullies and bosses and guides, tormentors and pseudo-angels, who'd made an imprint on us thus far in life. We not only reacted to him, we reacted to some archetypal form of authority that lived in the farther reaches of each of us.

And if the teacher awakens images of tyrants past—and for Tommy Buller, most of the authorities past were probably tyrants—then there is nothing to do but attack, try to get some of your own back. In every early encounter between a teacher and a student there are multiple beings present, multiple ghosts, many of them not beneficent.

Great teachers react differently to this fact of pedagogical life. Some of them never show their hand. They always turn the question back on the student. They never declare themselves. This is the way of Socrates, as it is of the expert therapist (Socrates is, among many other things, the first deep analyst of the psyche, the spirit), who functions as a mirror, always showing the patient her own reflection back. But there is another way of proceeding too, and it can be no less transforming. That is to expose oneself fully as a teacher, to be receptive to everything, every resentment, fantasy, affection, and hatred the student brings forward. And once those passions are alive, once they are in play, then let the student use them as energy for intellectual inquiry and thence for change. Such teachers are human incandescences—they have ideas, then the ideas have them; they promulgate theories, they burn brilliantly with them, and they are always, always right. They create disciples, smaller versions of themselves. They found schools. Freud was such a teacher. So was Plato. So, in his way, was Jesus.

What Socrates wants is rather different. Socrates wants you to know yourself and to become yourself, to pursue the good as it's in your particular nature to realize it. So Socrates is very reluctant about voicing an opinion. His method is irony, questioning, hanging around, and being annoying. Lears, who was made for the Socratic mode, had just screwed up. He'd just laid his cards on the table and Buller had attacked. Lears was a beginner. He didn't quite have the moves down.

Lears gives a softly regretful look and swings his right wrist, which rests on his thigh, as though he's practicing his baseball card toss. I grew up flipping cards in games like farsies (furthest card wins), topsies (put one card atop another and win the pot; edgies don't count), and leansies (knock down a card propped against a concrete wall and take the lot), so I knew the motion. Unlike many of his movements, this one is not tentative; it's his standard nervous tic: He works at it all the time and has grown very adept.

Then comes Lears' interjection, which is one of his classroom mantras: "Well all right, Thomas. What do others think? What do people think?"

What do people think? He says it all the time. The phrase has circulated through the first week's class meetings, generally in the manner of a worthless coin, a counterfeit. Because, quite candidly, people don't think. No, thanks. No one but Sandra does the reading assignments. No one, except maybe Sandra, could understand more than the rudiments of the rather elementary Durant text. We sit there like deaf, dumb, and blind kids. We know nothing and couldn't care less. We're dwelling in Plato's cave, where people, chained in servile rows, see only imitations of imitations of life and never know enough to pine for the real thing, for Truth and

Beauty. We loved the show in the cave. In fact, we wanted it displaced further, made more illusory. Give us some TV, a movie—a film strip if that's all you can muster. Get us three removes from the real rather than the customary, disconcerting two.

If Lears' head had burst into flames, alight with inspiration, we would have sat like painted clay figures waiting for the clock to jump and for the bell to ring so that we could get back to homeroom (Lears' was our last class of the day), then out into the street, where we could talk about football and beer and proms and skirts and legs and money and pool, and where life could be reignited in earnest.

So we sit, thick and dim, in the circle where Lears can see us all and where it feels strange, as though some sort of ritual is supposed to happen. When Lears turns away for something or stares down into his book, some of us come to life, the way the toys— especially the malicious toys—are supposed to do on Christmas Eve after the family has gone to bed. We throw paper balls, poke and pinch each other, crack jokes, run small-time riot, until he looks up again. Then we return to our poses, stolid and uniform as a bunch of bowling pins. We dare the sage to knock us down, even to move us around a little bit.

There are two exceptions to this rule of dead silence. One is Tommy Buller, who talks frequently, often without invitation, to say how stupid and wasteful and tedious whatever Lears is going on about truly is. He is tremendously, spectacularly rude, like a cross between Jimmy Hoffa and Nikita Khrushchev. It was easy to imagine Tommy reaching down to pull off one of his shoes, letting loose the tattery argyle's overpowering stench, then slamming the desk a few times for order. He never did the reading; he barely knew what Lears was talking about. But Buller was one of the two most engaged students in the class.

As to the rest of us, we thought Buller was very, very funny. We'd crack up when he issued his Khrushchev ultimatums to Lears. He was a grotesque, greasy clown, to be sure, but he was doing our business for us. Rick Cirone, sitting judge of relative cool in the classroom, would smile a knowing smile, looking bemused and mildly disgusted, and speed up his production of "Wipe Out," played with hyperactive drumming index and middle fingers on the writing arm of the chair, when Buller popped off.

The other exception to the talking-in-class embargo, the thinking embargo, with which we hope to starve Frank Lears into some kind of submission, is Sandra Steinman, the hippie girl. Sandra comes to class prepared. She actually reads the book in a more than cursory way. And, give or take, she knows what's going on there.

Buller clearly hates her. My guess is that he has associated her from the start with everything that makes him quake internally—with money, with status, with intelligence, with bourgeois living rooms, where the couch is a work of art and the curtains are gripped back from the picture window by elegant cloth drape holders with mock-gold pins to secure them in place. But mostly, I think, he hates Sandra because she is associated with something he has heard about on TV—with hippies, and with a particularly noxious branch of hippiedom, something then called women's lib.

For though existentially, for want of a better word, we are buried deep in Middle America—where Sunbeam bread rules and Dad soaps the car luxuriously on Saturday before heading out to get loaded and run riot with the boys, forty-plus in age that night—we are also living in Greater Boston, not far from the Boston Common, which the summer before was colonized by the hippies. They came to Boston in unwashed multitudes, like the early Christians, to hang out and to display themselves. We saw them on the channel 4 news all summer. Almost no one from Medford actually goes into Boston, unless it is to visit a doctor or go to court; TV has to do.

And there they were, the hippies, smoking dope on the sly and giving each other weary, theatrical hugs, consoling hugs, as though someone had just died, and wearing their love beads and head scarves and sandals, doing a broke-Gypsy routine, even though we knew that they were all rich as can be. They turned the Common into a kind of lazy utopia, and no one could figure out how to kick them off. The household fathers went into a rage when the hippies appeared on the screen. They hollered out to them to get a job, to cut their hair, to go home to Wellesley, to cut the shit. My father, who was nonplussed when the sons of the doctor who used to live across the street from us in Malden returned from college and started going around barefoot on their front lawn—barefoot in Malden, Massachusetts!—was, to say the least, agitated by the invaders. He was not talking about a National Guard action or a vigilante assault as some other dads were, but he was surely not pleased.

And Sandra, it's pretty clear, has spent time with the Gypsy hordes. She walks differently than she used to, and than anyone else at the high school does. She has a dreamy, otherworldly sway to her approach, as though she's in a mild trance, on a ship maybe, sailing somewhere delicious, guided by perfumed winds. Her movements are slow and deliberate in their grace. She is always smiling a little bit and ready to expand slowly—not burst—into a larger, more embracing smile. She may or may not be literally stoned. But her ethos, the Boston Common ethos, is to go around cloud-walking, looking stoned whether you are or not.

She is also highly intelligent. She's articulate, modest, goes back and forth with Lears in an easy, often humorous way, simply not caring that the rest of us are enraged at her for breaking rank.

Sandra, from what I can gather, thinks Tommy Buller is a deeply annoying person but not past salvation. And by making the dismissive remark about Plato, he's put himself in the way for what might actually be an edifying exchange.

She does not look Buller in the eye. Locking eyes with Tommy is not a wise course. Sandra is no paragon of street smarts, but she does live in Me'ford. To make contact with opposition, even if not bodily opposition, if only the opposition of one psyche to another, might send Buller into a full-blown rage. The idea of such opposition coming from a female could make him combust spontaneously. He is a seriously pissed-off individual. So Sandra, her eyes down on her book, takes the Platonic-Buddhist line and runs with it.

She says that if you hurt someone, it throws you into disorder. The uglier passions triumph over the better parts, and once they've tasted this kind of triumph, it'll happen again and again. You'll start out hurting people and things you think you hate, and before long you'll be hurting things that are close to you, things you love. Because every faculty wants to dominate the others. Only reason knows how to dominate without suppression, stay on top without crushing the other desires.

She repeats herself (and Plato): "If you hurt others, you'll end up ruining yourself. It's always better to receive an injury than it is to do one."

To which Tommy mutters simply: "Bullshit."

And in my heart, if that is the place where such things occur, I all but second his response. On the football field, you have to deliver the first blow. You have to establish mastery, rob your opponent of his confidence, then ruin him if you can. Throw him down, send his helmet bouncing like a lopped head across the lovely grass. The latter-day Homeric warrior, the one who can hold his own with Tommy Sullivan or with Frank Ball—or with Le Duc

Thanh, who is practicing busily, getting ready for us with twenty-cent shoes made from castaway tire rubber and a thousand-dollar rifle—believes that after a line has been drawn, harm's got to be done. So I side with Buller. But.

But there is this. Walking to a class a few days later, I see Sandra sitting on the top step of a flight of stairs, looking into a book. I climb to a step or two from where she's perched, and she looks up and smiles sweetly, with unaffected, nonflirtatious goodwill. "Hi, Mark," she says. "What did you think of class the other day?"

I cannot answer. She is simply too much for me, in her work boots and her man's shirt and her sitting where people are not supposed to sit, damnit. And she is asking me an inane question, asking me to take school seriously. I cannot do it. I cannot answer her. I don't even shrug. I simply pretend that she is not there, and I walk on.

And I am aware enough to know that I have done her harm, have snubbed her—this good-humored, smart, and, most of all, kindly girl whom no one will talk to, whom nearly everyone writes off as absurd. She is against the war, and I am for it. She is a hippie; I am from Medford. (Which is no small distinction: A friend who lives down the block is picked up hitchhiking, and after a ten-minute conversation, the driver asks him if he might not by chance be from Medford. "How did you know?" "I'm not sure. I think it was the way you said 'mother.' ") Given the chance, I do Sandra harm. And for the rest of the day and for the week to follow, thanks to her and to Plato and to Frank Lears, I smart for it. And the truth is I would rather—far rather—that someone had treated me so. At least then I would not have to go around thinking myself a mean lout.

It's better to receive harm than to do it. It is very hard to get this idiotic idea out of my mind once it's lodged there. (But I will succeed eventually—I am determined to.) It is better to be Sandra, roundly humiliated, than to be me, the executor of the snub; better to be the Blind Girl that Paulie spins than to be prince of the poolroom; it's better to be Franklin Lears, despised by your students, than to be one of the circle of kids, one of the knowing herd with its designated scapegoats. Very peculiar this notion, very strange. It lives for a while in me—it does—but then, wise Medford kid that I am, I will, as they say at the poolroom, smarten the fuck up. I will cast the thought, knowingly, away.

Chapter Four

MY FATHER,

FRANK LEARS, TV, ME

About two months into the class, late October or thereabouts, a couple of odd things happened. The first was that my father, who never exhibited curiosity about much of anything, began to take a pronounced interest in Frank Lears and the philosophy class. The second was that we—me and Rick and Dubby and John Vincents, my pals in the course—began imitating Lears, mimicking his speech and gestures and doing it in ways that were, to say the least, peculiar.

The day when the imitation thing got into gear Tommy Buller was in a particularly foul mood, straining hard on his chain. We had begun the sitting-in-a-circle business sometime before, but whenever we entered the classroom we would feign forgetfulness about the new design and plunk down in the established rows. (Apparently, the prior class—whether it was Lears' or not I can't say—used the old detention pattern.) So we did on this particular day, not giving Lears the satisfaction of showing that we understood, much less welcomed, the teaching innovation he had cooked up for us.

It was a hot autumn day, and Lears, as I recall, was wearing an off-off-white rumpled suit, a size or two large as usual, and looking, particularly if you could have added a Panama hat, like a planter who had recently lost the plantation. He told us, wearily, to form a circle. Most of us sat still. We generally wanted to compel teachers to use the maximum force to get us to do anything, no matter how minor. But to Dubby and to John Vincents—a soccer and track star whom Dubby had nicknamed the Navajo, because his family once turned up at a soccer game wrapped in blankets— this was an opportunity. They began sliding their desks into each other, banging and ricocheting away so as to approximate the pleasures of a well-loved Revere Beach attraction, the bumper cars. Donald Bellmer, the reedy, pale kid Dubby had bopped with spitballs on the first day, joined tentatively in, and the Doober, seeing an opportunity, slammed him as hard as possible.

"Owwwww!" Bellmer cries, his blanched face going into a pained mask. We all watch and giggle. No one else moves.

So Lears, in a rare burst of physical action, a rare burst of motion that does not savor of the workings of a man in his fifth decade rather than at the start of his third, takes action. He delivers himself to the back of my chair, grasps it from behind, and leans away, so that he looks like a driver pulling back to balance a team of sled dogs. Then he gets his feet—the *Monitor* and the *Merrimack*— moving sloppily, haphazardly, and the chair begins to slide backward. I weigh about 190 pounds. On the football program, I'm listed at two hundred, having included the weight of my pads (wrongly, Jackie Lane, the only black kid on the team, has told me; we've argued the point no end, like a couple of Aquinian scholastics). Lears puffs and huffs theatrically.

"That's a lot of weight you're pulling there," says Rick Cirone. "He plays defensive tackle. Very hard to move."

I mumble something about playing lately with singular lack of

success. It's true. Despite the pronouncements about all my promise made at the end of last year by Mace Johnson—and even, with
some equivocation thrown in, by Rourke, who perhaps comes to
think I have better genes than were initially apparent—and despite
a murderous program of summer weight lifting, I've been relegated
to the position of all-purpose backup lineman, popping in and out
(much more out than in) of the games. I'm enraged. How could
this be?

Without my glasses, I could discern only glowing blurs flying here and there on the field. Every play, I would fire forward
and smack one of these blurs. Sometimes the blur would prove to
have the ball, sometimes not. My drawback had come clear to the
coaches one day in practice when, in a tackling drill, one on one, I
rampaged completely past the guy with the ball. Manly chuckles
all around. The next play, I locked the ballcarrier in the radar and
hit him so hard that it was truly surprising to see him rise again.
He walked around for five minutes like a man feeling out the effects of his new frontal lobotomy. But the damage was done. Football is not blindman's buff, or shouldn't be. One kid on the team,
Pooch, dubbed me a future all-pro blindbacker. My career was finished unless I could somehow afford contact lenses, to say nothing
of figuring out that I needed those rare and pricey objects.

On being told that my football hopes were in a state of ruin,
Lears simply said: "Still, I wouldn't want to run into you in a dark
alley." This was mockery. At least I was pretty sure it was. He had
been no less dismissive on seeing my copy of *Instant Replay: The
Green Bay Diary of Jerry Kramer,* by the Packers' formidable offensive guard. I had gotten the book free with a razor and shaving
cream. The most affecting passage in the book, at least as I saw it,
was the one where Kramer described himself as having lost a little
of his stature, maybe as much as an inch, from the beginning of his

pro career to the end. The shrinkage was the result of his neck being slammed back into his shoulders with repeated hits, so that his vertebrae contracted. I found the dedication that would result in this kind of thing very moving.

When Lears saw *Green Bay Diary* on top of my copy of Will Durant, instead of praising me for reading something, anything, he had simply said, "Are there pictures? I'm sure there are some pictures."

This was ridicule, to be sure. Had Lears aimed with a degree or two more subtlety, he would have missed me entirely. Henry James would have had no hope with us. We would have flummoxed the Master entirely. But to be chided in terms even as subtle as Lears' was a great novelty to me, who was accustomed to imprecations out of Bedlam from coaches and friends' fathers and neighborhood bullies and from other demented males of every description.

The little metaphysician took his seat and began to work away at the resisting stuff in front of him. He read aloud from the Durant script, he paraphrased, he tried to provoke. But nothing happened. Sandra was sleepy that day. The only one awake on the scene was Buller, who raised his hand and tried to get Lears to recognize him. But Lears, no doubt wanting to avoid a Buller collision, looked away. Finally Buller dissolved the protocols and began to harangue Lears. It was nonsense, idiocy, crap. He, Tommy Buller, had had enough.

"Ah, Thomas," said Lears, hand-swinging, head-nodding. "That doesn't seem at all germane to the question at hand." Germane! What the hell was *Germane*? A form of German? *German* as pronounced at Harvard?

As Lears talked, Dubby and Rick began routines, hand-swinging, head-wagging, tongue-tsking in Lears' peculiar way, and laughing at themselves, and at Lears, who was invited, of course, to look over and to observe, then to make of it what he would. If he saw, Lears was too shrewd to take the bait.

But this began the period of intense Franklin Lears imitations. I had one, Dubby and Rick did, John Vincents would do it, and so, ineptly, humanely, would Cap, who hadn't enough meanness in him to mock anyone with much success. A couple of modes of imitation were ascendant. In one of them, we would kick off with a Lears standard ("What do people think?" being the most common), and then go stumbling into Lears-like polysyllabics, as though we were learning incantations from a wizard: "Oh, Thomas, you have to consider the prosaic, propinquitous passions of Plato." And, to be fair, Lears *was* singularly attracted to enormous words. He remains the only human being I have heard use the word *propinquitous* in conversation. Rick wanted to buy him a pair of propinquities for Christmas.

But we had another mode of imitation, too, and this one at first seems weird beyond explanation. What we would do was to locate a subtext in Lears' polished, detached utterances. "Thomas, I think you ought to reconsider some of the premises of your argument" would become "Buller, you moron, why don't you go home and suck on the tailpipe of your old man's car until you perish, you piece of shit." That sort of thing. Or, from Dubby, doing Lears addressing the whole class: "You idiotic brutes, why don't you all just go screw yourself rectally right now?" All performed in the soft, lilting Learsese.

What were we doing? Maybe we were bringing him down to our level. Perhaps we needed to believe that this person, who seemed so markedly odd, was in no way different from us. We thought and spoke in the most vulgar ways—and perhaps underneath that's what Lears truly wanted to do. Maybe it was only his repressed high-class manners that inhibited him. Accordingly, we were better than he was, more honest, truer to the brutish human base.

But there was another possibility, too. Perhaps we were, in our bent way, identifying something we all felt but could not have expressed. We were conveying a simple fact: Lears obviously had a healthy dose of confidence. On some level, we sensed, he held us in contempt. There *was* a measure of derision there. He must have thought we were minor-league fools for not using this, our last chance before we were thrust live and whole into what was waiting for us. We had a final opportunity to think a little, to stand back and make assessments, before the powers in charge peeled back the lid of our tiny tin box of a school to pluck some for the factory, some for the office, some for the army, some for booze, some for dope. So with this odd mockery, odd imitation, we brought forward that part of Lears that was quietly at war with us.

This sort of derision was not absent from Socrates, either. Socrates "asked [his pupils] to open their souls to him," says the philosopher Alexander Nehamas, "and let them know he did not like what he saw. He did not so much reveal to them their dark, shameful underside as refuse to accept their surface as his own, as a mode of life he could follow. He needed courage not only because he made his contemporaries face some difficult truths but mostly because he displayed his own disdain toward them."

We were used to encountering teachers so shelled-out that they did not care one way or another how it went, or teachers who terrified us or whom we terrified. But to find someone who was actually engaged but wasn't there to curry our favor, who felt himself to be better than we were, or at least further along the road, and believed that we were lucky to have him—this was strange.

Surely, too, our imitations, which we began to perform everywhere—on the bus, in other classes, even a few times at football practice—meant that we wanted Lears to be present even when he wasn't physically on the scene. We wanted him on hand, to scrutinize and ponder. Somehow he'd colonized us, gotten inside our heads, and we didn't even realize it.

AT MY house, too, Lears was becoming a presence. My father began taking an interest. I believe it was the business about TV that got him going.

This interest of my father's in what was happening at school was, to put it mildly, unusual. My father was capable of driving his car, always a large one, a heavy-deco American whale, at least ten years beyond its Detroit vintage, past a scowling brick structure, constructed firm and fast lest the British make one more attempt on the old colony, and asking, in all innocence, what that particular building might be. On being told that the place was my school, or my brother Philip's, he would grunt, inhale noisily through the resounding caves of his crooked nostrils (he had a radically deviated septum), puff on his omnipresent Camel (his "coffin nail"/ "coughin' nail"), and file the information distantly away.

The only pre-Lears exception to this policy of school nonawareness came when I was in the eighth grade and struggling to learn French. Things got so bad that my father was summoned on the scene to talk. My teacher was named Miss Finkelman. Miss Finkelman was an enormous young woman who came at you like a large, heavily turned out vacation liner, someplace where they serve lunch nine times a day and irony is forbidden. She had yelping dyed-blond hair, great painted lips that bespoke prodigious oral interests, bulging eyes, de Gaulle's Gallic honker, and a gregarious, good-humored way of taking up the room.

We had nicknamed her Skater. Why? Because Finkelman gives

you *fink,* which gives you *rink,* which yields *skater.* Get it? That we had done no worse suggests in what general affection, or at least in what absence of blood hatred, she was held. And the temptation to flay her was considerable: This was during the time when Ed "Big Daddy" Roth, the dragster impresario, was making automotive hay with a car called the Rat Fink.

Anyhow, Miss Finkelman relayed to my parents the not inaccurate view that I was failing French because I never did any of the assignments and spent all of my time in class dreaming of she knew not what. My father was generally a proponent of fate: You got what you got in life, and that was that. One of his pet sayings was "You can never win," often said with considerable relish, as though he were secretly aligned with the forces in the universe that kept everyone, himself included, separate from victory. But this time, he claimed, he helped me out. He persuaded Miss Finkelman to relent and give me a D, a stigma, a sign of possible stupidity, but not a hold-'im-back-till-he-towers-like-Gulliver-over-the-class F.

My father was somehow charmed by Miss Finkelman, who was not the dully throat-sticking sort of pill the rest of my teachers seemed to him to be. He asked about Miss Finkelman from time to time, even when I was years beyond her class, had quit French, and had gone on to study Latin, a subject in which I could sustain consistent mediocrity without doing the homework.

(When I was in graduate school at Yale, I, braced by two years of college French and a visceral terror of having to pass the language requirement by studying *Beowulf* in Old English, signed up for a French literary theory course with the formidable Paul de Man. De Man was at the height of his reputation at the time. He and Jacques Derrida were the godfathers of deconstruction, which few academics could readily explain but was burning a hot path through American-literature departments nonetheless. De Man's early Nazi affiliations had yet to be revealed. When my father heard that I was taking French again, he slapped himself on the forehead and sighed. "Am I going to have to come down to New Haven and talk to this de Man guy the way I did Miss Finkelman?" An encounter I would like to have caught.)

Anyway, Miss Finkelman aside, my father generally took about as much interest in my education as he did in avant-garde painting and Husserlian phenomenology. But then Frank Lears came along and about his tendencies, tastes, and quirks my father, who was usually curious about nothing—for to be curious indicated that one was not omniscient, and every adult male of my father's generation seems at least to have toyed with the omniscience possibility—couldn't hear enough. The business about television started things off.

One day in class, Lears suggested to us, smoothly, in an indirect kind of way, a conversational wrist shot, that he had no television. We had become, without quite knowing it, students of Lears' personality, if only (we imagined) to use the information we collected the better to mock him. And, strategically or not, he was chary of giving out much by way of personal data. You had to keep your ears open, because a good deal was to be found in the intonation. This intonation business was very non-Medford. Medford spoke in one tone of voice—loud, assertive, fragrant, obscene. The intonation thing, the irony thing, suggested a combination of worldliness and modesty, and would eventually make the Medford yawp sound almost frightened, a way of worrying about what might be said in reply and an effort to shut off all replies, or rebuttals, including your own.

This time, Lears' intonation gave us to understand that he suspected that anyone who enjoyed watching the tube probably had suffered a touch of early brain damage, a quick drop and pickup from off the gray kitchen linoleum.

"Don't you even watch it for the news?" Nora Balakian had asked.

"You can read the newspaper," Lears said. "You can read the *Times.*" We were encountering someone, maybe for the first time, who was not immersed in the world of TV.

To all of us, TV was something like a third parent. We had grown up with it. At my house, the first person up on any given morning flipped on the set, which stood dead-center in our upstairs-apartment living room, and the magic box hummed, hollered, sang, wept, flattered, and cajoled all day and well into the night, often with one or two or three or four of us there gazing, but often not. Often the TV sounded and flashed away to an audience of no one in particular. Did the cave dwellers extinguish their communal fire when they weren't actually warming their hands in front of it? Then why should we flip off the box when we weren't actually watching?

"Mr. Lears hasn't got a TV," I announced one night to my father, pretty much out of the blue.

"Why not?" Then, adding a kick, because my father usually adds a kick when he can, even if it isn't well aimed or adroitly delivered: "Can't he afford one?"

Was this a probe on my part? Was it an unguided missile of resentment sent off toward my father to see what would happen? For my father loved TV. He also hated it, dearly.

I can see him still, standing in front of the television set, fresh from his shower, with a threadbare red bath towel cinched around his waist, his belly distended, statesman-style. Though his waist is thick, the rest of his body is very thin—sticklike, birdy legs; small, delicately boned arms. I have been able to beat him at arm wrestling since the sixth grade, but from the night when I defeated him at the kitchen table—slamming his fist against the wood, with a noise like a gun blast—he has never been willing to give it another go. The veins in his feet are a striking, almost frightening blue. He has a giant hawk nose—he calls it noble, aristocratic, Roman. His glasses are only half a generation removed in style from the heavy, black-rimmed GI specs that were standard issue in the army and maybe too in the National Guard unit where my father did his bit.

Wright Aukenhead Edmundson: forty years old, overweight, on the way to being worn to death from incessant work and from yet more devoted—and to him restorative—carousing (also known as galavantin' and calupin'). He's got his cigarette, the Camel straight, with which he is committing a pinch of suicide—self-destruction on the installment plan, for those who, for various reasons, can't manage to do it all at once—stuck in his mouth and he's puffing away, letting the ash extend itself to French-café length, then ordering me to procure an ashtray (children are servants in their parents' houses during this period; he has once clouted me so hard that I saw the galaxies born, expand, explode, and die for not hustling off to Charlie DeLuca's to get him a pack of his smokes) so he can tap the butt before the carpet is scattered with ash.

The TV is on, it's the news, and Wright—Wrightie, as he's called at Raytheon, at work—is denouncing virtually everyone bold enough to push his face into our living room. The sportscasters—in particular Curt Gowdy, the genial voice of the Red Sox, whom everyone else dotes on—the news anchors, the weatherman, the pundits, the guests: all are rounded up in a human clump, belted together, knotted tight, and cast away into the infernal pit as a plague of *morons,* and *geeks.* (Later, after *All in the Family* becomes popular, he'll insert *meatheads* into the repertoire.) And should a woman, any woman, hold forth knowingly on a subject unrelated to cooking, gardening, or the higher arts of gabbing the day away on the telephone, the roof is likely to lift from the eaves of 58 Clewley Road, Medford, Massachusetts. The DeMarias, who live downstairs and who own the house, loopy as they seem, while we, fraught with intelligence (maybe), pay ignominious rent, punch our floor, their ceiling, with a broomstick when my father launches stratospheric, powered by the highly combustible fuel of a pontificating TV presence. My father ignores the pop-pop-pops, the civil artillery barrage. For here, in his living room-den-dining room (his meals are often taken in front of the tube so that the morons will not be able to pull off anything egregious on the sly), my father is a lion of displeasure.

Does my father hate the announcers for being bland, flat-minded dispensers of vanilla good cheer? Yes, certainly. Does he also envy them their positions, their right to hold forth to the world on all and sundry topics, their self-importance, their well-chosen ties? Yes, yes. And which is ascendant in his railings, the envy or the apt critique? To this day I could not tell you.

Generally, my father's relation to the TV is an active one—he's almost always got a dialogue going with the box. But one thing shuts him up completely, turns him mordantly silent. And that is any mention of the Kennedys. He dislikes the Kennedys and always has. When JFK ran for president in 1959, my father referred to him exclusively as Black Jack. When the man's handsome face appeared on the box, my father would turn away in disgust. This was odd behavior in Massachusetts, where Kennedy worship was a minor religion, an adjunct to Catholicism, and to certain Jewish and Protestant strains, too. It wasn't at all uncommon to go into someone's house and find there a Kennedy shrine—a few photos of JFK, one of Bobby, a snap of sainted mother Rose, with devotional lighting on the peripheries. But about this distaste, which encompasses the whole Kennedy family, down to the newly born—and a new Kennedy seemed to pop into the world every three months or so—my father, who is not oppressively restrained about most of his views, is silent.

He changes the channel when a Kennedy homage comes on; he snorts and sneers when one of the royal clan is depicted on the news. But there is no accompanying tirade, no corresponding denunciation. He voted for Nixon in the 1960 election. Following his lead, I too was a Nixon man, size small—the only one, as I remember, in my third grade class. I wore a campaign button to school every day. Some of the Belmont School teachers—future Kennedy shrine-builders maybe—were shocked at my apostasy and took me aside in the halls to try to talk sense to me. In the fall of '69, though, my father was anything but enchanted with Nixon. He referred to him familiarly, disparagingly, but with a pinch of affection, as Tricky Dick. Generally, Nixon was subject to the blanket skepticism that Wright threw over all pretenders to truth and virtue. This would change.

MY OWN relation to TV is almost as long-standing as my father's, surely as enveloping, though much more complacent. From the time I was five years old, I have been a stone addict. I remember hopping out of bed early on Saturday mornings when I was very small, passing the closet where, I believed, my father hid his National Guard rifle, turning a swift pirouette at my parents' half-open bedroom door, the way the Lone Ranger, crossing the entrance to a bank, broke the aim of desperadoes holed up inside. From the pantry I snagged a handful of Fig Newtons, then took a slow-motion Ted Williams slide over the living room rug, pulled into Sioux powwow posture, and popped the on button. There I would sit, my breath softly held at the back of my throat, waiting for the cool, thoughtful hum, the pinhole of light, then the great eye dilating into wakefulness.

TV to me was everything: As various shut-ins are said to do, I cultivated personal relationships with the figures on the screen. I believed that I could talk to Roy Rogers and Clarabell the clown, the Hardy Boys and the Lone Ranger, and that they would hear me and understand. Walking to school, or on the border of sleep, I elaborated on the shows I watched, merging the characters with my friends and family, creating my own scenarios.

But by the time I was ten or so, I strained to see the underside of things, and in this my father was my guide. He let the air out of my favorite shows, one after another. It was like putting aside the things of childhood, to have them debunked this way. It was this century's equivalent of cutting the boy's curls and getting him out of short pants. He showed me how the Lone Ranger and Tonto were chasing the bandits around the same shrubbery prop time and time again, show after show. He pointed out how some elaborate combat footage from a film we'd seen together weeks before had been spliced into a Saturday-afternoon Hercules epic. He spotted a rip in Pinky Lee's pants.

But my father is not only a critic; he is also an authority in his own right. His field of expertise encompasses all things and everything. Whence does his authority come? Not from any formal education. My father dropped out of high school, then slipped back in and copped a degree by the skin of his teeth. Until I was about ten, he worked two jobs to support us (and a lot of wayward habits). He was a short-order cook on two contiguous eight-hour shifts, one at a restaurant called Perry's and another called the Chuck Wagon. (It was at Perry's that, family legend has it, I met two of the more prominent individuals ever to pass through Malden. One was the formidable future governor of Massachusetts, who then owned a construction company—this was the [soon-to-be] Honorable John A. Volpe. The other was Albert DeSalvo, the Boston Strangler, responsible for the horrible deaths of at least a dozen women.) Perry's was days; the Chuck Wagon, nights. He arrived home at three in the morning, smelling of booze and blistered, charred beef, turned on the TV medium loud, and hoisted *The Boston Globe* in front of him like an enormous white sail. He was off into the broad seas of knowledge.

Then and always, he read the newspaper with a flaming eye: the front page, the ads, the editorials, the stock quotes (though he had no stock), the obits, the sports, the columnists he could barely abide and the columnists he abhorred. No one ever got such value from a dime's worth of paper and ink. When he found something especially good—usually a story off the AP or UPI wire, a story, that is, that he did not have to credit to any other human being— or one particularly repugnant, he read it aloud to us, as though he were its creator or its appointed assassin. I believe he read aloud to us when we were asleep. After he read through an issue of the paper, you expected to see it cleansed, pure white, with no print remaining, as though it had been dunked in an acid bath.

My father needed no Bible; the paper was enough. Once, when I was ten or so, he went downstairs to repaint a chair. To begin, he spread the floor with old newspapers. Two hours later, I peered down the darkened stairs to see him under thin light, poised in what the yogis call child's position, down on his knees, buttocks resting on his ankles, head forward, eyes wide, chugging down the print. The paint can was unopened.

While he read the paper and snorted and groaned through his great damaged nose, my father would be glancing up at the tube, denouncing this figure or that, and sometimes praising one, too.

For despite the general mob of morons and geeks who bayed at him from every quadrant of the dial, there were also a few human paragons, whom it paid to observe closely and, when possible, to emulate.

Johnny Carson, who appears every weekday night at eleven-thirty to host *The Tonight Show,* he classes as one of the first among men. There is nothing that Carson cannot do. He can talk to anyone adroitly on any subject and do so modestly (that is, he—or his script writers—knows just about everything that, say, a truly dedicated reader of a solid metropolitan newspaper might know), and he has admirable physical proficiency. When the winner of the Alaskan Olympic Games decathlon (sled dog–related events predominate) comes on the show, Johnny beats him two times out of three at the sport of stick grappling, in which you try to wrest a four-foot-long engraved staff from the other contestant's hands. And then—pièce de résistance—when the world's female arm wrestling champ comes through the curtains and sits down in the guest chair and challenges Johnny, Johnny grits his inhumanly perfect teeth and whips her handily. Or so my father tells it.

These events took place before my Carson-watching period, which, in my senior year, has just begun. Sometimes, after my mother has gone to bed, my father will let me stay up late, past the monologue and into the show itself. And here we have some of our best times together. He is tired, ready to go to bed himself, and the fatigue, functioning like a soft drug, along with the TV's oddly lulling light, calms him down a little. He loses his edge, grows almost benevolent. He truly likes Johnny; he likes the way that without ever being rude or high-handed, Johnny stands up for the regular guy and calmly tames all the big-shot authors and movie stars who appear on the show, makes them lose their airs, relax—or face his low-key, softly flaying ridicule.

For my father, who is never relaxed, wants everyone else to be. He can't bear the agitation that any nervous, pulsating being adds to his considerable store of anxiety. He is always telling us, sometimes at impossibly high volume, that we must, individually and collectively, *relax*. "Relax!" At meals, where he is especially tight, he sometimes decrees complete silence. When we chatter too much, he slams the table and hits us with an old National Guard command, "Chuck it in!" Until I was about twenty, I half believed that talking at the dinner table was not a sign of cultivation but of pig-rudeness.

Johnny was relaxed. He was calm, sure, and also very much himself—a midwestern skeptic, Montaigne from Nebraska, without the classical quotations. He accepted nonsense from no one. So when Carson gets set to go into one of his standard routines— say, Carnak the Magnificent, his mock fortune-teller—my father will exhale hospitably through his great beak and say, "Listen, listen, listen, Mark. I think you're really going to like this." And this concern for what I might like, this willingness to put himself in my seventeen-year-old weird, blemished place and imagine a pleasure for me, warms me nearly to the point of tears.

To my father, Carson was the apogee of sophistication, and for my father to think that I might be capable of sharing this taste with him was no small tribute. My brother, Philip, seven years younger, was much too junior to enter the Carson circle. It was my father and I who together attended his television academy.

My father, up late at night, talking to Johnny, and through Johnny to me, told me what he thought the world was like and showed me what he most aspired to, which was a kind of balance, the balance that Carson had on camera, supported by his handlers and dressers and makeup men. It was a balance that my father wished for and perhaps thought he possessed. Such balance was achieved by being affable, witty, receptive, but only up to a point, for there a sharp if adroitly phrased skepticism had to come into play (Carson was no gull—ever). One was courteous without being stuffy; mildly curious, but never particularly surprised by anything; one was, above all, supremely relaxed, though one never needed to holler at other people to relax in their turn. Carson, at least the on-screen Carson, followed Jocasta's advice from *Oedipus Rex:* He lived lightly, not worrying himself about the big questions, taking in the passing show with detached ease, doing no philosophy, consulting his account books when need be, diverted by the world as it unfolded before him, but unimpressed by it, too.

It was not just my father and me in the living room (dining room, den) awake late at night. For with us there is a constant unseen presence that never sleeps. It is my sister, Barbara Anne, who died at the age of six, three years ago. She is rarely spoken about, rarely alluded to, though a small photograph of her sits on one of the end tables and the room is decorated with reproductions of famous paintings depicting innocent young girls. Renoir's *Girl with a Watering Can* has pride of place over our television set, presiding in melancholy grace over Carson as he runs through his shtick. Barbara's death, from a series of strokes, had been brutal, horribly painful to watch, as she slowly, slowly degenerated over time. First she lost what speech she had; then she could not walk without dragging her foot behind her. All the expressions of pleasure that come to pass in our living room are partial, muted: Every birthday party or Christmas celebration goes on beside a small unseen grave, barely covered over by the dense yellow carpet, the ornate couch, and the large patriarch's chair on which my father sits, pitched and ready for battle with the TV. In our house, we attend what seems to be a never-ending wake.

When I told my father about what I gathered to be Frank Lears' views on TV, did he take them as a slap at the medium only, a snob's dismissal of what the unwashed loved to drown their rages and pains in, a kind of ocular booze, or did he see it as a stroke against our tiny confraternity of Carson, which—who knows, for he would never have told me—might have meant as much to him as it did to me? When, two years later, I spent a summer working at Raytheon, one of my father's colleagues after another commended me for some past achievement that my father had described to them in pinprick detail, though he had not offered me a direct word of praise about it.

Carson is a credible figure, a plausible Nebraskan man of the world. When my father wants something more high-flying, he goes to Humphrey Bogart. *The Maltese Falcon* is by far the greatest movie ever made; and my father will wake us up at any time of the night to come in and watch the best scenes with him. He knows the film so well that he can run two or three lines ahead of the track, so the movie is less in stereo, as sometimes happens when an inveterate repeat watcher of this or that classic is on hand to recite the dialogue simultaneously, than it is simply out of sync. More than a "cocker," one of my father's highest terms of praise, *Falcon* qualifies as a "peachy cocker." But Bogart is a joy ride, a night of debauchery, liquored up in a black sedan. Carson— Carson is the unacknowledged anti–philosopher king of America. Though in my father's mind, Richard Nixon will eventually replace him.

For now, Wright, whose name bespeaks accuracy, truth, rigor, is comfortably in the saddle and he can afford to play a little with my puzzlement and his own about this Frank Lears character. So what is to be made of an unprepossessing guy who apparently has no use for the *Globe* but who reads the *Times,* which my father has heard of and knows something about, since the *Globe* refers to it occasionally and nothing that was or is or ever shall be in that paper seems exempt from being stored in my father's memory? But consider, if you read, truly read, a sound enough American newspaper (and the *Globe* was that, even if it had a predilection for stories about missing and found dogs and the like) and read it like a ferret, then took it and digested it and metabolized the whole business, and if you watched TV with hyperactive intelligence, you would know a good deal—all Johnny did and maybe more, though no little might escape you, too. Frank Lears may or may not have been a part of that no little. My father, oddly enough, was eager to know.

One night while we were discussing Lears my father became so interested that he threatened to turn up in class and break a lance or two with the guy, argue a few points about Plato, whom I was describing, raggedly enough, during a commercial. It would be the *Globe* against the *Times*, the Chuck Wagon versus Harvard. For, about Lears, I had already told my father other puzzling and tantalizing things.

I told him that Frank Lears liked rock and roll, despite his being a great reader of books. In fact, on a couple of occasions, Lears had indicated that there were things to be learned from listening to rock—that some kind of sloppy, fantastical vision was unfolding in the music. To me, rock was nothing but the kind of amped-up raucous noise exemplified by the Stones, a good prelude to a street brawl or a football game; or it was the agreeable surfer noodling that the Beach Boys and Jan and Dean provided. I didn't much care for the Beatles. That rock had any consequence beyond being a kind of additive that raced or quelled the engine a little—this was a peculiar idea to me. I turned it over in my head, then pushed it aside to think about the Somerville game and Abigail Glynn, who looked like the human equivalent of Ivory Snow but, rumor had it, did it all with her boyfriend, Johnny Contini.

My father detested rock and adored Beethoven. Each year he

asked us to present him with a bust of the composer for Christmas
or for his birthday. For twenty years, we never delivered the gift,
never really looked into it, in fact. Then, when it was finally found,
bought, wrapped, and opened, my father, who then was getting
old, though only in his fifties, simply looked at it ruefully and put
it aside.

As to books: My father, in my sight, read two of them in his life.
One was Yeats' complete poems, a gift to me for Christmas when I
was twenty-five or so; he stayed up all the night before Christmas
reading it, and my mother had to wrap it the next morning. He
pronounced it a cocker. The other was *Humboldt's Gift*, by Saul
Bellow: also a cocker but absurd, because the characters were un-
believable, too flagrant and power-packed—this from someone
who could have auditioned for a role as a minor Bellow figure.
Based on his affection for Yeats, I suggested that he try a few more
modern poets—Stevens, Frost, Elizabeth Bishop maybe. He looked
at me like I was nuts.

I told him that Frank Lears wore suits of fifty years' vintage. "We
got a guy at Raytheon who does that," my father replied. "Wears
hand-me-downs. He's got a tiny goat beard, a goatee, and he says
that it makes him look like an intellectual, so he's worth one or two
K extra at raise time."

I told him that Lears, as far as the class could figure, drank only
tea. Tea! A man who only drinks tea? My father was nonplussed. I
could almost read his thoughts. What about coffee? What about
Budweiser? Or Miller High Life, the champagne of bottled beers?
What about Jingle Bells, J&B scotch—a true challenge to the belly
and liver of the American male?

One habit of Lears' that my father seemed to approve of un-
equivocally was his way of conferring praise. There wasn't much
praise to be conferred, not at this point in the course, but it came

in an odd way. If Lears liked what someone said—that is, liked what Sandra or, occasionally, very occasionally, one of the rest of us, said—he would observe, grinning subtly, that the remark was "not too bad." Or sometimes he would observe that the comment at hand was "really not unintelligent at all" or "far from stupid." Over time—a long time, given the difficulty of the lesson for us— we learned that the more dire the word Lears negated, the more he liked the comment. So "Not in the least dumb" was better than "Not too bad." My father—whose favorite adjective was probably *atrocious*—found Lears' mode to be a reasonably dignified way of dispensing praise when there was no way of evading the job, and he probably began making use of it at Raytheon.

I told my father that Lears kept a journal. One day he had mentioned, apropos of not too much, that he often found it helpful when he was bothered by some issue, philosophic or personal, to sit down and lay his thoughts out in written form. Huh? The idea that someone would do this, like the idea that someone would eschew TV, would drink only tea, and would wear old clothes when he could afford new—these notions had me scratching my head, if only in passing. People I knew simply did not do these things. Who, for instance, would ever be faced with an issue so complex that it needed writing down? Then who could find the words to give it expression? I could maybe write a paragraph or two in English class under the rolling eye of Miss Cullen, but that would be about something we'd read, or should have. (I was rather good at guessing what the plot of a book might be from reading the first dozen pages or so, though sometimes this method failed, with me killing off many of the major figures in the end simply because they had rubbed me the wrong way on first encounter.) But using writing to make things clearer? I could not do it. I lived in a near phantasmagoria of feelings and illusions and hopes, with occasionally a stab of reasonable sunlight sliding in. If you had asked me to describe my family, my religious views, my politics, my likes and dislikes in music, I would have left the page empty or made something up. I was probably afraid of cogency, scared of what I'd see—didn't want any of that business at all.

To the information about the journal and the exploratory writing, my father just gave a grunt. He wrote only Raytheon reports, no essays in the manner of Emerson and Thoreau, but he did take himself to be a prose stylist of distinction. He periodically delivered a lecture that might have been titled "When You Write Something, You Must Never Make a Mistake." The lecture was an outgrowth of his central commandment about life, which, in digest form, was Never Make a Mistake, Period—Be Like Me. He talked with Ciceronian expansiveness about the rigors of punctuation, about the necessity for impeccable spelling. "Look it up if you don't know it! If you don't know it, look it *up*!" He was a similarly inspired professor of math or science. He would help me for a few minutes, then begin hollering his math-science slogan: "Either you know it or you don't! Either you know it or you don't!" When it came time to write my college applications, my father took control and composed them himself. When he was finished with one of the essays, he read it aloud to my mother and brother and me, then declared it worthy of Abraham Lincoln—which was true enough: It sounded a good deal like the Gettysburg Address.

What I was perhaps telling my father—unbeknownst to me, for at this point I would have told you that Frank Lears was a walking joke—was that I had found someone else to listen to, someone who seemed to be dealing cards from another deck. I wanted my father to see that though in the past I had rarely even made small shows of resisting his influence, I might now be open to someone else's, that a diminutive scholar was piquing my interest and that, strangely, slowly, I was waking up from what seemed years of sleep, sleep that only fatigued and dulled me further. These feelings flowed like a tentative underground stream. I knew virtually nothing of them; my father, perhaps less. He had not done his job well enough and was not doing it, but, I probably wished to say, come and take over the seemingly pointless and dull kid sitting absorbed by his woes and dreams; there's still time and, truth be told, there are few other contenders for the prize. What Frank Lears offered scared me, and I would rather have stayed home.

My father would eventually meet Lears in a dutiful sort of way, just as he went off dutifully to watch most of my football games— or, often, to watch me watching them from the bench. He watched us lose to Malden, his own high school, on Thanksgiving Day, watched me deck the opposing star fullback, sending him flying off the ground, a play that, I was told, found its way into highlight films for years after.

But generally my father had his own troubles and little attention left for me, who, at least on the surface, would have represented simply one trouble more. His own father had remarried after my grandmother died. (He told me once that though she died when he was one and a half years old, he was sure he could remember his mother's face—but he said this, ostensibly, not to underline the strength of his feelings but to celebrate a feat of memory.) My father was the last of my grandfather's children, the youngest, with three sisters and a brother. He was named after his father: He was Wright Aukenhead Edmundson, Junior. When my grandfather remarried, he sent all the children away, or the wicked stepmother did—the explanation was never clear to me. And, family legend has it, the first male child born to my father's father and his new wife was named nothing other than Wright Aukenhead Edmundson, Junior.

So somewhere in life my father had a double, a doppelgänger, walking around. I have never heard of anything quite like this—not in literature, where some shrewd novelist might have made some hay with it, much less in life. But how could it have felt to my father? It was as though *his* father had all but declared that he had gotten it wrong the first time, wrong with this first Wright, who had been something like an inept rough draft, marred and ill-made, and that he would forget this blot of a boy and go on and try to replace him with something better. A more promising creature needed to be summoned out of the darkness to carry the name of Wright A., Senior. It was a symbolic form of infanticide, I suppose. Or maybe, to look at it with a less dramatic eye, a simple hedging of the bet: With two Juniors out there, the chances that someone who bore his name would amount to something would increase.

But suppose the two men ever met, which as far as I know they never did? Wouldn't it be almost natural for them to fight to the death, to attack each other in some primal way? A Greek dramatist might have done something with this cruel happenstance—which could not possibly end well.

My father, disowned for no cause, no transgression of his own, was passed around from one sister to the next, then on to his brother, George, and his new wife. They doted on my father for his razory intelligence and his beautiful flute playing, but they had a family of their own. A strange, wayward, often charming younger brother didn't fit.

He had to take care of himself too early, my father. He skipped stages, skipped steps, became externally a man while inwardly the boy was still there, waiting for the face of his mother to loom again like a gorgeous moon and to tell him that life was softer and more protected than in fact it would ever be. That he made it into adulthood at all seems something of a triumph.

He may have played the flute exquisitely, but not well enough, he could see by the time he was seventeen, to make it into the Boston Symphony Orchestra. And if he could not be the best, why do it at all? He put the instrument aside.

He skipped school all the time and hung out in a poolroom and slipped back in for Latin class, because he liked it so much. He was president of the Latin club. He worked late at Perry's restaurant and used to sleep through German, with the teacher's approval. He was handsome then, and unbearably smart. He ran fast. He had bad teeth. Once, maybe twice, my uncle George pulled him from the Malden River, where he'd gotten caught in the weeds. He was called Boca, after a kind of coffee you could get back then, during the Depression. He could never remember how he'd gotten the nickname.

After years of double shifts cooking short order, my father got a job at Raytheon. I was about ten years old at the time. He was to be a janitor, but something a little better opened up; he became an inspector third class, looking over shipments fresh in at the loading dock. From there, he worked his way up to quality-control engineer, someone who hounded Raytheon's contractors until they did their jobs to spec. He made missiles, mass-murdering weapons, and he once said he couldn't believe all the time and energy that he and thousands of others put into making machines to destroy people. It was horrible, brutal. How could such a thing be so? Then he laughed in derision, as though someone else had been talking, and went on his way.

Money ran through his pockets, because once he was wound up, he needed to unspool himself—and that was not cheap. He could get by on two hours of sleep a night, then on Saturday he'd crash, like a copter falling dead out of the sky, and go unconscious for twelve hours straight. He blew up at people at work, called them geeks and morons to their faces. He never apologized. He laughed in nervous bursts. He loved small children. He was embarrassed by sex and by death. (After my sister died, I never heard him speak a word about her, though he had surely adored her.) He was virtually the only white man I knew growing up who never used the word *nigger.* I heard him swear only once in my life.

He had no time for a mis-made boy, beset with asthma—from his own Camels maybe—anxious, angry, strange. My father was living in a whirl of work and booze and sorrow and debt. He burned himself out, like a rag soaked in gasoline and wrapped round a stick, bright in the night air, and he died when he was fifty-five years old, not far from my age now. The last words of his I know of were words he wrote on a psychological evaluation that he had taken before he stepped into the car to drive home. On the way, his mind and body blew out in a fusillade of light and heat, a stroke and a heart attack at once. The assignment was to complete the sentence "A good father————." My father had ended it with the phrase "loves his children."

ONE NIGHT not long after I told him Lears' verdict on TV, I was lying on the bed in my room listening to the radio. The Jefferson Airplane was telling me about how one pill can make you larger and one pill make you small but how the ones that Mama gives you don't do anything at all, and trying to puzzle out what the words meant. Because Frank Lears had told us that they might mean something? Maybe so. On my wall was a poster of carousing Hell's Angels, which I was staring at longingly.

"Hey, Mark," my father said, poking his head through the door. "Why don't you come in and catch the monologue?" Johnny was on. He was, maybe, wearing a Nehru suit; it was about that period. He'd be saying a few mildly derisive things about President Nixon.

"Nah," I said. "I think I'll skip it tonight."

"It's gonna be good. He's supposed to do Carnak." When Johnny did Carnak the Magnificent, he put a soothsayer's turban on his head and draped himself in a flowing cape. Then he'd magically glean the contents of sealed envelopes and joke about them. The omniscience thing (writ small); my father loved it.

"That's okay. Thanks anyhow."

My father's tone changed. "Then go to bed. You're up way too late."

"All right," I said. Pointing out the contradiction—that it was not too late for Carson but was too late for the radio—would not have been wise. My father could detonate with any passing spark. As I slid into bed and turned out my Tensor lamp, radio turned not off but down low, I was not at all unhappy. In fact, I felt a certain inner glow.

My father was not easy for most people to read. He manifested many feelings—grief, fear, anxiety, even sometimes relative pleasure—in the form of anger. (On the day of my sister's death, he had burst into a rage at me for no discernible reason.) But I had studied him for years in no little awe, the way lower animals who group around the water hole carefully memorize the habits of a near-dwelling lion, and I knew that in the gaps of his anger tonight there was a dose of pain. I had hurt his feelings. I! For just a passing moment, the first one that I could remember since the night I'd beaten him arm wrestling, I was one up. I felt mildly elated, freer; not half bad.

When I got up the next morning, very early, he was still on the couch, still watching TV. He greeted me cheerfully, all things considered. He told me that he had been awake through the night. Carson was fabulous. There had been a Bogart movie, then another, both peachy cockers. He told me this in great triumph, as though a masked ball, replete with celebrities and sirens and swordsmen, famous statesmen, outlaw poets, and prodigious lovers, had taken place in our living room during the early hours and I had slept through the whole shebang. Then he heaved himself up and headed for the bathroom, for his morning ablutions. We had one bathroom, and he'd be in there, I knew, for about forty minutes. Until I figured out that drinking any liquids after say, seven o'clock, was a dumb thing to do at our house—until, that is, I was about ten—I spent many agonized interludes in front of the bathroom door while my father shaved and attacked his short-cropped hair, military style, with a pair of fast-flying brushes, saying all the while, like a genial torturer, "Just a sec, I'll be done in just a sec."

I went back to bed, turned on the radio, WMEX, and listened for a while to the Who and the Beatles and the Airplane, then fell back to sleep. When I woke up, my father was gone.

Chapter Five

FRANKLIN LEARS
FIGHTS BACK

Mid-November came, the air went frigid, frost took hold of
the ground, and Frank Lears apparently decided it was time to
fight back.

For some time, Lears had played by the rules. He had tried to be
a sane, dutiful teacher. He summarized the Durant book; he read
it to us when need be. He asked us questions and bore with the silence when we said nothing. Sometimes, when Sandra was tapped
out and Tom Buller was on the nod, the place was quiet for ten
minutes at a time. All you could hear was the irregular pop of the
classroom clock, which detonated like a tiny, eccentric bomb.
Things became so dull that the sense of smell took preeminence
from sight and hearing and we got lost in the aromas of very, very
inexpensive perfume and hair spray—lots of that—and gym reek,
from those who had kept the mandatory white socks on their feet
and hadn't changed their T-shirts after a wild game of crab soccer.
(Get on your backs, face and belly toward the ceiling, and scuttle
around on feet and palms trying to swat a part-dead volleyball into

the space between two cones: Do this with fifty guys on a side in a small gym, Jimmy Brown's worst nightmare, Dirty Ed Bush—"Go ahead. Kick him! Kick!"—presiding, and you *will* perspire.) Then after we had integrated the smells and flattened them out to nothing, to neutrality, as the sense will do for reasons of its own, we would relapse into light trances, docile, slouched, but also touchy, so that if a neighbor stirred us with an elbow or knee, we would leap at him in brief firecracker rage. And we would stare on and on at the clock as it did its funny jitterbug. We were starving Lears out, or trying to, we the herd without shepherd, who needed none, being free and certain in all that mattered. Soon he'd crack.

But I and the rest of us were in error. We had woefully underestimated our man. For unlike Miss Cullen of the stolen glasses, the purloined rank book, and the supply closet imprisonment, and Mr. Sweeney, of the flittering fingers and gushing invisible blood, and unlike even Mace Johnson, who never quite seemed sure that he was the one who should be leading the parade, invested as he was in higher authorities, always a little like an edgy noncom in search of the lieutenant, Frank Lears clearly thought extremely well of himself. And after a couple of months of our nonsense, he must have decided to hit back—though, to be sure, he fought us in a way that was entirely in our interest. But this much needs to be clear: He *was* fighting, taking some territory back.

He started by setting a trap. "Let me tell you a story," he said one day apropos of nothing much. The story was about an experiment that had been conducted not long ago in New Haven, Connecticut, at Yale University. This installment of the experiment was a preamble, it was worth pointing out. The whole show was to climax in Germany. Americans would act as what the social psychologist in charge of the operation, a man named Stanley Milgram, thought of as the control group. (Much later, I would teach verse writing to

Milgram's daughter. "I'm sure you know about my father," she said. I claimed innocence. "No," she insisted. "Everyone who's been to college knows about my father's experiment"—which is more or less true. But we in Medford knew nothing whatever of the man.)

The experiment involved pain—inflicting pain. But the people who participated in the experiment did not know this. They came in off the streets volunteering for an experiment in pedagogy. They thought they were going to be teachers. When they got there, they met a large, pleasant man, who was the student. After a few preliminaries, the "student" disappeared into an adjoining room, while the "teacher," directed by a supervisor in a lab coat, sat down in front of an impressive-looking console. The teacher understood that he was going to test the student on a memory exercise. The guy in the other room—the student—had to match terms accurately after hearing eight or ten pairs read to him in sequence just once. But the student was sometimes dull. He made mistakes. It was necessary to do something to enhance his concentration.

So when the learner made a mistake, he received a punishment— a jolt of electricity. Given a wrong answer, the teacher pushed a lever and administered a certain set voltage. With every mistake, the voltage rose. To some teachers this was a bit troubling. In the initial interview, the student, a man of about fifty, had claimed to have a heart condition. At three hundred volts, he began crying out about his heart "hurting." The supervisor said to ignore it. The shocks were painful, he said, but they were not dangerous. As the teacher inflicted more and more voltage, the student in the other room cried louder.

Of course the cries were coming from a confederate, someone who was in on the experiment. No real pain was being inflicted, though the teacher didn't know as much. When the teacher demurred about inflicting the pain, the supervisor would encourage him with a few words: It's all right. Go ahead. Don't worry. On many occasions, the arrow went into the red zone. Screams came from the adjoining room. Then, after the teacher reached 350 volts, there was no noise whatever. The lab supervisor encouraged the teacher to keep posing the questions. When the student didn't reply after five seconds, he got another dose. The top dose was five hundred volts.

Half the people who participated in the experiment went all the way—five hundred rousing American volts.

What was *supposed* to happen, Lears told us, was much different. The Americans in the experiment were supposed to be incensed at the whole idea. When someone told them to send an electric charge through a stranger's skin, they were supposed to swear at the experimenter, then storm out in rage, maybe ante up a punch in the jaw to the bad guy in the white coat.

In Germany, it would all be different. There, lulled by the banality of evil or subsumed by the totalitarian mind or whatever, the people would cheerfully goose the needle up as high as it could go, as fast as they could get it there.

The experiment never made its way to Germany. The control group failed to perform its function. Instead of providing a glowing image of American independence, many of the people in the experiment showed themselves remarkably eager to do what they were told and torture an innocent man for not being able to pair two words correctly.

"Well," said Lears (hand-swinging, a bit of tongue-clicking, the *tch-tch* sound having been recently added, whether because he was getting more comfortable or less, one couldn't say). "What do people think?" If they did that sort of experiment here at Medford High, what would the results be? Would all of us—Lears always included himself in a potential indictment—be eager to keep on pushing the buttons? Would we be good experimental confederates? Would we follow orders?

We had been quiet for a long time. We had provided Lears with deserts of silence, where he could straggle absurdly, trying to sustain himself in his wanderings on the manna of his own thoughts. We had given him the silent treatment. But now we had plenty to say. We bubbled with insight. We would *never*, under any conditions, be willing to push the plunger down while someone screamed in the next room. No way—not us.

"So how do you explain these other people doing it, then?"

Buller thought he knew. Maybe the thing was a stunt. Everyone in it was an actor. It was like the American moon landing as explained by the Chinese government to its people—a fat hoax. The experimenters had done it to get attention. Some respectful murmuring at this.

"I don't think so," Lears said. "I believe that they really did it."

We roared on, nobly defending ourselves, our compatriots, America and its way, and Lears nodded and smiled and listened to every word we said as though we were inspired prophets. I spoke up and said that most people I knew would never do such a thing— no way.

And I can still remember the way Lears settled his gaze on me as I talked. His soft brown eyes were mesmerizing; it was as if a deer had somehow acquired preternatural intelligence and could combine warmth with the greatest level of comprehension. It struck me then for the first time that when this guy listened to you, the experience was of a different order from when anyone else did. He wasn't thinking about anything else. He was completely poised on your thoughts.

What I said was dumb, neither here nor there. But one of kids' great inducements to say idiotic things is the deeply in-worked feeling that no one cares what it is they might have to say. If it doesn't matter, then what the hell? And if you're outrageous enough, then they will at last pay you some attention, though probably not of the sort that you hoped for at the beginning.

But when Lears listened—and this was probably my first full-length expostulation in class—it felt as though, odd to say but true, you were being fed something, something very good and sustaining. And when he stopped listening because your turn was up, it was as though earthly ambrosia was being taken from you. It was a beautiful drug he dispensed. I had never gotten it before.

And the harder and more humanely he listened, the more anxious we felt. The fact that he seemed ready to credit our inane reactions, to respond to them as though they were long-pondered elements of contoured philosophic systems, started out by making us feel better, more comfortable and self-assured. But the listening intensity also somehow threw the issue back onto us. Is this really what we believe? Is it what we think? If it's not, do we want this person, on whom nothing much seems to be lost, to see that we're trying to deceive ourselves and him both? It was not humiliating to lie to teachers—we did that all the time. What was humiliating was to be seen through by someone who felt not outrage about our deceptions but compassion, genuine pity that we couldn't actually think about matters and then speak our minds.

Lears gave us thirty full minutes to defend ourselves and the American way. Then, without a word of commentary, he let us go. But he was not through with the issue, not through with us. This was to be a play in two parts, and the second act was on its way.

ALWAYS AT school there was another world, a place for your thoughts to migrate, where you could loiter in vague, fantastical pleasure, one far from the humdrum mental assembly line you were traveling down. In a while, football would disappear and my world elsewhere, my Erewhon, would be the pool hall and the prospect of getting beer on Friday and Saturday nights. But during November, when Lears told us about Milgram's experiment, it was still football—that was the place where my thoughts loved to glide.

We had started the year with two wins, one over the redoubtable Boston Latin, an out-of-conference game, and the second against pushover Chelsea. But after that, the great chance had come: We had gotten our rematch with Somerville, the team that had broken the Mustangs' winning streak last year, stopped Medford's string of eleven in a row, and started us skidding into deep mediocrity.

They were big, tough Italian kids, the Somerville players, who came from a town where, it was said, there are more barrooms per capita than anywhere else in the world. They wore bloodred uniforms; they walked on the field like construction workers arriving at a site, coming on to do a job; most of them seemed to have heavy beards. The guy who played split end, usually a position for speedy flyweights, weighed 220 pounds. They had a tackle so strong that no one in the Greater Boston League could block him alone. He had to be handled by two or even three players. Their fullback, named Sal Cartelli, was a compressed meteor, tight and strong and crazy. ("The kid's fuckin' crazy": That phrase was a major tribute in Medford and environs.) They came to Hormel Stadium to kick us around, slap their hands together a few times, workmen at the end of the day shift, traipse off together for a few brews, then home, maybe, for a pop at the wife.

Before the game, they kept their linemen in the locker room so that we could stand around and imagine how big and tough they were, like Beowulf hearing the lays about fearsome Grendel, before their match. As soon as the game began, Somerville set to work on us. An early play from scrimmage went to the huge flanker. Tiny Medford defensive backs hit him and flew off like bugs. He looked like a moving popcorn popper. He gained forty yards. Then they smashed the ball up the middle time and again. Their points were quick and easy—they were sure there would be plenty more to come.

They were so big and mean and fast—how could we win? But as fast as they were, none of them was quite as fast as our quarterback and fellow philosopher Tom Capallano. Cap grabbed a kickoff and flew down the sidelines—we had a special play, featuring a line of blockers that, having thrown an initial shot, would set up like a picket fence, each player a post, along the edge of the field. Once the returner made it in behind that fence, he could fly.

From scrimmage, Cap was also a terror. He ran around the ends; he ran up the middle on quarterback draws. He scrambled away from their pass rush and picked up eight, ten, fifteen yards. And suddenly the feeling hit everyone that Somerville wasn't invincible, and the Somerville team, which had believed all the hype about itself, began to leak slowly like a sad red balloon. As good as they were, they had no one who could catch Cap and no one who, on his own, could tackle our running back, Mo Murphy. Murphy was hurt nearly every day of every game for his whole high school career, except that day. He was like a huge white stallion, with muscles standing out, magnificently contoured. All over his pale, pale face were vicious pustules; his skin was tracing paper–thin, you could see every vein in his body; but other than that, he was a study in physical perfection. He ran so hard that his knees nearly bumped his chest. Tackling him once was like getting into a bad poolroom fight.

Suddenly, at the end of the first quarter, the conviction descended on us like a rogue blessing: We could win. They were better in almost every way, but they were afraid now, nervous, embarrassed, executing poorly. And they were out of shape. No grass drills for them under the roaring sun, Mace Johnson striding through the rows. We could beat them.

The game turned into war. It got dirtier and dirtier. In every pileup, the Somerville players kicked and clawed; they punched. One of our linebackers, I can't recall who it was, caught Cartelli coming around the end on a sweep and hit him so hard that on the bench, and probably in the stands, too, you could feel the fillings in your back teeth jolt. Cartelli was, as the announcers say, slow in getting up.

At a certain point, the contest became so intense, bitter, and hard fought that the cheerleaders stopped cheering full-time and began watching the game. That's right—the cheerleaders actually began taking an interest in the football game.

In the mythology of high school, the links between the cheerleaders and the football players are established and understood: The cheerleaders are the most beautiful girls in the school, and they live and breathe to serve the studs who play on the squad. As to the cheerleaders being beautiful, that was true enough, at least for our group. They were chosen by a shop teacher—a rotund, grinning fellow named Mr. Pelagrino—and Mr. Pelagrino might as well have been a Persian sultan who had been borne through the ranks of the four hundred–odd girls in the senior class and emerged with the most comely. He was drawn to blondes, was Mr. P., as he was to dark, impossibly lovely Italian girls. It's likely that all our cheerleaders could jump and kick and spin, but it's certain that they were quite close to being the fourteen most alluring girls in the school.

As to their being the love slaves of the football team, or even the team's dedicated admirers, that was another matter. The morning of the Somerville game, I'd arrived at Hormel Stadium the usual three hours before the whistle, so as to get taped, squeeze into the absurdly tight dress pants, and hang around doing endless nothing. The cheerleaders were practicing on the running track in front of our bench, and Rick, with a couple of backfield associates, was looking on, hanging on the chain-link fence, apparently trying to strike a standard cowboy let's-evaluate-the-mares pose. Rick was wearing a blinding white T-shirt, double-bleached and ironed; his pants fit impeccably; his hair was perfect. From his taped hand hung his Gayle Sayres–style helmet, with the signature white face guard, and a couple of hawk decals—rewards for interceptions and exquisite grabs.

The girls were executing what had to qualify as their most inane cheer: "A touchdown, a touchdown, a touchdown, boys. You make the touchdowns, we'll make the noise."

Rick, his mind most likely on the Somerville behemoths now curled up, deep in the back of fetid caves, chewing morning bones, no doubt: "Hey, hey, girls, I got an idea. How 'bout this time you make the touchdowns and we . . ." Rick trailed off. He must have known this was far from his best shot.

Cathy Leslie made a face as though Rick had just become ill in proximity. He shrugged and ambled off. This was about as intimate and friendly as things got between the two groups, at least when both were in uniform.

Who got the idea of having cheerleaders? Where did the practice of having young women hop, dance, and urge the boys on come from? Was it another classical throwback? Were the girls there playing the roles of the women who looked down from the battlements and cheered on their men, cheered them on lustily, because if the men on the plains flagged and the city was taken, the women would be raped and killed, their children sold off as slaves? That, at least, was the objective in Homeric times.

But the Medford High cheerleaders were not quite one with the Mustang warriors. On the contrary, they spent most of the game with their backs to us, facing the crowd. And their objective, unspoken but clear enough to any observer, was to bring the attention from the field onto themselves. They chanted and leaped and sent their short, short skirts flying up, exposing their tight blue underpants. And very often they won the tacit battle for attention. The crowd, or some significant portion of it, males mainly, zoomed in on them and lost contact with the impossible sprawl that was the football game. We fought with the girls for attention most days, and often they came out on top. Sometimes we emerged from the game victorious, little knowing that they had won the ratings war.

But that day, in the game against Somerville, they stopped cheering in unison, put their gloved hands to their mouths, and bit their folded knuckles—or clasped their palms together in prayer-like suspense—and stood stunned as the game went on. When the Mustangs gained a few yards or stopped a sweep, they jumped spontaneously, without any choreographed plan. They were for once—and for the only time all year that I saw—on no one's side but ours.

With about a minute left in the game—the score 20 to 14, Somerville ahead—we had the ball on their twenty-yard line. Handoff to Mo Murphy, a simple dive between the guard and the center. Murphy broke through the Somerville line, spinning off the big tackle, the moose, who was too tired from chasing Cap all day to wrap Murphy up. Stan Rutollo, another meteor, who played linebacker, was there waiting, perfectly positioned, feet apart, arms wide, neck bulled, ready to make the tackle. Murphy got his knees churning ("like pistons," as our radio announcer liked to say). But instead of running into Rutollo and creating a red smash like two spheres colliding in space, Murphy reared back a little on his right foot, kicked with his left, and jumped clean over him, like a great horse making an impossible leap. I don't believe Rutollo touched him. When Murphy was in the end zone, the linebacker was still standing there, position unchanged, poised and ready to hit, as though he were posing for a publicity still. He looked like one of those stone gnomes that people use to decorate, if that's the word, their country gardens.

With twenty seconds left, Chewy DiCarlo, big Chewy, the tackle, who weighed nearly 250 pounds and who was really a gentle boy, went jiggle-trotting into the game. Chewy was called forth by Frank Ireland, a screaming skull who coached the line and had no business determining how we'd handle the conversion after a touchdown. That was the head coach Ed Connoly's call. And usually we went for the two-point conversion, with a run or a passing play. Connoly, with his froggy voice, croaked from the sidelines, trying to get Chewy off the field. ("Yeah, I heard him," Chewy said later. "But no way I was comin' back.")

The hike went to Cap, the quarterback, the ball handler. He put it effortlessly down. He was, he told me, smiling as he placed the ball. "It was our game. We deserved it," he said. (Like all latter-day knights, Cap believed that the universe was a justly wired operation.) Chewy stumbled forward like he'd been shoved in the lunch line, nearly lost his feet, righted himself, and gave the ball a boot. It rose up, up, up, then began to descend, hurt and ungainly, like a waterfowl winged by a hunter from his blind. The football seemed to hover in the air for a full minute. Then it dropped dead down, slapping the mucky ground so hard you felt it must have been logged with water. The referees raised their arms over their heads, the ground crew welcoming a small plane to the runway. The game was over. Medford 21, Somerville 20.

And though I hadn't played in the game, I went mad, embracing Tony Lincoln, a black defensive back who'd graduated the year before—his stutter aside, Tony was a ringer for Little Richard. Tony had squirted illegally down onto the sidelines to watch us exact revenge. "We'll get them for you next year," I'd said to Tony when he was brought, near crazy with pain, out of the game at Somerville the year before. "F-f-f-f-fuck next year" was Tony's judicious reply. But Tony was now in ecstasy.

We all were. We could have gone on from there and sacked the entire city of Somerville, burning and looting and howling our way through town, stopping at each of the two hundred or so taverns to hatchet open the beer kegs and toast our victory. The enemy was as good as dead. After Chewy's ball went through, many of them fell to the ground in shock: the big guys, the shavers, the working men; they were crying like children unjustly slapped.

In the clubhouse we were silent, amazed at what we'd done, thanking powers on high. Usually the coaches gave out the game ball after a win. Today, we simply found it, took it, and put it in Cap's hand: There were no protests from the authorities.

Coach Connoly, he of the diminished froggy voice, probably the worst clubhouse speaker in the game of football, croaked, "Now you see what can sometimes happen if you stick with a thing and don't give up." Which kept the joint quiet for another few minutes. Then we exploded again.

And what had Frank Lears, with his little black book filled with digests of the philosophers, to compare with this? Plato could go on all night about the rhapsodies of pure contemplation and how love of the beautiful in women and men passes on to love of beautiful ideas, then to love of the Good. But this was too tame, too serene. Plato's plot to offer something more alluring than Homer's battle joy looks, from the perspective of a bitter winning fight, like so much polite nonsense, sanctified jive. It's all stay-at-home, all tame. A school thing, a church thing, a tiddle-taddle of teacup-clinking voices. "We are skin drums which nature beats," says a latter-day Dionysian, and when nature lays down its rhythm, you have to move.

It sometimes seems that men love only one thing, and it is not women or family or home, much less fine ideas. It is war. And the closer you can come to war at any time, the better, particularly if you survive. The philosopher William James made a big deal out of concocting something called the moral equivalent of war, a condition in which we could rally all the energies and powers that come with rank belligerence and put them to some civilizing use. But it is a futile exercise, I would have said that day, a Harvard man's pipe dream. Because victory, achieved by the body over other bodies, the stripping of the armor, the taking of prizes, the humiliation of the foe—that is what the heart wants. Once you've had the feeling of total warrior triumph, nothing else exists.

ONE COLD late-autumn day, on the cusp of oncoming New England winter, not long after the Somerville game, when we could still taste the rich, briny flavor of the win, not long after Lears had laid down the riff about Milgram and his experiment, he began class by sending Rick Cirone off to run an interminable errand.

Rick had a high-arching spring in his step during those days—guys in a good mood often did; the bouncing walk was part of their élan—but Rick, being Rick, not only did the bounce, but parodied it, apparently enjoying its pleasures and its deflation at the same time. Rick had been catching passes. Cap's primary receiver the first few games, Tom Danton, was now getting double coverage. And Rick, who had been playing ball with Cap since grammar school, was snagging pass after pass. Number 49 was ascendant. He flew like his favorite player, Gale Sayers, flourishing the single-bar white face guard ("go ahead, land a shot and knock my teeth out, but you gotta catch me first")—blithe, quick, wind-propelled.

Lears sent him, Mercury-like, off to the main office, then the library, and then the gym—a ten-minute odyssey, even with the bounce turned up high. As soon as Rick left the room, Lears, sly look on, walking up and down in front of us like a physician pondering the intricacies of a case, laid out his plan. When Richard, as he called Rick, came back, there would be a surprise for him. We were going to play a game. The game would have some counters—a few pieces, as it were. These would be paired sets of lines drawn on the blackboard. There would be about ten of these pairs. Sometimes the lines would be the same length exactly; at other times they would be unequal.

When Rick returned, Lears would get the game going. He would ask us to designate, by a show of hands, whether the lines were equal in length or different. We were, he instructed us, nearly rubbing his hands together, always to answer incorrectly. If the lines were of equal length, well then, a roomful of arms should sprout at the moment when Lears asked how many thought that they were unequal. Get that? Are you ready? Kids?

Rick, bounce and all, took a long time to complete the errand. And while he was gone, we had the chance to writhe and shake in delight. Oh how delicious to see how he'd react to this gambit. What a singular pleasure for school to yield. For this was one of those rare moments—akin to a fight in gym class, a urinary accident in study hall, the sudden gross illness of a teacher—when school became as interesting as life outside its confines could, at its best, become. Rick—well liked, good-humored, funny, intelligent—was about to drop into the scapegoat's role. We were all well pleased.

In ten or so minutes Rick returned. Still on the bounce, he cut the corner toward his desk with a mock head-fake and resumed his seat. Then the games began. Lears actually made like the exercise was already in full swing and that Rick had arrived at something like the beginning of the second quarter.

"And how many think that both lines are equal?" says Lears, looking out mildly at us all. The lines are different in size, though not outrageously so. Hands grab for the ceiling.

"How many think they are different?" Up, with almost no hesitation, goes the hand of Rick Cirone, one of the pass-catching mitts.

The sole hand is up. Lears looks at Rick balefully.

"How many take them to be equal?" he says, pointing to a perfectly matched couple, lines that would go through life in a state of geometric bliss. No one lifts a hand. Rick sees them, obviously knows they are the same, hesitates. "Different?" Up fly the arms, like salutes at the rally. Rick, after a moment's hesitation, joins in. Now he's ours.

It is amazing how good we are at this game. It is splendid how well we restrain ourselves from staring at Rick or laughing or coughing obtrusively; it's striking how ready his friends and teammates are not to feed him the critical info and let him in on the trick. This is something that Lears will remark: We have a talent for this kind of thing that seems natural, seems innate almost. We are pros at this art, whatever precisely this art might be.

On Lears goes, from one set of lines to the next. Does Rick cave? Does he go trotting along with the herd, off to the next watering place? No, not quite. But he doesn't stand up to us consistently, either. He about splits the rest. Sometimes he manages to hang tough and to say that the two obviously equal lines are so, even in the face of complete opposition from the class. But other times he gives in, mistrusts his own vision and goes clop-clopping with the group, a stray who's seen the advantages in getting with the program.

Lears is patient. He takes Rick and the class all the way to the end. And only then does he offer the explanation and let Rick in on the secret, the way the experimenters in the Milgram scam do. Rick doesn't seem crushed, exactly—just very, very nonplussed. He blushes—something I've never seen him do—and moves around uncomfortably in his chair.

But Lears isn't finished yet. He has a little more salt to shake on the wound. He looks out at us and poses a very simple question. He does it deadpan, Charlie Chaplin–style: "Do any of you think that you might have fared better on this experiment than Richard did?"

This is not, it turns out, a rhetorical question. He asks it once, then again. No hand goes up. We all burrow as far as we can go into our private molehills. We scatter dirt over our heads and wait. "Mark?" He's on me. "How do you think it would have gone with you?" I say nothing. I feel that the room has gotten about twenty degrees hotter. All my efforts go into holding on and giving no clue as to the thermal pressures I'm suffering. He hits a few more of us, with similar results.

But then it's time for dessert. And after what Lears has put up with on this front, how is he to be blamed? "Thomas?" No noise. "Thomas? What would you have done?" Buller snorts and chews his scabrous paw, but he will not even emit a grunt. The clock jumps and waits, dozes, sleeps, jumps again as Lears asks every one of us how it would go. He asks Dubby and John Vincents and Nora Balakian and Cecilia Doe and Carolyn Cummer. And no one has anything of substance to say. Because, really, we all know that Rick is the best we can offer. Not one of us has the ease and smooth high school élan that he has, and no one combines his level of smarts with his genuine confidence. And he, it turns out, had only partial staying power.

Finally the clock hops for the last time. The bell rings, and we are free.

On the way out, Lears stops Rick to thank him for taking it all so well. "I needed someone with an even temper," he says. "I'm terrified to imagine what might have happened if I'd chosen Tom Capallano."

Maybe Lears thought that Cap would have blown up when he saw the trick, having been so roundly humiliated. And what he assumed, of course, is that Cap, herd animal that he was, would have been duped every time. I'm not so sure, even now.

It took about a week, maybe more, for the implications of this seemingly trivial event to dawn on me. For even now, one says, Oh yes, of course that's how it would go. People are like that, group animals. Groupthink always prevails. We've all taken Sociology 101 or encountered some equivalent lesson in this or that magazine article. But the effect of these displaced encounters with the phenomenon is to jade you, to draw the poison out of the stinger.

Really, what went down that day, and probably will anytime you stage an experiment like this, is something to make you stand and gape. Asked to choose between their own eyes, which have made few if any simple mistakes up to now, and the will of the group, many people (nearly all?) will cave in and join. They will push that whole stack of chips, the individual freestanding I, tottering as it might be, to the center and merge it with the rest. It happens so easily. It is hard to believe.

Which of us would have clung to the truth? The answer was clear enough to me. Not a single blessed one—probably not even Sandra, or bulldog Buller, J. Edgar Hoover's little brother. No one, with the possible exception, I realized, of the unprepossessing little fellow up front. He would have wagged his hand and stroked his mustache and nodded his head and looked at the gunboats, and he would have gone his own way. Just as, faced with the Milgram experiment, he would have turned to the fellow in the lab coat and told him, in the most decorous possible way, that he, Frank Lears, was not going to send a single volt of electricity into another human being. And, further, that the whole idea of trying to teach anyone through electric shock was obscene.

That, I would come to understand, is what he had to offer. He could give you the pleasure and pain of sticking to your way, of seeing things as truly as a human being can, of not going around lying, at least most of the time. And for it, what would you get? Stones maybe, spitballs perhaps, or looks from your coevals that were equivalent. (Socrates, they killed—don't forget.) But you'd carry with you the sense that you told the truth, didn't conform to the tribal usages for convenience or gain. Noble enough.

But over at Hormel Stadium, it is Medford 21, Somerville 20 and we are blazing in triumph. Or it is the end of the Revere game, another hard-fought victory. We have come back to the stadium by bus, followed by the cheerleaders. In the locker room, we're celebrating the win when suddenly there arises a clatter like the waking of the dead.

It was beating, wild beating, on the gray locker-room door. The door squeaked its way open about a foot. In the gap, I saw the face of Marianne Campbell, a cheerleader; she was weeping and laughing at once. The girls, the cheerleaders, were slamming the locker room door and screaming. They wanted to come in, cried for it. Frank Ireland, the screamer, threw his body against the door and tried to force it back. No dice. The girls pushed harder. Chuck Mallory, a backfield coach, flung himself into the fight; still the door barely moved. The screaming got louder.

What was coming if the girls had made it in? An orgy, I half believed: ripping and snarling and tearing and unmeasurable, painful bliss in the Mustangs' sanctum amidst shower steam-clouds and the stench of sweat and the green muscle concoction, Atomic Balm, that we slathered on our injuries and that made us reek like rotting flowers. The noise outside the locker-room door was the most frightening and exhilarating thing I had heard in my life. I was terrified. I was alive. I wanted the coaches, with their Puritan manly muscle, to fall away from that door and disappear.

The girls are yelling, and our helmets are raised over our heads; they look like gleaming, streamlined skulls, emanating death-beauty; we are winning warriors, we Mustangs. After Revere, after Somerville, I screamed so loud in triumph I felt that I must have shaken the whole world.

Chapter Six

CUTE

One day, well after the debacle with Rick, Frank Lears walked into the room with what, by the standards he had so far set, had to qualify as a bounce in *his* walk. It was early December, a cold, gray day as I recall it, the sort of melancholy weather that Lears seemed to prefer. The sunlight just played an unwelcome contrast on your own brown-leaf mood—what good was it? He stood this time rather than edging himself into the wood and metal confinement chairs, punishment seats.

He told us to pass forward the Durant books. We would not be using them anymore. Dubby O'Day piped up immediately to inform all and sundry, and particularly Lears, that it was fine with him, since he was finished with the Durant book, finished, that is, coloring in the *o*'s. (It couldn't have been true, could it? Is it possible that the Dub colored in all the *o*'s in only a few months' time?) So up to the front of the room—there was still a gunmetal gray desk up there—went the books. Fine. No more books. Just free-and-easy discussions, empty nothing. Excellent. Maybe the teacher would disappear next, as in the pseudo–nursery rhyme about no more pencils, no more books, etc. Bliss.

But that was not quite how it was going to be. Lears, without having asked for or received anyone's permission but his own, had decided to revamp the curriculum in a stroke. He was going to replace the Durant, which even he clearly could no longer bear, with a sequence of books chosen exclusively by himself. These books had a focus; they had a design. In fact they were quite aggressively chosen—a rude whap at all our practices and pieties. But that would not be clear to me for some time.

He let us know that the books would come from the Harvard Coop and that we would have to pay for them ourselves, unless we couldn't afford to, in which case he'd pick up the tab. Buller intervened quickly to say that he didn't want the books, didn't have to have them, wasn't paying, and would not read them this side of the infernal pit. Lears softened his expression and said, as he would say approximately seven hundred times that year, "Ahhhhh, Thomas," as though the young man had just succumbed after a long illness.

At Medford High, this bringing in of books from the outer world counted as real innovation, genuine breakthrough thinking. No one before Lears would have conceived it or dared to do it. All books used in classrooms had to be approved by the school board and probably a dozen or so other state and local regulatory agencies. Lears ignored them. He probably saw that the place was so chaos-ridden that he could do pretty much as he chose and that it would take them a year or so to catch up with him. By then, he'd no doubt be on to something else. Whatever the reason, in this, as in all things, Lears went his own way.

He told us the names of the books, though he seemed sure that none of us but Sandra, who was nodding a bit madly as he went through the list, could possibly have heard of them. They were Freud's *Group Psychology*, Camus' *The Stranger*, Hesse's *Siddhartha*, and Ken Kesey's *One Flew Over the Cuckoo's Nest*. I remember hearing him say these names with an easy familiarity, as though there were something nearly predictable about them. But to me, this was not so. I felt irritated by the ease of the catalog, strangely left out of something that should perhaps have been my business.

No time was to be wasted. Our first book was going to be Freud's *Group Psychology*, and Lears launched directly into an account of what we would find there. And the account was, I had to admit, fairly engrossing. It bore directly on my condition at the time. But something else was going on of no little interest in that same class. Two surprising revelations were unfolding simultaneously, one of an intellectual sort, the other emphatically more carnal. At any given moment, that first day of Freud, it was not easy for me to decide which one to attend to.

I had come late to class that day, so I was compelled to sit on the outside of the circle. I slid my seat up behind two of the girls (I can't recall for certain which ones—Nora and Carolyn, maybe), who seemed not to know, or more likely not to care, that I was close by. Their subject for the day, addressed in the subtlest whispers, was who was and who was not cute. The conversation was a game, played a little like tennis. One of the girls would serve up a boy's name, and the other would acquiesce and say that yes indeed, he was cute—that is, attractive, sexy, desirable (1950s euphemisms were still in play, though, so *cute* was the word), and thus the server would pick up a point. If the other girl blanched and cringed or offered an expression proximate to vomiting, then the point was lost. It was clear that they were going to rack up the obvious points first. Cap was up top. Rick followed soon after. But then it was a matter of creativity and surprise, of placing a spinning trick serve past the other girl, making her admit that some boy whom she, and her friends too, probably, had never considered for the accolade was actually deserving.

The male version of this discussion was, as you might imagine, a few degrees cruder. The operative question wasn't "Is she cute?" but "Does she give?" In other words, Does she put out sexually? One of the more revelatory, or pseudo-revelatory, strolls I took at Medford High was through the halls with Jonathan Zucker. He was a large-lipped, large-eyed boy who claimed first- or at worst secondhand knowledge of the sexual proclivities of the MHS girls. So as we climbed the stairs passing the prim, back-straightened, blond Laura Croft, Jonathan whispered to me, "She gives. She gives like crazy. You just have to be her boyfriend, that's all. And she has *lots* of boyfriends."

But these tours were artful, full of surprises. Passing Rhonda Tantaglia—black stockings, fishnet, black bra strap dangling down the shoulder from under her sleeveless blouse—Jonathan would snort, "Nope, she don't give. [The word *doesn't* was never used in this oft-iterated sentence.] People spread a lot of rumors about her, but they're not true."

FRANK LEARS was discussing authority, and gradually he pushed the girls' discussion out of my mind. "What I want to talk to you about," said Lears, "is something called the psychological poverty of groups." Groups are poor, Lears averred, because those who join them, or who get forced into them without knowing what it is they're doing, surrender a major part of themselves as the price of admission. Every group, you see, has a leader, or a small circle of leaders, and in order to join the group, you've got to recognize the leader and perform a little internal operation. To put it bluntly, you set the leader up as an agent of authority, a miniature internal monarch, a little king or queen, and at the same time you depose the element of yourself that up till now has been calling the shots. What the leader values, you value. Effectively, you stop thinking. You turn that onerous function over to the other guy, and you begin saluting or goose-stepping or falling on your knees before the anointed one or simply conforming in what looks like harmless, standard ways. Your will is no longer quite your own.

Why should anyone this side of sane want that? Why does it feel good to deliver your autonomy, your freedom (for that is what it comes down to), over to someone else?

This question hung for a while in the air, joining a throng of previous Lears questions that had undergone the same fate. The atmosphere of the classroom, could you regard it with the right pair of revealing lenses, was laden with multiple unanswered, and often unregarded or uncomprehended, questions. They swam there, waiting to be attended to, like the poor souls that blow around the edges of purgatory, not quite damned, but far from redemption.

I left this question suspended with the rest and tuned in closely to the girls. Cuteness was still the issue. They were considering the relative merits of Donny Perkins, *a* class clown—we had not one but a circus-size supply of these—who was outgoing, a little round, and infinitely likable, who always wore an expression indicating that some prank had just been played, that it was minor but original, that he had done it, and was proud. He was soft-bodied, had red hair and an amiable face; he looked like a cross between Satan and Burl Ives. Donny used to greet you in the hall by asking his standard question: "Do you putt-it?" To which the answer was, or was supposed to be, "Do you?" Then Donny: "Of course I putt-it. Don't be silly. And so do you. Everyone knows it." *Putt-it* meant masturbate—in all probability.

They were having a tough time with Donny. And who could

blame them? Did they want to be spirited off to the Sheepfold, the make-out parking spot, by someone who might slip a whoopee cushion under their seat? They did not say as much. All deliberation was carried out with oohs and aahs and negating exhalations and the like. But one got the idea. Donny was a case of postmodern indeterminacy; he was to cute what a few choice, funny lines from *Finnegans Wake* are likely to be to meaning.

Of course, personally I didn't give much of a damn about how the two Fates would come to regard Donny Perkins. I was waiting, skulking, unwilling to say a word and blow my cover, to see if I myself might be mentioned. Where did I fit in, in this great amorous chain? Around the bottom, I suspected. But one always lives in hope.

LEARS, FOR his part, didn't hear, or ignored the whispers between the Fates, and went on. Why do we pine for external authority? That was his question. Why do we want to put others in the place of our own minds? Because doing as much immediately makes doubt disappear. Suddenly you know what to do. You know what to value. There are no questions anymore. Thinking hurts, and to stop thinking confers considerable pleasure.

That, I sensed to be true, having avoided all such activity since I could recall. And even though the girls were now past the hockey team, from which they'd selected the redoubtable Tom McQue as the most savory morsel, and were moving on to other matters, I turned their volume down lower and tried to bring in Lears. He was working against tough competition, yet somehow something he was saying was winning out.

"Now, where do you suppose this urge to get rid of thinking comes from? How do we know that not thinking is going to be pleasurable?" Lears looks at Buller and grins a rare cards-up-the-sleeve grin. No one has anything to say, least of all Buller. We sit, mud settling into solid, sound earth, as it was our duty and seeming destiny to do. Dubby puts his head down on his desk and commences a mock nap. John Vincents gets intimate with the dirt clumped between his soccer cleats, which he unaccountably wears to class.

"We've all already experienced this sensation," Lears says. "We had it as children. When you're a child, before you reach the age of reason, or some approximation thereof"—he adds this in deference to Buller, I suppose, but maybe in deference to us all—"you're completely protected. Others tend you, watch out for you, put you in a position of dependence." And, as Lears outlines it, we all want to go back to that state, the condition in which we're fully protected, where we always know what's right and wrong, where someone does all our thinking for us.

Early in life, don't forget, we're surrounded by giants, great figures, who seem omnipotent and omniscient. All our needs will be taken care of. All will be well. It's as though we were born in paradise and for the rest of life, memories of that place stay alive. When someone comes along and offers reentry, a shortcut back into the garden, slipping past the angel with his flaming sword, then it's likely that our eyes are going to glaze over with sugary hope.

And then he began with his questions—ceaseless, annoying questions. But he was getting a little better at it, coming up with some new techniques.

What groups are you yourselves a part of? Go ahead, take a minute, write their names down. Your church, your sports team, your neighborhood friends, school friends, family, camps, clubs, what have you. How about a country? How about the United States of America—is that a group too? Surely there is a leader.

Then think if you will, think if you can, about what kinds of leaders, what kinds of directing fathers and stand-in mothers, these groups offer. And think too of what you lose when you join one of these operations. Think of what, if anything, you might gain.

The girls became quiet. We all—well, maybe Buller excepted—did what he asked. We wrote, the fifteen or so self-selected seniors clumped in an almost-circle (I was the radical electron, the loose particle maybe about to fly away from the atom) in a well-lit room on the top floor of the old Medford High building, while December subtly modulated its grays outside. It was easy. It was list making and didn't require the labor of composing full sentences.

I made my own list, writing down the names of the track and football teams, my church, St. Raphael's, along with the names of its priests and Sunday school teachers; I included America in the list, and Richard Nixon, too. Then we all stopped and Lears made us stand up and stretch, take a little rest. Because even this much mind-work was to us the equivalent of a dozen or so wind sprints.

Then Lears began to talk about the qualities of a leader. Some leaders, he said, rule reasonably. They lay out their ideas, they tell you what they value, and then they put you in a position to make a choice. They feel sure that what they have to impart can be of some help and that people will recognize their own advantage in it. But there are other sorts of leaders, too. These leaders play on people's longing for the old fatherly (or maybe motherly) certainties. They have what's called charisma, the glow that comes off someone who exudes perfect confidence in what he believes. These people are warm externally. They seem to offer love equally to anyone who is ready to follow them. But inside they are ice. They love no one but themselves. They are indifferent to every other being. A leader of this sort looks completely self-reliant. He needs no one. So everyone tries to get next to him, get a boost from his confidence. He is the one who knows it all, the magus, the prophet, the orator, the dictator, the great helmsman.

Here, when he had laid these things out, Lears, it seems to me, took a step into becoming the kind of teacher that would change me, and some of the other people in the room, around. Don't forget, we had been busy driving him crazy. We had imitated him, teased him, in the case of Buller had insulted him; he'd thrown his most valuable pearls in front of us, and we'd coughed dismissively a few times and fallen back to the familiar swinish drowse.

With this narrative, and after the routine with Rick, he had us cornered. He could have gone at us full tilt. Why didn't he just command us to look at our dull religious lives—most of us went to church the way we went to school; it was a place to snore and make an occasional social linkup. But more than that, he could have assaulted us for the herd behavior that made us as wearisome to teach as we were. Who is the boss on the football team, who sets the tone? And in the sororities that dominate the school, who are the alpha girls? How do they enforce their petty tyrannies?

And as to the government—this was 1969, remember—how do they enforce such idiot acquiescence from you? How have they talked you into waging an unjust, useless war in Vietnam? How did they perpetrate the Red scare on your moms and dads? How did they get them into nine degrees of paranoid ecstasy about the Communist threat?

But he never posed these questions. He never ranted, never got in our faces. He controlled what must have been his utter angry humiliation at the way his class had been going. He laid off. He trusted us. For the first time, he put us in a position to examine ourselves. It was a chance to become explorers in our own lives. We could raise the spyglass and see ourselves as from a distance. But we could reject the invitation, too.

You could imagine how great the temptation to grab the helm and steer us where he needed us to go might have been. There sitting in front of Lears was Cap, who was his bane. Much more than Buller, who was just a mobile annoyance, Cap must have come across to him as something of a spiritual enemy, to use Blake's language. Cap, with his beard, heavier than most men's, the ropey muscles up and down his arms, and his handsome face, with his slight underbite and dramatic jawline. His teeth were carnivorously white, the white you saw on tigers; he had lovely hazel eyes that only came into certain focus when he was pinpointing a pass or laying up a basketball.

Lears must have looked at him and seen what the magisterial historian Henry Adams saw when he encountered Ulysses Simpson Grant in the president's office. To Adams, Grant seemed a crude throwback to some other, primitive time. Could civilization be spinning in reverse?

But what Lears didn't do was foist his view on us. He didn't address the whole bit about alpha males to Cap the way he might have, or torment him with a sequence of questions that Cap never could have answered about the place of the authoritative other in his own life. No, he put that sort of thing aside. He erased himself from the exchange as much as he could, and in doing so started to become the teacher he was destined, however briefly, to be.

Frank Lears seemed to be in the process of stepping over and becoming something of a Socratic figure. Socrates, as opposed to his disciple Plato, does not teach a system. He has no portable wisdom. What he offers instead is simply freedom from illusion. He will turn and criticize anything, no matter how exalted. Socrates is a questioner, who leaves no belief untouched. Family, religion, state—whatever it is, he asks you to consider what you owe it and what, if anything, it might owe you. He asks what evidence you have that the esteemed thing is good. He is relentless, and he never stops talking, won't stop asking. As Kierkegaard says, "His irony was not the instrument he used in the service of an idea—irony was his position, more he did not have." Lears had more—he had his beliefs, his ideas—but for the most part he held them in abeyance and simply asked us to take a first stab at knowing ourselves.

Lears asked us to consider whether the groups we had listed had leaders and whether they led by delivering us from doubt and bringing us back to the old certainties. He gave us thirty full minutes to do this, and we all sat silently and pondered, or at least I did. It was the first time I had ever actually sat and *thought,* at least insofar as I can recall. It was a first, a quiet enough one, one hard to render dramatic in the way a football game, a whipping laid on Somerville by the mighty Mustangs, can be. But it was a major moment for me nonetheless.

WHAT I thought about when he gave us our half-hour or so of silence was religion.

It started with a memory. When I was a boy, eight or nine years old, I was praying one day at the altar at the Sacred Heart church. It must have been after confession. When I went outside, a kid was waiting. He was a grade or two behind me, gawky, big-eared, wearing ripped corduroy pants and standing beside a rusted bike. He came up to me diffidently and asked, with no perceptible irony or anything even mildly toxic in his voice, if I was going to become a saint. Why did he ask? "Because you prayed so beautiful."

And, truth be told, I was a pious little boy. I loved church; though the sainthood business hadn't occurred to me, I was more than interested in becoming a priest. The life of renunciation looked very good to me. I could enter the rectory and be left alone. I could get rid of school, family, friends, the whole works, and just lower myself into a completely protecting, completely prescribing environment. And then too, I loved God a great deal and Jesus, if possible, more. I also feared hell.

For a long time, I wore faith like a deep coat. I worshiped the Christian doctrine, believed fervently in angels and the Blessed Virgin, who would intercede for us at the throne of the almighty, and fiercely retributive, Father. My initiation scene was in the Sacred Heart church, Malden, Massachusetts. There in the lower chapel, dank and frightening as any catacomb where the first Christians practiced their outlaw faith, I listened to Father O'Hara, known to us boys as the Fat Father—awful, gregarious, bluff, and sly—intone his favorite Bible passage, the one where the sinner in hell, burning, begs to be permitted to lick water from the finger of Lazarus, a poor, righteous man who is with Abraham in heaven. "Never," cries the Fat Father, becoming for a moment a burning pillar of wrath and thus temporarily losing his resemblance to the fat sergeant, Sergeant Garcia, the buffoon on the TV show *Zorro*, from whom he has acquired his nickname. The sinner was left to roar in everlasting fires.

Daily I felt hell's breath. I confessed my sins, did penance, made good acts of contrition, as the priest told me to do after confession, when I read out my partly fabricated list of transgressions. I disobeyed my parents four times, lied six times. I teased Joey Merrill, our neighbor, four years younger than myself. The Joey Merrill teasing was always last on my list: I phrased it ambiguously—so it could have meant either that I had done it just once or that it was perpetual—hoping the priest would imagine option A. B was closer to the truth.

Obsessively, I imagined eternal punishment, conceiving of eter-

nity not unlike the way Joyce rendered it in *Portrait of the Artist*:
A bird comes every million years to lift a grain of sand from an
endless mountain. In many eons the mountain will disappear. And
that whole time will be but one instant, a flashing evanescent tick,
in the course of the eternal. Late on summer nights, as fireflies
popped their spooky, subaqueous green, my friends and I envisioned
heaven and hell, impressed on each other the facts of eternal
damnation and everlasting bliss.

I remembered the nuns who taught me at Sunday school as hu-
mours out of Ben Jonson: There were the crones, crabbed, thin,
and zealous; and the stalwarts, grand battleships alight with rectitude; and then the seemingly benevolent ones, portly and content.
Yet even the most kindly could break into furious rants. Sister Eu-
lalie, with her benevolent, moony face gently framed by her wim-
ple, and her sweet milk-white hands, once told us that when a girl
dyed her hair, the poison from the dye seeped through the roots
and slowly, slowly built up in her brain. Then one day the fragile
organ would start to decompose into polluted gobs, until the brain-
pan itself became a horrible vat, bubbling and spitting.

Over time I moved in and out of churchgoing, pulled from the
church's orbit by the likes of Johnny Kavanaugh, who became,
when I was eleven years old, Father O'Hara's replacement. Johnny
was the way, the truth, and the life. He owned a doughnut and sub
shop, where he also took, or pretended to take, numbers over the
phone. (In my Malden neighborhood, being a bookie was high-
prestige work.) Johnny screened stag movies for us, told us about
oral sex, and claimed to have gotten it on with one of the Supremes
(not Diana Ross, he added with some humility, but a backup
singer, backup). Johnny's friend Durante, an ambulance driver
about whose sanity even Johnny had doubts, demonstrated basic
fornication for us using an empty juice bottle and his semi-erect

item. Johnny—apprehended by all sane adults as a yammering buffoon—was practiced in the ways of the world.

But despite my waywardness, I knew for a long time that there was a God. I knew it in part because of my horrendous sense of guilt. Whenever I did something wrong—terrorized a younger cousin, spoke harshly to a teacher, lied, or cheated—I quivered under the flying lash of my conscience. I became physically ill at the thought of my sins. And where could this guilt and suffering come from if not from the Lord on high?

In better moods, on better days, I knew God through the magnificence of his creation—not its beauty or its goodness or pleasure but the overpowering presence of what *was,* the massive thereness of the world. How could all this grandeur be, I asked myself, if there was no God to send it into light? I acknowledged the God of creation but I believed, tremblingly, in the God of pain.

Almost everyone I knew believed in God, or professed to. There were atheists in existence, I knew. But they were damaged individuals, like my childhood friend DeFazio, who would walk down the street hollering out to God to prove his existence by striking him, DeFazio, down with a bolt of lightning from the sky. I recall debating with Fran and Mikey O'Rourke whether we ought to scatter when DeFazio issued such Homeric dares, lest the Almighty cast general death in DeFazio's direction. A lot of talk ensued. Eventually we agreed that anyone who could create the world in six days had enough fine-motor skill to take DeFazio out with a precise stroke while leaving the rest of us standing by unscathed, if maybe a little smoke-stained.

But then my sister, Barbara Anne, died an excruciating death, after half a dozen strokes that befell her over a period of two years. She was a sweet, pale, beautiful child, with soft blue eyes. At three, she could barely talk, though all else was normal. Soon afterward, she had her first stroke—so rare in children that a number of doctors at Massachusetts General Hospital had never seen it happen—and came home dragging one foot when she walked, her face drooping on the left side. Then another stroke came, and another, and another.

I recall that when she was in the hospital for the last time—I must have been in the ninth grade—I prayed incessantly to the Lord above to spare her. I made lists of all the things I would do, the pleasures I would surrender: no more TV, no more desserts— and I would follow through on these things for weeks on end. Nothing would change. Then I would go back to my past harmless habits. Nothing would change for her. Or she would get worse. And I would blame my own waywardness, my own lack of faith. I blamed myself but never the God above, who, despite all of His claims for being merciful and good and His need to be worshiped slavishly for those things, could preside so serenely over Barbara's slow, horrible death.

On the day she died it was black outside and poured rain, and I pretended that this was heaven's acknowledgment of our grief. The sky weeps for you, a friend said. And I took this temporarily to heart with remarkable, foolish tenacity. I listened to other stories, too, like the one that held that the soul of a sinless child like Barbara would flare straight to heaven and abide there in glory, waiting for us to join her when the time came. But I could not fully believe any of it. Could a God who looked down upon the agony and death of a child be a God worth worshiping?

Yet I clung to the outward forms. I went to church, attended confession, made good acts of contrition. And the habit of hypocrisy grew in me. In church I felt voided, as though I were an empty thing, hollow, my heart and lungs and inner organs removed in some horrid trick. I was a shadow walking and kneeling and mumbling prayers and observing the rites. I didn't have the simple courage of my conviction to turn and say that whatever the truth might be about God and faith, it was not to be found here.

Lears' implication—and of course, being who he was, he did no more than imply—that religion, like every activity that involved a Big Other, an ultimate power, was bogus, a lie, shocked me. It was such a blow that I could barely absorb it. Here was someone, fully grown and mature, not a skittery whelp like DeFazio, who could suggest that we might laugh in the face of belief.

Yet I was also tempted by the possibility that Lears (and Freud) held out. That my sister had suffered and died and that there was no explanation for it but bad luck, horrible chance—that was an insult. But then to cover that horror over with pious stories that I could not honestly believe—and that no one, from what I could see, did—that was too much.

I'm not sure I went this far in the thirty minutes of silence that Lears gave us, though in days to come I would. But as freeing as what Lears said might be—for exploding an illusion, or what's taken for one, is always initially liberating—another question obtruded. What were you left with once you stopped taking anything on faith? What did you have once the illusions were cleansed? I couldn't answer the question at all clearly then; I only know that it scared me. What you got was freedom, of course—you reclaimed your own mind. But you cut yourself off from all the forms—churches and schools and governments—that made it their business to dispense the truth and, with it, some measured comfort. You became, in short, something like Franklin Lears—and like Socrates, that other eternal questioner and annoyance: an orphan adrift in the world.

But the class did not end in spiritual angst for me. When the clock made its last leap, the minute hand hurdling over the final numeral between us and freedom, and we all got up to trundle to the door, I caught the tail end of the two girls' conversation.

Directly in front of me, in unmistakable tones, one turned in the direction of the other and said, "Isn't Mr. Lears cute?"

"Yeah, he is, he really is."

Lears cute? Lears desirable? How could this be? He was a composite of many things the girls had agreed, in invisible congresses, it seemed, to find repulsive. He was a "brain," and no girl at Medford High could get herself worked up over a brain. A brain was—well, what else?—someone who was all head and no body, no spirit, no heart, no equipment, just gray matter and maybe a pair of glasses stuck on to keep the world in focus. A brain cute?

But I didn't dismiss it out of hand. I didn't laugh it off. Because the girls had rebelled once before on the matter of who was and wasn't attractive. I could date the event, the great seismic shift in American erotics, with some precision. It was the day after the Beatles appeared on *The Ed Sullivan Show* for the first time, in February 1964. I was in sixth grade then, and I remember how the girls had returned to school that Monday in a state of primal rhapsody. They sang "She Loves You" and "I Wanna Hold Your Hand" at top volume from the girls' bathroom. You heard it blasting through the vents that connected the two lavatories, ours and theirs, as though through a badly made speaker system. You heard it in the corridors and out at recess. What had a few days before been starched tight little girls, who went to mass at Sacred Heart and whose most daring style of in-school transgression was to stand suddenly and turn a soft ballet pirouette beside their desks, were now tiny, leaping maenads, who talked about how much they'd like to get their hands on John or George or Paul or (even) Ringo and punctuated their expostulations about the four with shrieks and yelps. When the erotic provocateur Charlie Musselman—the kid who had brought pornographic postcards to sixth grade, cards given to him *by his father*—asked Janet Gianelli where exactly she'd like to be with Paul (her particular favorite), she screamed, "Where else? In a bed!"

This sort of thing happened all across America, all at once. Suddenly Elvis and Dean Martin and Sammy Davis, Jr., were old hat. They were too weighty, too ponderous, too slow and cool. They were selfish, closed-down, too male. Their place was taken in the national dream life by tiny mop-headed boy-girls, whose presence was so collectively light that a sharp breeze, you felt, might have picked them all up and sent them floating off the stage, up and away. They'd grin and wave bye-bye. It had taken place in one revolutionary night, under the aegis of the knuckle-popping funeral home director Ed Sullivan.

As time went on, the macho clan won back a little territory: America could hardly do without grizzled pioneers and slouching, brave GIs. But the inroads the Beatles made never disappeared. They repealed large codes of fraud and woe, as the poet puts it. A new world of erotics came into being, where women expected to see something of themselves mirrored back in the men they loved, something not opaque and solid but freewheeling, mercurial, complicated, felt. This world came spinning into existence in a trice and was never wholly eclipsed or destroyed. And in it there was room for Franklin Lears, who was clearly in the Beatles anti-macho mode. And if there was room for Lears, for the brain, who knows what other opportunities this brave and still reasonably new world might offer, even—after a certain amount of personal shape-shifting thrown in—for me?

Chapter Seven

THE WALRUS

But in my life things got not better but worse over the course of that winter. I sniffed at the orphan state prescribed by Lears and by Socrates—or, more optimistically, the liberated condition, in which one becomes, as Goethe put it, a free artist of oneself—and got nervous; terrified, really. I was left with the psychological poverty of being outside the group, outside the pack. Football was over and life seemed to be, too. So rather than going over to Frank Lears—who, unlike Mace Johnson and the Fat Father and all the other fathers abroad, didn't really want me, or who wanted me, and the rest of us, only to become ourselves, whatever that might mean—I found myself another guiding light, a new prophet, and a new, more literal kind of high than anything produced on the football field.

To put it a little less obliquely, I started getting drunk as often as I could, and I put myself under the tutelage of a new mentor, an anti-Lears in most ways. I became a disciple of the amateur but inspired philosopher we nicknamed the Walrus.

I got drunk for the first time at the end of the football season. I went down to Playstead Park, an enormous preserve with a soccer field, a baseball diamond, tennis courts (vandalized), and swings (same) to commiserate with some of the other players and a few hangers-on after Malden, the Greater Boston League champions, ruined us on Thanksgiving Day. When ordering time came, rather than holding back as I usually did, I jingled four quarters and called for two quarts of Schlitz. They returned soon in a car piled with illegal booze, and there, standing on crusty, frozen ground, I chugged them down in a fraction of an hour. I had them both open at once, the quarts, slugging from one bottle then from the other.

I took to liquor like a duck to the pond. Heidi ho! I had to yell. Sounded like a hillbilly. Heidi ho!

Whatever invisible weight had been draped like lead bags on my shoulders was instantly lifted. This, I remember thinking, is what it feels like to be young.

And wasn't I young the rest of the time? Apparently not. For now I was ripsnortingly alive, feeling as though I'd just thrown a perfect cross-body block and were ambling, free and easy, back to the huddle, the pack. I walked on air; I breathed an intoxicating ether. Nothing hurt—nothing. I thought I could dance, sing. I did both. I thought that my utter failure—no, it was not failure, because I had never even brought myself to the testing point—with girls must be a matter of pronounced shyness. If only I could drop the mask of foolish propriety, cast off my inhibiting skin like the slough it was. Drop the mask and let the sweetness stream in, in and out. I was a mortal god, standing in cruciform in Playstead Park, Medford, Massachusetts, flourishing a quart bottle in each outstretched hand, mass-produced nectar of the masses, Schlitz lager. Heidi ho!

All the grief I felt at having been separated from the closest thing to a tribe I'd yet known ("best years of your lives, boys!") was suddenly dispelled. I was not separate anymore. I was part of everything. I belonged, here, among these people, and on this earth. Whatever it is that holds one aloof and apart lifted from me, licked clean away by the warm tongue of the booze. Good-bye to all that self-inflicted pain and a toast to the glorious drunken nights to come.

But they were not all conducive to sweet Keatsian flights, those nights, not all about winking bubbles and sweet draughts of Hippocrene and fading blissfully away. Booze is tricky stuff, a mystery drug. It lifts the curtain of inhibition and defense, quiets the sometimes raving inner figure of authority that Lears had told us all about—at least it did for me that first night—but every time there is something different behind the curtain. So sometimes I went around exultant, spreading gurgly joy. But other times the curtain lifted and strange things slouched forward.

Outside a burger joint one night, some unwise kid gave our carload the finger when we cut his car off in the parking lot. Ryan, another football lineman turned hockey team enforcer, and I tore out of our car, ripped the other car's doors open and grabbed two astonished guys from out of the backseat. There were two girls up front. We went to work.

Every other weekend I'd find myself in a brawl of some sort, drunk and mean. I didn't care so much if I lost, just as long as I could get down into the mud and onto the concrete and give and take in a chaos of self-forgetting punches and kicks.

For I had tasted the sweetest mix that there was. I had administered slamming straight-on hits, helmet first. And I could not easily say good-bye to the feelings that came with them. I took pleasure in the bruises, in the sore Sunday morning face, nearly as much as I did in victory's smashed-up knuckles. I liked being hit nearly as much as delivering blows, though (luckily) not quite.

Listening to Lears talking about groups and their hypnotic function, I began to see, dimly enough, that I was in sorrow because I was in exile from my pack. There was little I could do about it, though. Where else could I go? Where else find the feeling that I had lost when football ended if not in the guys' drunken pack and in the brawl?

I did not go too far in thinking about these questions, or about the answers Lears might offer to them, in part because I was in the position of what you might call a contrast gainer. Dubby, the Doober, was genuinely in bad straits. Dubby was—no great surprise here—failing math, and he was doing it with gusto. Mr. Repucci had taken to making an object lesson of him, including him prominently when he preached his sermons to the class about how, without proper application, they would amount to nothing. "Now, take Donawd here. He is a smart enough boy and not a bad-wooking boy. But he fails to do his homework, and so he wiww fail geomtwy ober and ober again." Donald did the imitation with glee, trying to force his face into the correct rodent-sniffing-for-the-last-cheese-crumb squinch.

Dubby's mother was making regular visits to the school now, in fear that Donny would fail and fail forever, and she was falling into league with Mr. Repucci. Always hard-edged, she was beginning to take Leo's version of the Doober as gospel. The two of them were teaming up, becoming a sort of unholy Gothic parentage for the Dub. Donny's mother was a nurse. She'd seen death and disease in all guises and it had not softened her heart for those who labored under something as comparatively slight as math-induced sorrow. She'd seen how powerful the forces of fate were, and somewhat in my father's mode, she'd gotten herself on their side. She could preach at length on how if I didn't stop lifting weights and bulking up for football, packing on muscular pounds, my asthma would blossom and I'd die panting at the age of twenty-three. She said this with some gusto, as though she'd entered into long-term alliance with the asthma.

Dubby's literal disease (the math thing was supposedly all in his head and in his deplorable spirit) over which Mrs. O'Day presided and whose strength she touted when she could was diabetes. Dubby often traveled with his syringe and his transparent life-giving juice and delighted in flourishing his works at unexpected times, tying off and shooting up. So standing in line, waiting to buy a submarine sandwich, as "heroes" are called in Boston, I turned around to see Dubby, with a gesture he'd learned from watching some junkie-featuring TV show, dramatically tying his arm off with a rubber tube, cinching it with his teeth, then setting up the needle, squirting a little of its contents into the air, and taking a violent jab at his arm. Then he sank into an apparent puddle of bliss, "Ahhhhh" and grinning toward heaven. I had to talk the sub-maker out of calling the cops.

Anyway, Dubby's mother actually loved him lavishly, wanted him to possess the world, and so headed off her disappointments by loudly telling the world (and herself) why this would not, could not, be. She could get rhapsodic on the impending mortal effects of the Doober's disease.

Dubby's father, Jack, was the counterweight to the formidable Mrs. O'Day. Jack O'Day was a salesman for the Hershey company; he hawked chocolates from town to town, and evidently with success. Dubby's house on Rondel Ave was a model of Medford bourgeois decorum. They had twin living rooms, and even a second bathroom. They were what the residents of Southie, Boston's Irish ghetto, disparagingly referred to as two-toilet Irish.

When Mrs. O'Day was rampant, Jack would invite Donny and his sister, nicknamed Sweetie, to mount invisible horses and ride away with him. They collectively mounted up and created giddyap noises and hoof-pops with their tongues and teeth, and thence were gone.

Jack was the kids' advocate in all things. One day he was driving me to Cape Cod, to visit with the Doober, when he went into an aria on the tribulations of Dubby O'Day. "This boy," he intoned, "has not led a normal life. He's been deprived of the pleasure that other children have as a birthright. Imagine never having tasted a piece of candy. Imagine not being able to eat your own birthday cake. Imagine that you can never, never eat the way that other people do." And as he said this, a tear coursed down the good man's cheek. He became eloquent about the joys of sweets, in the way that he would have had to do to be the successful chocolate salesman he was. But rather than an inducement to buy, this lyric was on the order of a funeral oration about the death of Dubby's youth from insufficient sugar intake.

I had all I could do not to spit the truth out like a peach pit. For Dubby ate everything in sight, then sought more. He ate cookies and pies and cakes—and not just a slice here and there but, the better to chuck the finger at fate, he ate them in apocalyptic quantities. He'd die, he believed, with icing on his face.

Not only did Dubby eat in profusion, he also became a devoted drinker of beer, his brand being Schlitz, the beer that made Milwaukee famous, and his standard order being two six-packs, usually with a half-pint of bourbon to sip on between cans. He could drink two beers, sometimes three, in ten minutes' time, by "shooting" them. That is, he would use a can opener to put a tiny hole down toward the bottom of the can, place a finger over it, put the hole to his mouth, then pop the top. The beer flowed like a small geyser down his throat. In this way you can drink a Falstaffian amount of liquor in record time.

Dubby was a fine dispatcher of booze, but he did not hold it well.

It was like being hit with Circe's wand; it turned him into a low, snorting creature in seconds. Liquor sent him on ferocious eating binges, in which he'd declare the need for, say, a dozen cheeseburgers, the small kind, purchased at White Castle. I remember him there one Saturday night, coming around the corner on hands and knees, crawling and barking, a bag of burgers hanging from his mouth, looking like a Saint Bernard. He refreshed himself with nine, ten, eleven, and then threw up in a huge blast all over the concrete apron of the establishment.

When he had cleaned himself off, he demanded the final cheeseburger, on the premise that Dubby always completed the feats he had planned for himself, something like Hercules with his labors. Art Mondello and I, part sadistically, part not wishing to witness another eruption of vomit, withheld the burger, whereupon Dubby hit the concrete again and roared, "Dear Jesus, help me, I just gotta eat one more cheeseburger!"

Artie and I suddenly became solicitous. We told Dubby that given his medical history, further cheeseburger eating would not be in his interest. Then one of us—Artie, I'm 90 percent sure—heaved the remaining burger to the edge of the parking lot. Dubby, always well monied from his poolroom exploits, snorted at us and returned to the cheeseburger window.

Closed! Cat howls, mock weeping, professions of undying love to the troll who commands the window. Then vicious threats. No dice. Dubby, undaunted, hustles across the parking lot. There, amidst glass and cans and general detritus, he recovers one more cheeseburger, dusts it off, and consumes it. Artie and I shrug. We have done our best to protect Dubby from himself.

Dubby needed saving more than once, and as I've suggested, I could always look at his tall form and handsome onion-shaped head to persuade myself that I was in pretty fine condition, at least by contrast. Artie and I frequently took the occasion to remind the Doob of all we had done for him. Whenever we needed him to drive us somewhere exotic—that is to say, outside of Medford—or to spot us five dollars for a game of action at the poolroom or to do one or another errand, we simply reminded him that we had saved his life.

We had done it on an extremely drunken night, when we were all three urinating off a small walkway bridge over the Mystic River. Artie and I were weaving and laughing and telling jokes. Dubby was in Hamlet-like dudgeon, in part because it had been a miserable week in math. "What's going to become of me?" he said suddenly. "I'm a complete failure. A complete fuckup." At which point, Artie turned to me and, behind Dubby's down-pointed aiming head, mouthed the words *my poor mother*.

"My poor mother," said the D. "My poor, poor, poor mother. Can you believe what she has to put up with? Look at me. I'm worthless. I'm a piece of human shit." He started intoning some lines from *Hamlet*—he'd played the lead in ninth grade—about his too sullied flesh melting away.

Then the next thing I knew, Dubby was no longer on our side of the bridge but the other. Then he was no longer standing facing us but dropped down to about ankle level, hanging over some very dark and February-cold New England water. Here, where the molasses had come in from Jamaica and the rum had gone out, Dubby was about to take what might have been a mortal dunk.

"Why not," he cried. "My life is ruined anyway."

Artie and I dropped down together and grabbed Dubby by the wrists and began to haul him up. He struggled against us. "Come on, it's no big deal. Just a little swim." Dubby was a fabulous swimmer, but the water was ice, and within he was more alcohol than blood.

As soon as we got him yanked over the pole, the argument began with Artie, who was to become a highly successful lawyer, announcing that we had saved the Doober's life and that henceforth he was our slave-robot as well as friend and the Doober insisting that it had all been a play, with his lines from *Hamlet* about the sullied flesh being part of the act. He said we were getting way too cranked up about nothing. We said he was a suicidal psychopath and owed us his life, or in any event owed us a share of his remaining beer—Dubby always bought more than we did. Having made no oath to the gods to consume a certain set amount that evening, Dubby relinquished the cans and we let him alone, for a while.

So I had Dubby to look down on as he tried to slide out of life like a snake from its skin. (Maybe.) And then, too, I had some other tricks to hold back my fear—the fear that was in part Frank Lears' creation, for it was he who, with my hardly realizing it, was beginning to make me mistrust everything around me, he who was destroying my equanimity, my peace of mind.

AFTER A time, I found my little surrogate community, and my debauched high priest, too, to replace football and the coaches. For the world teems with people who will impart wisdom free. Though, to be fair, it is often the people who have most soundly screwed up their own lives who are convinced that they have the most insight to offer the young.

My new sachem, replacement to Mace Johnson and Johnny Kavanaugh and the Fat Father, alternative to the maddeningly nonconclusive Franklin Lears, is the Walrus.

The Walrus is actually named Walter, but he has been given his nickname in a timid burst of counterattack. He has been given the nickname because he has given many of us—workers for Boston Distributing Incorporated, BDI—nicknames of a less flattering sort. Johnny Edsel, the Walrus's right-hand man, whom we have always called Ed and who has the distinction of taking the BDI truck home on Friday nights, has been renamed Fat Eddie by the Walrus. And the Walrus likes Edsel, whom we all now refer to simply as Fat, a good deal.

The Walrus himself is hardly svelte. He is thirtyish, smooth and sleek and imposing, with a handsome, slightly aristocratic face, a large nose, and soft hazel eyes. Better dressed, he would play well enough in Vegas. He is regal in his walrusdom, not old or hoary or sadly gray, but rich in presence.

Somewhat like Lears, the Walrus is a philosopher of life. As Plato celebrated the forms that exist on high, as Schopenhauer endorsed the life-spirit, as Socrates (and, in his way, Lears) favored open-minded doubt, ignorance of all things, as Hegel touted the zeitgeist, in order to begin to explain what mattered, the Walrus too has a key to experience: It is sex in general and fellatio in particular.

The Walrus has hired us, about a dozen Medford High guys—me and Rick and Cap and Dubby and Johnny Edsel (now Fat), Johnny "Gumshoes" Patello (nickname courtesy of the Walrus, in honor of Johnny's reluctant pace), and a few more to roll up inky advertising circulars with rubber bands, the kind of things that Lechmere Sales and Mal's Market put out, and distribute them, on Wednesday afternoons and Saturdays, all day, to the porches of homes through greater Boston. We strolled down the streets like monarchs, flipping these rolled-up batons of paper onto the doorsteps of the working class. Occasionally, displeased at the arrival of unwanted paper, they toss them back, occasionally with advice that involves their intimate repositioning. The best place to toss the circulars is at storm doors, which, on a direct hit, make the noise of the Last Judgment.

Cap, who could break the storm doors to smithereens, never does this sort of thing. He lopes along, chuckling to himself, singing softly, and tossing the papers from behind his back or between his legs; when he misses, which is not often, he hops onto what there is of a lawn, recovers the circular, and puts it where it ought to be.

The best time to execute the crack-of-doom maneuver is on a Saturday morning, early. The best place from which to execute it is not the sidewalk, particularly if you are neither large nor fast, but from the front seat, the shotgun spot, of the Walrus' panel truck, with the Walrus driving at a steady tilt.

Dubby is spectacularly good at this. It's a matter of hand-eye coordination, not unrelated to his poolroom skills. He can make a street in Jamaica Plain ring like the inside of a pinball machine as the Walrus cruises along, bellowing in delight at each score. Dubby is also superb at engaging passersby in mutually improving discourse, hollering random insults out the truck window.

If the traffic is female and young, the Walrus generally takes over, leaning across Dubby's seat, resting companionably over the D's lap, while he lays down his patter. The Walrus never has much success with these women—he never, that is, lures them into the truck or even gets a phone number from them, though he does manage to hold their attention for spectacular amounts of time. As he says, "I'm in a delivery truck with ten guys yapping like monkeys in the back. It's a miracle they listen at all." Which is true enough.

Dubby has been catapulted into bliss. He hops into the truck on a Saturday morning with a dozen lemon doughnuts, and by the time we are in Jamaica Plain or West Roxbury or wherever, he has eaten them all, being sure to leave a massive ring of white

powder around his face. Though few of us can abide lemon doughnuts, we begin insisting that he share them. No way. He seems to
have made a dozen-doughnut vow to the god of gluttony. Instead,
Dubby prevails on the Walrus to stop the truck and buys two dozen
more for general distribution. The sacrament of doughnuts completed, we settle down to the most important part of the BDI day,
which is not the rolling and the throwing, or even the pay, which is
outrageously high by going rates, but the Walrus' sermon.

The sermon can take many forms, and will draw with varying degrees of intimacy on personal experience but, like the sermons of
Jonathan Edwards and Cotton Mather and all the great preachers
before him, the Walrus has one major subject, a central topos to
which he relentlessly returns. This is salvation through blow jobs.

The Walrus, by his account, is a sexual high priest of the first
order. He requests and receives numberless blow jobs from great
varieties of women. They are married and single, young and middle-
aged, pretty and (he is willing to admit) sometimes ill-favored. But
they are united in their willingness to bring the handsome, sleek,
overweight Walrus to the headlands of bliss.

Doughnuts consumed, sitting on the wheel wells and atop great
heaps of circulars back in the truck, we go silent. The moment of
revelation is at hand. "So, Walrus," Dubby intones. "Whadja do
last night?"

"Well, it's interesting you should ask," Walrus says in his
imitation–W. C. Fields barroom raconteur voice. "Last night I
hooked up with Courthouse Karen." We all know who Courthouse
Karen is. But we must ask again. It's part of the ritual.

"Courthouse Karen," the Walrus begins—and with zest; he is
never weary of retelling the tales—"is the daughter of a judge. If
you'll take her out someplace nice for dinner, then bring her to the
lawn of the courthouse, provided the weather's not so bad, she'll

do anything. Anything! But she'll only do it on the courthouse lawn. Ain't that something?"

We agree that it is. And then, in chorus, we ask, "So what did she do?"

"So what did she do? What do you think she did?"

Silence. It is that point in the mass.

"Courthouse Karen blew my socks off!"

The van erupts in cheers. Screams, hollers, loud halloos, general din. The communicants are in bliss. And then the Walrus goes on to explicate the pleasures of the particular b.j. This takes some time and involves detailed and intimate description, reference to various advanced techniques.

"But, Walrus," screams Dubby. "Didn't you get laid?"

The Walrus predictably, exuberantly declaims, "Did I get laid? I got laid, relayed, parleyed," at which point we all join in as a chorus: "Marmalade, Band-Aid, first aid, prepaid, Gatorade, orange-ade ["root beer," someone screams], unmade, Kool-Aid . . ." and on it goes through a vast litany that you'd think only a shaman could keep straight. And of course, among other things, this is a parody of Mace Johnson's old football litany—lean, mean, agile, mobile, etc. We've got a new master now; out with the old. The truck is roaring inside like a madhouse, rocking on its greasy shocks as it cruises through Jamaica Plain. Inspired by the Walrus, lifted on the wings of his tale, we have gone to banana heaven.

The Walrus knows the secret of life. It is having sex as often as possible—and at seventeen, we know that can be often indeed. If you do succeed in having sex with Walrus-like frequency, if you do it with a great variety of high-spirited, willing girls, who never get hurt or mad or seriously want to get married, then the rest of life will be quite bearable, more than bearable in fact, because you can anticipate the sex and you can become a raconteur of great sex acts past. You can work in a broken-down truck, in the company of testosterone-racked, terminally screwy high school kids and you can sustain your high spirits, your feeling of ongoing *élan vital*, nonalcoholic inebriation.

The Walrus didn't drink, and had contempt for booze. It was, in his philosophy, a substitute for sex, indulged in by the terminally timid or the absurdly ugly. The *absurdly* ugly: because the Walrus believed that virtually any guy who made sex his major interest could always find someone to couple with, and if he stayed at it and treated the women well, he'd be surprised at how many willing votives he'd acquire. You can imagine how welcome this piece of news was to us.

"There's not a guy in this truck," he once said in his sincere voice, "who is so ugly that he couldn't get laid all the time if he wanted to, if he'd just put his mind to it."

The Walrus, for his part, was partial to pretty girls. If you could find a pretty girl to have sex with you, well and good. But plain girls were fine, and even girls whom everyone in high school said were ugly could, if you looked at them long enough and spent some time in their company, be found to have redeeming features. The Walrus repeatedly told us that one of the bullshit aspects of high school consensus was that it cordoned off the supposedly desirable girls, the cheerleader types, and told you you had to chase them and only them and leave the other girls home to do their homework and, in time, to marry boring guys. And that was too bad. Because what girls wanted most wasn't handsome guys or rich guys but guys who weren't boring, guys who had something to say and who knew how to have a good time, guys who could make them laugh, and who could produce a half-dozen or so negotiable hard-ons a day.

"Even you, Dubby," he once bellowed. "You got a sensahumor. You could get all the girls you want with that. Girls love to laugh."

Dubby had earned this accolade by pointing out the window a few minutes before, spotting a pair of socks wagging on a clothesline, and crying out, "Hey, Walrus, those socks belong to you?" Banana heaven ensued.

But the Walrus didn't just seek to liberate us into the kingdom of the higher orgasm. He had another pedagogic function, too. He was in charge of a certain kind of group discipline, discipline through humiliation.

We're cruising along the Alewife Brook Parkway, say, on the way to a delivery site. The truck is relatively quiet. The Walrus leans back in the driver's seat and calls out a name. "Poochie!" Mack Puccinello is a football player—bulky, intelligent, clean-cut, and clear-featured, with a face full of probity, like one of Cromwell's Roundheads. To hear one's name bellowed in this way by the Walrus is to shake with fear. It means that it is your turn to withstand whatever carping, cruelty, and random unpleasantness the Walrus, or the rest of the truck, might care to dispense.

"He's Pooch-Boots now. That's his new name," says the Walrus, as though he's an explorer naming freshly discovered land. Pooch has made the mistake of showing up for work wearing a pair of Timberland-type work boots that are colored an absurdly raw yellow. It is as though all of Poochie's own rank inexperience, his unworldly character, is embodied in the shoes. The van fires up with echoes of the new nickname. Pooch-Boots! Pooch-Boots! Poooooooch-Boooooots! Yeah! Puccinello blushes and says nothing.

There are two schools of thought on how to handle a Walrus rank-out session. One is to retaliate (my philosophy). The other is to fold your psyche into the fetal position and let it all beat off your back.

Now the truck is comparing Poochie to the Pillsbury Doughboy. Now the truck reminds him of a dumb question he asked at a football chalk session more than a year ago. He had inquired in all earnestness how we would block a particular play if the enemy configured itself in a defense that, a year before, the coaches had referred to as "Chinese." So the word *Chinese* begins to bang around the truck, sometimes distended, sometimes compressed. Poochie purses his lips, nods his head, and tries to form an expression more mature than anything the Walrus can muster. "You guys," he intones again and again. "You guys."

What one must not do under these circumstances is get mad. Because if you lose it, the teasing will never stop. You will be driven crazy by it and forced to quit the job, which pays nearly twice as well as anything else around—"five balloons an hour," in Walrusese.

The rank-out sessions are of course the Walrus's way of keeping us under control. Once he draws a little blood, we all dive in pecking, with insults and anecdotes that have been accumulating for the last decade. The Walrus learns a great deal about us in these sessions (we know nothing about him—except what he chooses to tell us), and with this information he enforces his rule. When someone gets insubordinate—doesn't want to hop off the truck in a particularly foul neighborhood, for instance—the Walrus will draw on the litany of insults that come from the pecking sessions and drive him out. And then, too, the Walrus uses the info simply for kicks, to see us squirm and shake.

But in his way, he is preparing us for life. We are bound to be insulted, all of us. We'll get it in the army, at the factory, in the office. And if you can't handle it, can't hold your own, and if you can't dish it out occasionally, you will probably not survive. You'll burst into tears someday, working on Route 93, picking up trash on the median strip, and you won't be able to come back to the truck. The skill the Walrus is imparting, with no particular sense of altruism, is probably more important to survival in Medford and environs than a rigorous class in geometry or world history will prove to be.

The Walrus may come off as an unsavory piece of work, I suppose. Perhaps he seems a sort of rogue male, trying to desocialize the kids, tear them away from a humane, responsible life. And there's truth in that diagnosis. The rank-out sessions were rampantly mean; the sex chatter could border on misogyny.

But the Walrus was himself something of a philosopher, if you mean by that someone who had gone ahead and, without society's encouragement, indeed even against its dictates, figured out a way to live. He understood, in his terms, what use to make of the world. The Walrus was resigned to life as it was. He was driving a truck. He would be for some time—off to Jamaica Plain, back to Medford, a swing through Malden. He was, from a certain point of view, a loser, turning around on Ixion's Wheel. No future, no horizons. And so were many of us going to be. How could anyone doubt it?

But rather than going into a tight cocoon of misery over the whole thing, camping out, as I had seen myself doing in the basement apartment, swilling the Tall Boys, the Walrus had declared himself eligible for some intensity, some life. No second-class citizen, the Walrus. Though the genteel might choke on his presence, Walrus would not have cared: He was going to enjoy his life as well as he could. He was going to try to do little harm. A lot of his coarsest talk about sex was self-protective. You could tell that he actually liked women; he took pleasure in their company—he enjoyed kibitzing with them as well as coupling. And he wasn't going to accept the standing social wisdom, gleaned from *Playboy* magazine and the like, about who was desirable and who wasn't. The Walrus was going to savor, and also spread, the only pleasure that was in his compass.

SOCRATES, the Walrus' fellow philosopher, was not too good to admit to having a pronounced sexual itch. Though married, he was drawn to beautiful young men. He once said, in talking of someone he loved, "When we touched shoulders and brought our heads together while looking at the same book I felt, I can assure you, a sudden jab in my shoulder, like an insect's sting: It went on irritating for five whole days and poured into my mind a ceaseless longing."

In *The Symposium,* the dialogue that takes place at a raucous Greek dinner party, Socrates gets teased for wanting to sit next to the beautiful young men and enjoy their company, as they enjoyed his. But Socrates was also prone to restraint. Alcibiades, one of the richest, most beautiful, dangerous, and alluring men in Athens, wanted to sleep with the sage. Alcibiades "lived a life of prodigious luxury," Plutarch, the great historian and moralist, says, of "drunkenness, debauchery and insolence. He was effeminate in his dress and would walk through the market-place trailing his long purple robes, and he spent extravagantly." For his part, Socrates was surely interested; Alcibiades was one of the sexiest men ever to live.

But ultimately, though they spent a night together in bed, nothing worth reporting came to pass. It was Socrates who held back. Why? Because he believed that erotic enchantment is a wonderful thing but that what we truly want when we fall in love with beauty isn't sex, isn't carnal consummation, but rather knowledge of the beautiful, which leads then to knowledge of the good, itself beautiful in its perfection. When we become obsessed with a beautiful face and body, we're getting stuck on the way to a better knowledge about how to live. Socrates didn't want to get stuck there himself.

And he didn't want Alcibiades, whom he truly cared for, to get stuck either. (Would Frank Lears have shown a similar restraint if one of the beauties who found him so "cute" had come on to him? I suspect he would have, and probably for good Socratic reasons too.)

Alcibiades admits that the only person who can get him to stop and examine his life is Socrates. If they became lovers, Socrates would be disenchanted; he'd sacrifice his sway. So Socrates couldn't let Alcibiades lose his last chance for wisdom by burning up that questing energy in a night of sex.

To which the Walrus says what? The Walrus really hasn't thought all that far into these matters. Pretty quickly, he runs up against the thick abutment that is the border of his own active, intense, sex-drugged brain. So the Walrus, never wholly at a loss, simply rears back in his overloaded driver's seat and begins to spin another sexual fantasia, or, in a less obliging mood, decides that Dubby or Fat or Pooch would profit from a quick rank-out session. "Fat!" he bellows. (Seated on his stack of circulars, Johnny Edsel begins to twist and squirm.) "What's this I hear about how you . . ." And the good times begin again.

Chapter Eight

SDS COMES TO CALL

Communists, or something like them, were due to show up in Franklin Lears' class the next day. He told us as much as we were walking out the door on a chilly Thursday afternoon in winter. Word spread around the school. Everyone wanted to hear more. This was a first: Something was happening at Medford High that was not a projected one-on-one brawl or an all-in rumble, a football game, or a dance, and we were looking forward to it.

The first person I ever heard say a word on behalf of communism—and it was an extended word, a rhetorical aria that took place over the period of about half an hour—was my father, Wright Aukenhead Edmundson. This was in 1962. I was ten years old. The second Eisenhower installment had closed out and Kennedy, Black Jack to my father, was in the White House. Everyone then knew—just as everyone knew that there was a God who reigned above and intervened on America's behalf in all significant matters—that communism was a horrible thing. Communists were godless fanatics who created earthly hell wherever they went.

Where I grew up, to speak even a neutral word about communism was considered a sign of insanity.

In New York in 1962, the *Partisan Review* intellectuals were still tussling about when it had been appropriate to turn against the Party. Intellectuals everywhere were having their ambivalent, splintering sentiments about the god that might or might not ultimately fail. But in Medford and neighboring Malden, where we lived at the time, the case was closed before it could be opened. Communism was death. We ducked under our desks at lunchtime drills to practice protecting ourselves from its oncoming missiles, Red death from Cuba.

In grade five, I was a rabid Cold Warrior. I inveighed against the Berlin Wall and the evils of totalitarian life. The adults thought I was something of a prodigy, a Metternich in the making. Everyone seemed to agree with me on this matter, and of course all I was doing was repeating the views of my father. I wore his brown-rimmed no-nonsense glasses, sported the same stylish buzz cut (he called it a whiffle), and said and thought pretty much what he did. Until the night my father began orating on the subject, I was sure—based in large measure on his edicts—that anyone who was at all sympathetic to communism could simply be written off as a rabid moron or geek.

The oration came one night, late, when our car was broken down. This is not quite as determinate a designation as it might seem. Our car (always at least a decade old) was perpetually breaking down. To be fair, cars, even new ones, broke down with regularity then. We were parked at the curb, waiting for one of my father's pals to show up and charge the battery or remesh the gears or yank the distributor or do whatever needed to be done. Then, in the era of major automotive dysfunction, men spent about 10 percent of their lives administering to the broken-down cars of their buddies or giving their careless friends rides, often to eccentric destinations.

I recall my father hopping out of bed at two o'clock one morning to ferry someone from Malden to Providence, Rhode Island, a place forty-five minutes away, where my father had never been in his life. You never refused a friend help fixing his car—or help standing around in wonderment at what could be wrong this time—and never denied a buddy a ride. Anywhere. Of course once you were out of the house and had discharged the favor, there might be other things to attend to, bars that needed to be shut down or opened, dog tracks to inspect, poker games to look in on.

Anyway, we were parked on the side of the road this time, and for some reason the designated buddy didn't arrive in the usual nine minutes flat. So when the subject of Vietnam came up, there was opportunity for expansion. America, then under Kennedy, was sending troops. You had to fight communism where it cropped up ("anytime, anyplace, anywhere," as the local redundant phrasing went)—that was the general consensus in Malden and environs, and I was saying as much in the backseat of the car, sitting beside my sleeping brother.

Fathers then were often like small-scale thunder gods, Joves in miniature. Usually you could predict their tendencies, often you could placate them with entreaty, with sacrifice, and through the simple expedient of staying out of their way at the right times. But not always. Sometimes they detonated out of the blue.

From nowhere, my father was off and running with a highly informed and madly emphatic account of how well collective life could be grafted onto the kind of village life that the people in Vietnam and most of the rest of Asia lived. "They're very nearly Communist anyway," my father said. "What's the big deal if they go all the way?"

He also talked a little about Buddhism, the predominant religion in Vietnam. (How did he know anything about Buddhism? Had the *Globe* run a "Religions of the World" feature twenty or so years before, for him to commit to memory?) He said that Buddhism was a philosophy of renunciation. You accepted the idea that life was pain, and tolerated whatever came along. What you desired as a Buddhist was peace, and anything that roiled that peace was bad news. Right now we, America, were roilers of Vietnam's Buddhist calm. Much more along these lines followed. Had the Viet Cong needed an American lobbyist, my father, at that moment, would not have been a half-bad candidate.

Then, dropping from the skies of religious anthropology, he issued a shocker. "Besides"—a blast from the grand, badly wrought nose—"what business is it of ours anyway?"

"We promised them," I averred.

"Malarkey," came the response. "We promised their leaders, who are nothing but a bunch of crooks."

I sat in the back of the car speechless, in a state of shock. Then—in 1962 and thereabouts—no one we knew said such things, ever. The mental grooves down which such a line of thinking could flow hardly existed, except in my father, where such grooves could appear, then disappear with lightning speed.

The next time the matter came up, it was as though our conversation in the car had never taken place. My father was a tried-and-true patriot then, though it couldn't have been more than three months after our talk. My country right or wrong. We needed to keep our promises, damnit. We needed to show our allies what we were made of. To a child, it often looks as if the world is terminally mad, but the less said about it the better.

*　　　*　　　*

THE COMMUNISTS, if that's what they were, who were to descend on our classroom were coming from Harvard. They were
going to talk to us about Vietnam. They were, Lears said with the
Socratic grin, coming to try to "radicalize" us. Did Lears agree with
them? Sandra was the first to ask. Were they going to come and lay
out ideas too hot for Lears to own to without putting himself and
his job at risk?

But it was foolish to ask Lears that sort of a question. He just
shook his head, did the wrist business, and told us that we'd see,
we'd see.

Three people, guys probably, coming from Harvard to radicalize
us. I didn't say a word to anyone in authority (if you could really
call what Fran Todesco and Jingles possessed *authority*, a word that
has some dignified connotations) at the high school. I knew what
would happen. They would intervene in some way, stop the whole
business. I couldn't resist informing my parents, though. There
was a collective shaking of heads at the dinner table as my family—
my mother, father, brother, and I—gazed down mentally on our images of the interlopers. Harvard types, we could take them in
stride. We knew all about them.

To Medford, Harvard meant unkempt, crinkly-haired professors
who closed their umbrellas in the rain or attempted to use their
walking sticks, Moses-like, to part the baying traffic in Harvard
Square so that they could make their way across the street. These
were people aptly fixed by a standard grammar school insight: He's
so smart he's stupid. They were school-smart, in other words, the
Harvard types, but in terms of worldly intelligence, Medford had
them beaten hands down.

The actual fact of Harvard's enormous power, we chose never to
contemplate. We preferred to think of the place in terms of a daft,
Anglophilic, who-snatched-my-trousers silliness, a warren of bum-

bling physical incompetence that, as can-do Americans, we disdained.

We did not wish to know, or to recall, that from the spartan privilege of the brick barracks on the Charles there issued the socially, then educationally, advantaged young men—predominantly men at the time—who would rule the world in general and our own tiny domain in particular. They would preside over our factories, represent us—or pretend to—in the state legislature. When we broke the law, they would sit on the judge's bench and mete out our punishment; if we were lucky and mortgaged everything we had, we could retain one of them as a lawyer to represent our interests to his classmate. And that was just the local division, the preserve of the small-time Harvard types. Operating in the greater world, they would send us off to war when the fancy took them, cut us loose from unemployment comp or carry us for a few more necessary weeks or months; they would rule like lords from the White House, surrounding their sun-loving, smiling president, around whose manifold flaws they flocked like protective retainers. It was easier to joke about such people when the alternative was to admit what they were and what place we, accordingly, maintained in the overall scheme.

Recently, I had made my own breakthrough on the subject of Harvard. I discovered that I was doubly connected to the place. There was the Henry Wadsworth Longfellow business, but there was another, more immediate tie as well. For a few years, when I was five, six, seven, my grandmother used to talk about her sojourns at a place called Cumlaude. Cumlaude was the source of quite a bit of women's clothing that worked its way through my family. The stuff was very elegant; some had a bohemian air—do I recall a few all-black outfits, maybe a beret?—and it was all treasured. So naturally I took Cumlaude, pronounced Cum Lawdie, as in praise the Lawd(ie), to be a big-time Boston department store akin to Filene's and Jordan Marsh but much more pricey, a major in-town establishment, purveyor of the finest.

I was both right and wrong on this matter. Cumlaude was a big-scale in-town operation and much, much more venerable than Filene's or Jordan Marsh. For it turned out, as I learned ten or so years after my family's commerce with it had ended, that Cumlaude was nothing other than Radcliffe College, Harvard's sister institution. Cumlaude was *cum laude,* the designation from the diploma, "with honors." My grandmother and her sisters, Rose and Alice and Cathy, had been chambermaids at Radcliffe. Sometimes the young women gave them their castaway clothes rather than sending them off to the local Goodwill.

This had been a family secret for some time, from me and my brother, who might have been ashamed that our dear grandmother was a servant to the quality, and even maybe from my grandmother's husband, Phil, a stone Yankee, who worked maintaining the engines at General Electric and who might not have been pleased by the notion of his wife picking up a few extra dollars tucking in the corners of rich girls' beds. (The word on the intimate habits of the Radcliffe girls? Sloppy, very sloppy. "Slobovian," my great-aunt Rose said.) For my grandfather was, after all, Philip Wadsworth Benton, direct lineal descendant (as I was, my grandfather often reminded me—but not my father, no, not Wright) of Henry Wadsworth Longfellow, renowned fireside poet, author of "Evangeline" and "Paul Revere's Ride" and—not least of his achievements—professor of modern languages at Harvard. Supposedly somewhere up in New Hampshire there was a book at the Longfellow family estate. Supposedly my grandfather's name was recorded in this book. Mine too might be added. We were perpetually making plans to head up there and claim our place, but somehow we never made the trip.

My grandfather was also purportedly the descendant of Horace
Greeley, or, as he was called in our house, Horace-Greeley-Go-
West-Young-Man-Go-West. Greeley, a nineteenth-century newspaper editor, who seems to have been on the right side of every
pertinent question of his day, eventually ran for president, lost, and
went mad.

Look how far my family had fallen in the world. During the Depression, my grandfather, carrier of the Longfellow and Greeley
heritage ("and someone else famous too," my grandmother used to
say, "but I can't remember who it is"), was compelled to catch fish
with a couple of poles off a bridge in Lynn. He did this for a living,
literally. No fish, no dinner. Or so my grandmother once confided
to me.

My grandmother was, or should have been, an education in herself. She was a woman who flourished in her fifties—flourished as
a grandmother. Her generosity was infinite. When she came to our
house, she emptied her pocketbook of all monetary contents, coins
and bills, so that my brother and I could scamper off to the local
drugstore and buy whatever toys we might have our eyes on. She
had to be cautioned to do her grocery shopping before she arrived.
She told three stories about Ireland, where her parents had grown
up, but told them so well that we never ceased wanting to hear
them. One, the one I remember best, culminated in a dialogue between two cats, one of which, at the close, heatedly ordered the
other to "go tell Paulro that Maulro's dead." We puzzled over this
tale for hours running.

At my grandmother's house, we were surfeited with ginger-ale
floats, with bread, butter, and sugar, and with French toast, cooked
to a perfection unreachable even by my mother, who was no slouch
in the art. My grandmother had no training at all, but she was
quite a good draftsman, able to render freehand anything she
looked at, though she refused, as she often said, "to draw things

out of my head." She could play the piano, by ear, and sang many songs, some composed by others, some by herself, extemporaneously. She sang and drew with a high good humor and with the fondest wish that we would follow her and take pleasures akin to hers. She lived for benevolent pleasures, and for seeing others she cared for enjoy their lives as well. She had only one major grief—the endless travails of the Boston Red Sox, who could never win a World Series. Her last sentences to me on her deathbed involved the afterlife, in which, despite being a lifetime practicing Catholic, she expressed rank disbelief, and the local team. "It's too bad about the Red Sox," she sighed, "but I think *you* may live to see them win the World Series." (I abide in hope.)

Searching for a guide to life, I could have done worse. In fact, I probably could have done no better than have tried to emulate my grandmother in most everything. She was an artist of generous and vital pleasures, a free artist of herself, without the angst or Sturm und Drang. But as Wilde says in *The Importance of Being Ernest*, nearly all women take after their mothers, and that is their tragedy; men never do, and that, alas, is theirs. The same, I suppose, goes for one's grandmother. Perhaps in some better days to come men will have the option of learning life from wise women, but in this world, despite whatever advances humanity's advocates claim to have seen and wrought, I do not think that is how things generally go. Young men learn from, and struggle with, older, more potent and adept ones. In this, they seem to have little choice.

SO, ARMED with this double-barreled Harvard lineage—my grandmother the chambermaid and Longfellow the distinguished professor—I hurried to get to Frank Lears' classroom to see what Harvard, this time, would produce.

There were three of them there, representatives invited by Lears from Students for a Democratic Society, SDS. Two have faded from my memory, but one, the preeminent member of the group, remains. I recall him as a sharp-featured, predatory-looking guy with an aggressive nose and large, arching brows. He wore a paisley shirt with a swooping collar, blue jeans, and boots. The other two guys, white, intelligent-looking, recessive, were clearly second-tier. Hawk was the boss, the propaganda minister out from the center of wisdom to illumine the hinterlands, eight or so miles away.

Lears had already told us something about SDS. He'd let us know how the group was founded in 1960 but really came to life a couple of years later, when it put out something called the Port Huron Statement. The SDSers had called America to account for being conformist and bland, for putting more emphasis on prosperity than on freedom and self-cultivation, and most of all—this part of the indictment caught my attention—for being far too boring a place to live. The statement came out against excessive conditioning, institutionalizing, the folding, spindling, and mutilating of persons.

What did the SDSers want? Lears said that it was something called participatory democracy. In participatory democracy, people got into politics on a day-to-day basis. They debated all the main issues that touched them and then voted—and their vote, the popular vote, was binding. The SDSers seemed to think that heaven was a protracted meeting, where everyone got to pop off interminably. But at least, as Lears described it, the document came from a reasonably benevolent group of people. They wanted everyone to have a better life. Sometimes they seemed a little milquetoasty, like a lot of former high school class presidents who'd grown their hair long but still wanted to impress the principal with their seriousness and command of parliamentary procedure. But they could be impressive as well. Lears read us a high point or two: "We would replace power rooted in possession, privilege, or circumstance by power and uniqueness rooted in love, reflectiveness, reason, and creativity. As a *social system* we seek the establishment of a democracy of individual participation, governed by two central aims: that the individual share in those social decisions determining the quality and direction of his life; that society be organized to encourage independence in men and provide the media for their common participation."

Was Lears himself an SDSer? He presented their views with some conviction, but then he tended to make any ideas he was presenting seem, temporarily, to be his own. We would debate the question of his SDS membership pretty hotly in the time to come.

My guess was no. He was too strange a character, too indrawn and eccentric, to fit into any group smoothly. He was a party of one.

The Hawk Man who came with SDS was nothing that you could have predicted based on what we'd heard about the Port Huron Statement. To give Hawk his due, he blew us away. By 1970, I had heard a few people on TV argue against the Vietnam War. They were bland, pasty men in bland suits talking to and past other bland men in dark suits, who thought the war either a national obligation or an exalted mission. Drone, drone, drone. But everyone held virtually the same premises, premises that did not even need to be brought to the fore. They were that the United States was a nation good to its core, that we had invented liberty and self-government, that we had saved old Europe from itself, twice, and thence had become, against our own will, default guardians of the world.

We made an occasional mistake, let this be granted. There were times when our naïveté, our combined goodness and lack of guile, might get us into trouble. But we learned from every stumble, righted ourselves, and quickly got back to being what we were: the best hope of the free world. Liberals, that is, saw and recorded the stumbles. To the conservatives we were all right all the time, nothing to worry much about. Or, a stealthy Kissingeresque step forward, we were one of many sovereign nations pursuing our national interests—except that with our national interest generally coincided the interests of the world.

In the winter of 1970, when the SDSers came to radicalize us, the war seemed to be winding down. The North Vietnamese had changed their strategy. With the Tet offensive of 1968, they had tried to end the war with a stroke. They had attacked cities all through central South Vietnam, including Saigon itself, the capital, where fighting ran on for two weeks. Tet shocked people at home in the States. No one could believe that the Viet Cong, who had been depicted as a side-bet operation, were strong enough to get South Vietnam in their grip and shake it.

But for their part, the Cong were nearly ruined by the operation. They suffered hideous casualties, and they failed in their ultimate intent, which was to get the people of South Vietnam to join them in rebelling against the Americans and their Vietnamese lackeys. So General Giap changed course, shifting from a war of conquest to a war of attrition. Though there were still plenty of ground casualties, by 1970 there hadn't been a major battle in Vietnam for about a year.

Nixon had promised peace with honor; he'd been elected on the assurance that he had a plan to bring the war to an end—a plan that he did not possess. By the winter of 1970, the battle was being turned over to the loyal South Vietnamese—Vietnamization had begun—and American troops were, it seemed, receding from the fray.

In November 1969, Nixon had given his most successful speech, next to the Checkers performance—in which he'd fought off imputations of graft, pointed to his wife's good Republican cloth coat, and averred that under no conditions would he give back the gift of a small lovable dog named Checkers. The Checkers speech had saved Nixon's career; the speech of November 3, 1969, galvanized his presidency. This was the "silent majority" oration, where Nixon, driven nearly mad by the war protesters, called out to the great American middle, the majority, who did their duty noiselessly, who never whined, who believed in America and a star-spangled God, to come to his aid. And they did. Calls and letters and telegrams hit the White House and Congress like a tidal surge of red, white, and blue. Nixon was driving again.

The war-protest movement had gone into a lower key; the war itself seemed to be fading. Many people who thought about it—I didn't, not unless compelled—believed that peace was near. This was, of course, dead wrong. Up ahead were the bombing and invasion of Cambodia; the burning of thirty ROTC buildings at American colleges; the deaths at Kent State and Jackson State. The Hawk Man—give him his due—was not at all lulled by recent events.

Three desks had been hauled to the front of the room, and the Hawk Man sat in the middle one, flanked by his minions. Our usual conversational circle was broken; we students were seated in a mass (Lears in our midst, as I recall), waiting to hear the word. The room was filled with about twice its normal population. The interlopers had skipped a class of their own in order to be here.

This was a first. Not the skipping of a class; kids at Medford High skipped class whenever they could get away with it. If a teacher rarely took attendance or did it only half the time, then some fraction of the class would daily execute the local and dimin-

ished version of the Great Escape. They would hang out in parking
lots behind the school, smoke cigarettes, drink, slap-fight with
each other, cruise around in a spiffed up Chevy or a low-to-the-
ground Buick, address one another as shithead, sometimes in an
amiable way, sometimes not, and otherwise do as much nothing as
was humanly possible.

But here was a first—kids were skipping class to go to another
class. It's possible that in the history of the institution this had
never happened before. There were a few predictable interlopers,
smart kids from the honors classes, kids who may have been turning up to see if they couldn't get to know more about Harvard to
help them augment their applications. These were kids who traveled through the high school in discreet bubbles of rectitude,
treating Medford High as though it were a real school: jollying it
up with their favorite teachers; pretending they themselves were
invisible as they sped from one class to the next, chatting with each
other about the *Lord of the Rings* trilogy and a bracing game of
Risk they had left unfinished; looking down at their respectable
tie-shoes, picked and purchased by Mom, when a gang of blacks
or South Medford Italians approached; gathering up their books
without complaint when they'd been knocked flying by a fast-
moving hand; never engaging the enemy.

But some other kids had shown up as well. Sitting across from
the Peace Hawk and his deputies was Jonesy. He was not sitting at
a desk but insouciantly balanced up on top of the chair back, feet
on the seat. He was poised to listen to what the SDSers said, because Jonesy, Peter Jones, observed the usages. He could be
courtly, polite. But I knew Jonesy well and I knew that he was not
going to like what he heard and that when his turn came, he would
not hold back.

The Hawk Man launched into his rap. His view, to put it concisely and make it cruder than it was, though it was crude enough, was that America had been a criminal nation from day one. We lived on an enormous and invisible grave site, taking our guilty repose over the bodies of the slain and despoiled. We never looked down, never knew that the corpses were there. What Germany had done to the Jews, America had done to the Indians, done to our African slaves, done to the Filipinos, was doing now to the Vietnamese and would do to any poor, inconvenient people who lay between the arrogant republic and its hunger for more.

"This is a criminal nation," I heard the Hawk Man say, "and the only solution when you're faced with a criminal is to bring it to justice."

Put America behind bars? In its entirety?

What the Hawk Man seemed to have in mind were war-crimes tribunals on the order of the one conducted at Nuremberg—punishment, then, for the main living perpetrators and judicious reparations for those who had survived America's maniac wrath but had been damaged by it nonetheless.

Was he kidding? Was the rant this guy's idea of a show of some kind, a put-on, as it was then called? Not in the least. He meant it. He thought he was living in the vitals of a murderous beast, and he wanted to poison it, or maybe mangle its guts from within—in any event, bring it down in a great heap of scales and talons.

This idea is all but commonplace now—commonplace in the sense that everyone has heard it, though only the rare few uphold it—yet at the time it was a brute shock, a hard punch in the face of a piety that I did not know I sustained. When you are in high school, and generally disaffected, it's possible to think of yourself as alienated from every standing opinion. But there is a difference between being disaffected, which is lazy and confused, and being opposed, which, however wrongheaded it might be, nonetheless involves the affirmation of strong and often unpopular ideas. I was disaffected. But I was no figure of opposition—Hawk Man was.

It is very hard, perhaps it is not possible, to re-create the feeling of American pride that reigned in the 1950s and 1960s, particularly for children. This or that nation could preen about its moral fiber—the Swiss probably enjoyed this sort of thing; the Brits, perhaps, too. Other countries could puff themselves up over their might: One thinks of the parades of tanks rolling down the boulevards in Moscow and Beijing. But we were a nation that possessed both. Our military power was unparalleled. (To our minds, we had *won* the Second World War almost single-handedly; we knew little of the massive Russian victories.) And we were good. We wanted freedom, self-determination, democracy for everyone in the world. With the war in Vietnam, those of us who had grown up on this faith, which was instilled as fiercely as any religion, had to contend with the possibility that we were not omnipotent, and far from pure. It was quite simply too much to assimilate.

I recall that when Castro took power in Cuba and threw his lot in with the Russians, I took it as a personal affront. I was hurt, mad, uncomprehending. It was 1961. I was at the time *nine* years old. On the day that Castro rolled in triumph into Havana, I heard the story on the radio and compelled my grandmother to swear not once but three times that Castro's forces, victorious though they were, would be no match, none, for the American Army.

So when the SDS Hawk, with his razory voice and his arrogant mien, began laying down this alien gospel, it threw me into confusion. I too was angry at the world as it stood. But that anger had no content; it was something that barely entered words, something that could be discharged by a hard smash on the football field. I looked to Lears for a clue about how to take all this, but the Socratic demeanor was on. He looked intent and slightly, just slightly, bemused. Let them make of it what they will, his expression seemed to say, just so long as they make something.

THE HAWK MAN riffed about "scenarios" and what was and would be going down, and he spoke of the military-industrial complex. ROTC was something called "Rot-C" to him. He was smart, Hawk-Dove, and he had endless facts on file, but he was also as brittle and iced-over as any of the best and the brightest, any of the Pentagon or State Department types he so despised.

You could discern from the strains of his yelp that it truly was all about him, and that, right as he may have been, he cared nothing for the rest of us at all. He was simply shocked, stricken in his pride, by the fact that the government, which had previously been a few songs and parades and diversions for the menials and the mentally overtaxed, had now taken an interest in him and was considering fracturing his well-greased life. Now the machine wanted to give *him* a mandatory graduation present, a close haircut, an unstylish uniform, day-to-day commerce with people who'd grown up on farms and in urban shitholes and never heard of Hegel, and, most of all, the chance to get his ass blown off by devilish Asians. No, thanks—that was someone else's destiny, not what Peace Hawk saw in *his* crystal ball.

Jonesy would have counted in the Peace Hawk's estimation as one of the shrunken members of the herd, and Jonesy would have sensed as much. Jones was the football team's preeminent hitter. He was about five-feet-ten and 160 pounds. He was our middle guard, the nose tackle, and when he unloaded on some fat-assed offensive lineman, he could send him off like a beach ball bouncing in big loops down the highway.

Jonesy had about seven brothers and, from what I could gather, about four of these were in the army, a couple maybe in Vietnam. Jonesy loved these brothers, though when they were home I suspect they fought each other—kicking, biting, and gouging encouraged— if only to keep the dull times at bay.

Jonesy loved his football pals, too, though he made a distinction between those who liked to hit and who made it to practice every day, for whom he would have done anything, particularly if it involved damaging a third party, and the skills players, ends and backs, who did not savor contact and who were *faggots* (the word pronounced with some irony, not always that much).

I knew something about Jonesy's views on Vietnam because they'd come out at football practice. Of course, everyone knows how it was bound to be with a bunch of football players from a working-class high school in 1969 when they got to the subject of Vietnam. Football players are supposed, in all social mythology, to be the school reactionaries, abusing and beating those who step out of line, going off to the peace marches to help their hard-hat dads attack the doves. But that's not how it went with us.

On October 15, the day of the first Vietnam Moratorium demonstration, we looked up over our heads to see a plane writing in the sky. We were running what was called team offense, practicing the plays we'd use in the game the next week, going at three-quarters speed. They were the same old plays; it didn't require much concentration. The major activity was speculating on what the skywriter was trying to create on the blue canvas overhead. It looked like the beginnings of a woman. Naked maybe? No. An animal then, a whale? A camel? Nope. Soon it became clear that it was a peace sign, a celestial totem for the crowd on the Boston Common protesting the war. Jonesy screamed out that what we were seeing was the footprint of the great American chicken. But Rick Cirone and Fred Tommasso, the class president, and Jackie

Lane, the black kid on the team, threw their hands up and flashed the peace sign back. Jonesy and a fair number of the lineman in turn gave the sign the middle finger, upraised. It seemed, to put it a little crudely, that the defensive backfield was pretty solidly against the war, that much of the interior line was pro-, and that there was a great unsaluting middle, of which I was a part.

For the next three weeks or so, the war got constant discussion in the locker room, and if the discourse never reached the heights of the Platonic academy, it was not the stupidest talk one could hear in America on the subject. For some time, at Medford High, the only place that I heard any opposition to the war was from football players. Strange? After up-downs and after head-banging block-and-tackle drills that left you bleeding from the nose and mouth and, if you were very unlucky, the ears, it wasn't likely you'd back off an opinion for fear of what someone might decide to say to you by way of rebuttal. In any event, if you look at the MHS football team photos, fall 1969, you can see Fred, and perhaps Rick, too, laying two splayed fingers out over their bent knees—the peace sign.

Jonesy now told the Peace Hawk what he'd told us in the locker room before. First, he gave barely two shits about the justice of the Vietnam conflict. A couple of other principles were uppermost in his mind, and he described them with bitter fluency to the Hawk Man and his cadre. He admitted that it was a stupid conflict to be in, but when you are in a fight, you win. Or you destroy yourself trying—you destroy yourself rather than quit. If you quit, you sacrifice your honor, and without honor, it is, as Achilles knew, not possible to live.

Second point: Joneses were involved, Joneses actual and Joneses metaphorical. He had friends in Asia. Other people he knew had friends and brothers and husbands there. The Cong and the NVA were trying to kill these guys; ergo, fuck the Cong. Let them burn in screaming napalm hell.

When the Hawk Man got explicit about his support for the NVA, talking about the impending victory of the forces of national liberation, Jonesy became furious.

"Do you have anyone," he said, keeping his voice under control, keeping from roaring, "do you have a single real friend who is in Vietnam? Do you have any relatives there?"

The war was hitting Medford much more directly than Harvard. In the *Medford Daily Mercury* you read about kids coming home dead who not long ago had been high school athletes.

A few nights before, I'd seen Rat Pelagrino, a hard guy from Barry Park, in front of Brigham's. He had just met up with a friend of his back from Asia. The guy was in a wheelchair, minus a leg and an arm, with a ruined face, and not much time to live. Rat caught this sight while high on mescaline. His friend's face, a horror as it was, had seemed to turn grotesque shades, yellow and green and pink, Rat said, and begun to melt before his eyes. Rat, wearing his friend's army jacket, was huddled into a ball, knees to his chest, face down, weeping furiously in the doorway of Brigham's. His body shook, as though a horrible wind were blasting through and only he felt it. "I can't believe what they fuckin' did to him," he said. "We used to be kids."

Back apparently untouched was a guy named Frank Politian, who had been a Ranger up in the mountains, fighting alongside the Hmong. He was in fine fettle, it seemed, handsome and strong and obscenely fit. But in the middle of Brigham's parking lot one afternoon, he invited me, for no particular reason, to fight him to the death, bare-handed. A pleasure, but no thanks. It turned out he was issuing this invitation fairly regularly. No one, as far as I know, took him up on it.

As the year went on, kids kept coming back, maimed in one way or another. They were drunk all the time and fighting, often in crazy brawls, where they seemed desperate to lose, take some punishment. They were grossly ashamed of something, it often turned out, but it took a while before we all had any idea what it might be.

As for me, I was getting calls from a marine recruiter; my pal Ryan, fellow lineman, drinking buddy, and brawling friend, had given him my name. It looked to him, the recruiter said, like we could get the whole offensive line there in a unit. We could go in on the buddy plan. Ryan said the recruiter was an amazing guy—he could do thirty pull-ups and he told fabulous stories about Chesty Puller, the most formidable marine in history, and how mangy (the reigning word for tough, crazy, indomitable) all marines were. I promised that I'd stop by to talk. What else did I have to do?

The Peace Hawk and his cadre wouldn't answer Jonesy. They tried to engage other students. Sandra had a question. Buller had a word or two to drop in. But Jonesy was a middle guard, and what you do as a nose tackle is to keep coming at the center and the guards on either side of them. You keep it up, and in the beginning, the first quarter maybe, they push you all over the place, because you're always being double- and triple-teamed. But you apply your fist to their helmets and make their heads ring like the inside of Notre Dame when the hunchback pulls the bells, and eventually they lose heart. They see that you wear a helmet cage to protect them, not your own precious face, because in piles you would gladly bite them, tear at their throats if you could.

Jonesy kept badgering the SDSers with the same question. "Is there anyone in your family in Vietnam? Because if there was, I'm not sure you'd go on about the impending victory of the glorious revolution or any of that other horseshit. I'm not sure you'd say that."

And finally, pushed to the wall, the politburo had to admit that it had no people in Vietnam but that this did not make the war any more just or true or good or what have you. What they should have said, perhaps, was that all people were brothers and sisters, all men and women out of a human family, and that they cared for the fate of the Americans on the ground as much as they did for the Vietnamese. But these words coming from the mouth of the Peace Hawk would have turned to ashes on the floor. For the boss man gave not one damn for anyone but himself and other mental alphas. Jonesy—"Thanks, that's all I wanted to hear"—climbed off the top of the chair and sat down in it, stretched his legs out, and looked like someone who has just succeeded in sending the corrupt judges off to jail.

How did Lears take all this? Was he angry that his SDS pals had been buzz-sawed by an honorable junkyard dog who would probably end up climbing poles for the electric company, if he didn't join and head to Asia to help his brothers out? For it was probable, from words that Lears dropped from time to time and that we puzzled over like Gypsies competing to interpret a scattering of tea leaves, that he himself was not in favor of the war.

But it seemed to me he was nearly gleeful—by his standard, that is—the day the commies came. People who usually did not think, who hardly ever talked, were doing both. Buller finally piped up to ask why the hell they didn't go and join the North Vietnamese if they loved them so much. Sandra asked why the antiwar movement was getting violent. Dubby wanted to know if there was any kind of war they would fight in. Rick asked what they thought of hippies who just turned on and dropped out, got high, listened to music, and ignored the government and the war. A lot of the kids were silent, sure, but they all looked like a current was running through them, as if they were replete with juice, instead of zombie-walking it through the day, asleep in the inner life, as they usually were.

So my guess is that Lears was getting a contact high off the exchange. He wasn't especially interested in making people think the way he did. He didn't look for converts. What Lears really wanted, I believe, was simply for people to think. He wanted them to examine their old ways of doing things, and if the result of the examination was that they liked those ways well enough or that they wanted to get more conservative, more government-loyal, more institutionally acclimated, that was all right. So long as they took up a distanced position from their beliefs and had a look.

To do this kind of teaching, you need a vigorous discipline. You've got to hold your own thoughts in abeyance. Never show your cards, never lose your temper, do not help people cut to the chase. You care about a process, not the results. So most of the time your students leave you as works in progress, works that may never be completed. You can't think of yourself as a craftsman who shapes beautiful souls.

For there are teachers, and they can be great ones, who aim to do just that. They've considered things from all sides, contemplated all the major questions, and they believe they know what's what. Plato, Socrates' greatest student, was one of those teachers. He knew how to craft that beautiful soul—reason ascendant, the passions and the appetites subordinate—so one could live contentedly and do no harm. Everything in moderation for Plato, except his conviction that he knew the transcendental score. On the subject of truth, Plato was immoderate in the extreme. For Socrates, of course, it was very different. Irony was his position— he had no more to offer. Lears did have more. Few of us, especially in our twenties, have the strength to go through life without any investments of the spirit. But at least while he was in class, Lears worked as hard as he could not to dispense any truth. He offered freedom of mind, and loneliness, too.

The Plato-style teacher, the great dispenser of truths, creates disciples. He is surrounded with smaller versions of himself, who vie for his love and spread his word. And, too, he creates apostates, people who fall in love with him and his works, then out of that love with a violent crash. Such people often have vengeance in mind. The Plato-style teacher must be preternaturally strong in spirit, in that he is constantly calling up all the dreams and hopes of his students, stimulating their long-suppressed wishes for perfect authority. He needs to fight against becoming a small-time deity or a demagogue: Often he fails. The ironist needs to fight against resignation that borders on despair when he sees where his students, left to unfold their own minds, can end up.

Yet often, as Coleridge liked to say, extremes meet. The teacher who dispenses truth finds his best pupil not in a disciple but in someone who needs to concoct a potent but very different countertruth. So Aristotle did in response to Plato.

Or the great truthteller finds himself lumped together with other great truthtellers, to be just one color in an extensive palette, from which the student draws to concoct her own eclectic vision. Or the ironist finds people who both adore him and rebel against his never-ending skepticism by creating a great system of their own. The permutations never end.

But this much may be true: If you would be a genuinely great teacher, you may have to pick one path, that of the ironist or that of the truthteller. For those are the ways to push your students into full mental gear. Most of us waffle. Most of us take the easy middle way, not having the discipline to keep the ironist's game going or the strength to lay our truth out to the insults of the world.

*   *   *

THE NEXT day of school, Lears came into class in a grand mood. He was primed for a splendid discussion. He had jolted us into life with the SDS class, like Victor Frankenstein rousing the lump of inert human stuff lying flat on the slab. But now, everything was different. It was a Monday, and it had snowed over the weekend. Boston snow—great, huge drifts, to make the all too familiar world into another planet, someplace virgin, inhospitable, resistant. Yet it was another planet that somehow manifested the cold essence of our own. This is what it really comes down to, this unwanting earth, and us, alien, running on top of it, hopping and blinking and trying to find our way.

What did people think of the SDS invasion?

Think? Come on? Give us a break. Let us be. We'd performed once, right? Now it was time for a rest, a long winter's nap.

The snow had narcotized us, like mind-flattening smack, and we had gone under willingly. All the tumult the visitors had brought with them to Me'ford was hard to bear, and we had shed it, most of us, when we walked out of school that Friday, to think about the poolroom or a date or a quart bottle of beer, maybe three or four.

Buller, of course, was never at a loss. He worked his acne and brayed at Lears that the guys from SDS were losers and fools, with nothing to say. When there was a war, you went to it. (Though one could have bet that Buller was a ready candidate for 4F; his genes were not blended happily into one Darwinian triumph. Flat feet would probably be his ticket out, but there would be more besides.)

Buller always brayed, perpetually cried out like an angry, put-upon beast. But the pity was the rest of us. We had nothing to say. And given that Lears must have dreamed, as I, a teacher, today still do, that one fine class will send people spinning into intellectual life and that they'll never fade or fail thereafter, never come down, he must have felt flat misery at what was unfolding in front of his kind, always tired looking eyes.

Buller would not stop. And after fifteen minutes of it, Lears came through with an idea. "Let's go outside," he laughed. "Let's go out in the snow."

The teacher calls for an escape from school! A jailbreak! What could have been happier, more cage-rattling than that?

So we shot off to our lockers, pulled on our coats—all as sur-reptitiously as possible, so as not to wake the drowsing authorities, the prematurely aged archons of Medford High—and headed out behind the burned-out section of the high school. Lears was in the lead, jabbering away with Sandra, maybe about a concert at the Boston Tea Party, the place you could go to hear the Byrds or the Jefferson Airplane or Big Brother and the Holding Company. By the time he arrived, everyone was standing around with no idea what to do.

But Lears knew exactly what he had brought us out there for. He was well dressed for it, wearing a big black frock coat and a padre's hat. He held the hat on his head with one unsteady hand, bent over, and with the other hand, the free one, he scooped up some of the dense snow. He stood and packed it together. He clomped his pale hands at each other in a clumsy way while we all looked on, perplexed, as though someone were cooking something that we were going to have to eat soon but that was, as of now, impossible to identify. Lears stared down into his now reddened mitts and—behold—what he had seemed to surprise him nearly as much as it did us. It was a snowball, a singularly malformed one.

He gave a what-the-hell shrug, or the Harvard variant of one, reared back, and—of course, he threw like a girl—heaved it with what force he could muster at Dubby O'Day.

Suddenly everything was clear. Frank Lears had brought us out not for a Thoreauvian walk in the pristine or, magnifying glass in hand, for an inquiry into the variegated and glorious geometries of the snow crystal. No, we were here for nothing other than a snowball fight. I can't imagine he knew what he was getting into.

We boys were snowball warriors nearly from birth. When I was eight years old and living in Malden, my friends and I would stand up on a little bluff close to my house on Main Street. The traffic flowing by was very heavy—getting across the street as a pedestrian could be an Olympic event. There were cars, buses, and trucks, mostly moving, by what was then one of the more direct routes to or from Boston. From that glorious promontory, we would chuck snowball after snowball. It was especially prestigious to sight a bus driver or a truck driver with his window open and paste him across the cheek.

Sometimes, to our unequivocal pleasure, the driver would pull over and give chase. We'd fly over backyard fences and be a block away before he'd pulled his road-stiffened bulk out the door. We were selective in our assaults, bombing some kinds of vehicles and leaving others untouched, daily creating a treaty amongst ourselves, a Malden concordat, elaborately negotiated each time, as to what constituted fair game and what did not. Trucks bearing the Roadway logo were sacrosanct, because Michael Lundell Hansen loved them with an irrational passion, and Mike, who got his way on nothing else, somehow prevailed in this. Roadway trucks were greeted with a hollered "Yay, Roadway!" B&N Corkum's vehicles we pounded mercilessly. Buses were a delight, because always, somewhere, there was an open window. Michael Hansen, Paul Rizzo, and I once thwacked a bus driver so hard and so many times that he stopped the loaded bus, got out, and ran for us—a futile gambit usually reserved only for truck drivers. But the driver left a whole busload of commuters stranded in their seats watching him lumber up the hill after us.

Did our parents disapprove? Were we punished for putting lives at risk? On the contrary. Far from prohibiting the sport— "You'll cause an accident! We'll get sued!"—they often watched with amusement from their windows. My father would rap the glass with glee when we got off a large-scale fusillade at a bus.

And of course we fought each other for hours in numberless snowball versions of the OK Corral. These sometimes lasted two or three hours, and involved major-size snow fortresses, charges and countercharges, and hand-to-hand combat, where heads were pushed into the snow and kept there.

Snowball was integrally linked with baseball, and by the age of sixteen most American boys—as though they were preparing to heave javelins or boomerangs on the prehistoric savannah—can let a ball fly like a bullet. Then there was Cap, the football quarterback, who also, for this is almost requisite, played shortstop for the baseball team. When he threw a ball, flame licks came from the surface. I had caught a few throws of his at first base. You saw an arcing blur, like a tracer shell coming in, but no ball per se. There followed a sound like a shotgun going off in the palm of your glove.

There was gender rancor to contend with. Here was a chance to whap the girls for saying no, for saying maybe, for saying sure, for being female, for saying things that were way too hard to comprehend, period, for judging us more coldly than anyone in their position—our mothers, I mean—had ever done before. I'm not sure that Lears knew what sort of bottle he'd pulled the cork from.

We went to work, lumping snowballs together, but all our eyes, all the boys' eyes, anyway, were on Cap. This was his chance for assassination. And truth be told, he had not been treated terribly well by Lears. He had reasons for payback.

But before Cap could load and aim, Buller was into a number of his own. A plow had been by and left lots of snow chunks. Buller immediately grabbed a massive, black-encrusted boulderlike mass in both hands. He heaved it over his head as though he were a caveman going off to brain his foe before battening down to wreck some celebratory havoc on the corpse. Buller's human features, such as they were, disappeared, and all you could see was a hunch-backed silhouette against the darkened sky. There *was* something unmistakably primitive about the form. Buller, *Pithecanthropus erectus,* headed in Lears' direction.

Everyone watched in breath-held silence as Buller brought the mock boulder crashing down at Lears—the way Diomedes might have done it on the windy plains outside Troy. Lears just managed an ungainly slide to the left, which sent his padre's hat flying but absolved him of the blow's full force. He took it off the back and shoulders, not across the head, where Buller presumably wanted the great ugly chunk to fall. So Buller didn't score the full nose-bleed, off-to-the-nurse, let's-think-about-the-hospital hit that he probably had in mind.

Lears took the blow gamely, laughed a cosmetic laugh, then went after Buller to try to push him into a snowbank. Things took on the aura of a science-fiction story, time machine–style; the caveman was now being assaulted by the avatar of modern humanity. Lears was not skilled in the art of push-and-shove, but he was surely game, and Buller, to say the least, had been cruising for it for a long time. Lears spun, got low (the essence of the football assault—get lower than the opposition—maybe he'd been reading Jerry Kramer on the sly), and sent Buller stumblebumming into a drift. Buller fell in a sloppy, limbs-amok way that evoked scenes outside a Somerville bar, the Jumbo maybe, where they served any-one who could reach the counter and where, on a February night, when the street was glassed over with ice, the patrons enacted pachyderm ballet outside. Down Buller went.

The class broke into a huge blast of applause. "Awwright!" Rick screamed. Dubby did an appreciative combination of a war dance and the boogaloo.

But he came up angry, Buller, looking for all the world like a club fighter who's taken one to the chops and rather liked it and now wants to even things up. He had murder in his face, or more murder than usual.

Mine may have been the first snowball to hit Buller, but there were a lot of others, including shaky salvos from Carolyn and from Nora. (He's cute, Frank Lears, remember.) Rick, who played third base on the team, sent one at Buller with a little smoke on it—you heard a thud on his greasy green parka, the kind trimmed with fake wolf fur. Then Cap, arm cocked, catches Buller's eye. And even Buller, who is almost blackly noble at times in his recklessness, clearly does not want a piece of this. One full in the face from Cap—throwing all-out—and you will lose teeth, probably worse. And the chances of his missing are small. Buller backs off.

A general melee begins, with Lears pelting everyone in sight, including, to his peril, Cap. But Cap is knightly, a gentleman, and keeps all his throws at three-quarters speed, if that. The girls especially want to tag him, want any relation they can get with him. But he just responds with fumbly, soft lobs in their direction. He packs the snow so loosely, the balls fall apart a bit en route. Then all the rest of us, Dubby and Rick and John Vincents and I, knowing our better—herd behavior, would Lears call it?—follow suit. We do it the way Cap does, for fun, kindly, with ease. I'm not sure Lears, sharp as he was, ever saw it, caught the dynamic, and knew what was going on.

"Nor did he refuse to play five stones with the boys," says Montaigne of his hero, Socrates, "nor to run about with them astride a hobby horse. And he did it with good grace: for Philosophy says that all actions are equally becoming in a wise man, all equally honor him." To be fair, Socrates was a reasonably accomplished athlete; he'd been a soldier of some repute. He'd have known how to throw much better than Lears did. But there was Franklin Lears, running gamely enough in Socrates' tracks, doing the most undignified and childish thing and thereby enhancing his dignity no end.

In ten minutes it is over and Lears and all of us are bending over panting, panting and laughing. It's the first time in a long time at school that I've had something that you could call fun, the first time I've laughed this hard without someone being humiliated.

Does Lears see how much he's triumphed today? Does he understand what it meant when the class refused to take this chance—for he had offered it—to smash him, like those poor bus drivers and B&N Corkum guys of yore, to run the scapegoat number? With those snowballs, we could have done much more than erode Lears' dignity. There was a hospital not far away.

When the time had come, when Buller had started out to initiate the big payback, things had worked out much differently. It was Lears, really, who had taken out a little aggression on us. As to our aggression toward him, well, Buller aside, we didn't really seem to have much. We had, or were beginning to have, a dose of gratitude and affection for the strange little man in the padre's hat. Cap and Rick, Nora and Carolyn, and I and Dubby, too (Sandra, true to herself, pretty much stayed out of the missile blizzard), had expressed that gratitude as well as we could.

And from that point, the class began turning around.

Chapter Nine

BLACK AND WHITE

"Hey, what you lookin' at, boy?" This question is issued by the guy sitting across from me on the bus. His tone is not friendly.

The answer to his question is in one sense obvious. What I'm looking at is his outfit—his pants, yellow as a plastic sun, and his shoes, pink, with ribbons on them. I'm also checking out his cape, which is trimmed in velvet. He's William Billings; he is seventeen years old and in my class at Medford High. He is black.

It's Saturday night and we're on the West Medford bus, heading to Medford Square. I'll be stopping there to shoot pool at Stag's and hang out in the parking lot of Brigham's ice cream parlor, maybe sit around in my friend Ryan's new car, a gold Plymouth Duster with all the trimmings, and demolish a few Schlitz Tall Boys. William, I suspect, is going farther down the Mass Transit line, to Roxbury probably, for what looks like a party.

William's face is almost spectacularly ugly. He's got an enormous nose, unformed, like a smooshed fruit, and a vast mouth full of huge, widely spaced teeth. But the face is also somehow very appealing, the calm, easily bemused face of someone who has figured himself out early, said yes to the whole eccentric package, and doesn't much care what the rest of the world thinks. He was a kind of male version of what the French call a *jolie laide,* a beautiful ugly woman.

Beside William is his best friend, Edgar Lincoln, also black, a little less flamboyantly attired, serene in presence, courtly in his movements. Both are very thin, refined-looking. The two of them together outweigh me, but not by much. I could massacre them both at once, with little effort. But that is not where things would end. They know this, and wait with suppressed glee for my reply. "What you lookin' at, boy?"

"Nothing" is not a wise response. It incites a standard Medford comeback: "Callin' me nothin'?" Matters degenerated from there.

I have a history with Billings and Lincoln, and it is not bright. Once, in ninth grade, when I first moved to Medford, we had an unfortunate run-in on the playground. Billings and Lincoln were in my gym class, and that day we'd played softball. I had struck out twice, hit a double, made a bad fielding play.

"You good at softball," Billings said.

"Very good, very good, I hafta say," Lincoln added. Both had all they could do to lift the bat; they were more swung by it than swinging. But they joked about the game and made the best of things.

Their intonation sounded nasty, carping. What to them was a playful tone, campy and a little affectionate, was to me aggressive. I had no ear for their art. I got mad and told them to fuck off or something equally original. They tried to explain themselves and preserve their dignity, too. I got madder. They left in what seemed to me an embarrassing, purse-swishing huff.

The next day after school, I had a compulsory chat with a representative of theirs named Johnny Malloy. Johnny was in no way similar to William and Edgar, and I'm not even sure he liked them much. What he did like was trouble. I was new to the school, unconnected to the tough Italian kids who ran it, at least on the playground, and thus fair game.

Johnny was the kind of guy who only has to fill in a few of the bubbles on the psychology test before he wins the sociopath rating. He was wiry, very quick, underweight, and dangerous. He had well-sculpted, handsome features; he'd have looked like African royalty if not for the leering expression he generally wore. On the second day of school, in ancient-history class, he took the time to inform me that he always carried a blade and that he was very, very good with it.

During the conversation about Billings and Lincoln, I was pretty sure I saw the switchblade open and down by Johnny's thigh. I listened to him tell me what would happen if I messed with his "boys" again. I agreed with everything Johnny had to say.

Later, on a basketball court—we both were going out for the school team; neither of us made it—I drove into the lane for a layup with habitual Humvee grace, saw Johnny, and laid my shoulder into him, catching him squarely above the sternum. He fell away and skidded off on his butt toward the basket, not without some style, like a pat of butter sliding across a hot griddle. He grinned the psycho-kid grin and did a knife-across-the-throat gesture.

I walked around in terror for a few weeks, but ultimately nothing came of it. By then I was partway connected to the Italians. I was semi-friends with Paul Vincenzo, probably the toughest kid in the school. On the offensive line, I played guard next to Paul, who was in the tackle slot. By rights I should have been the tackle, since I outweighed Paul by thirty pounds and he had about twice my mobility. (Guards need to pull out of the line and head upfield to block.) But he insisted that he was going to be the tackle and the coaches went along with him. Why he needed to be tackle I'm not sure. It might simply have been that the word "guard" sounded too passive, too stand-around-at-the-palace-gates-and-salute, for someone of Paul's temperament. Anyway, with Paul and a few others of his ilk as semi-friends, if Johnny had done something to me, there would have been an echo.

My last run-in with William had been fairly recent. Walking to Medford Square, I'd met up with him; he was with another guy this time, not Edgar. I, too, was with a friend, who got along okay with William. Still, it was not what you would call a cordial encounter. William had a dog, a German shepherd, which he said was a trained attack dog. I suppose experience should have told me to listen carefully to what William had to say. But no, I expressed doubt about the dog's credentials. William whispered a phrase to the dog—it sounded like German as intoned on the TV show *Combat*—and the shepherd flew at me, straining the chain, yellow eyes popping, staring lovingly at my throat. "Do you believe me now? Or shall I let him go?" I confessed full credence.

Supposedly—but this was white kids' lore; I never got it confirmed—William did the same thing a while later to a guy named Dickie McGuire, a weight lifter and star hockey player, who went to Boston College High. When William asked the signal question about whether he should let the dog loose, Dickie said, "Sure." Purportedly, Dickie caught the German shepherd in full flight, one hand wrapped around the jaw, one arm around his belly, and threw him—the dog was a scrawny, mangy version of the breed—into a passing bus. No more dog.

So there sat William, dogless, on the West Medford bus, staring me down and waiting for my reply. "What you lookin' at, boy?"

"William," I said. "How you been?"

Silence. Slow time passes. I'm conscious of the dingy, tired smell of the bus, acquired from carrying too many people too often to places they do not wish to go, and back to places they've no desire to return to. I begin reading the UNICEF poster across from me to calm myself down.

Then from nowhere a grin and a laugh. "I been good," William says. "In fact I been very fine." Then he and Edgar go off in a storm of giggles, falling all over each other, goofing on the straight white guy in his football jacket and white track shoes. (I had unscrewed the cleats from the bottoms of my sprinter's shoes—I ran the quarter-mile occasionally on the track team, though I was mainly a shot-putter—and when I walked, the metal cleat-holders played an ungodly tattoo on the pavement. But I took the shoes to be the epitome of jock cool.) William and Edgar were high and jittery as bats, pleased with themselves, and having a very good time. The mood shifted. We talked a little. No big deal.

But it could have been a big deal, at least to me. If you went to Medford High, and particularly if you lived in West Medford, where the city's black section was, your life was likely to be punctuated by this sort of black-to-white, white-to-black exchange. From time to time, one of these encounters blossomed, and you'd hear about how one of the South Medford Bears, the city's premier Italian street gang, had gotten jumped by a crew of blacks. Then the Bears would get into their cars and drive to West Medford and something large-scale and bad would go down. But usually things stayed on the level of petty annoyance, petty squabble, scuffle, intimidation, and retreat.

Blacks made up about 10 percent of the high school. And all of them, without any exception that I knew, lived in West Medford, in about a ten-block area, of modest, well kept up houses. In a way, it was the most solid neighborhood in the city, surely the most long-standing. A lot of the Italians, for instance, the parents of my class-mates, were first-generation Medfordites; they had made enough money to leave the North End of Boston, get out of their triple-decker houses in a neighborhood where, whatever the culinary attractions and general high spirits, the candy store was owned by a bookie-loan shark and Mob enforcers recently brought in from Sicily slept two to a bed in fetid rooming houses. The children of these North End expatriates, my classmates, would, if all went well, make a few more dollars than their parents and move away to Winchester or Newton or Melrose, places where people walked their dogs on leashes and Republicans occasionally got elected to the city council.

For the blacks, things were much different. Blacks started settling in West Medford at the beginning of the Civil War, around 1860. At first it was just a few families, headed by carpenters, blacksmiths, skilled laborers of various sorts. Over time the neighborhood grew and became a haven for enterprising, churchgoing black people who seem to have looked out for each other pretty well and sustained dignified, slightly aloof relations with the mass of whites around them. Among the parents and grandparents of my classmates were a lot of "firsts"—the first black man to get a dental degree from Tufts, the first black to work in management at General Electric, Raytheon, or some other major corporation. They were people who won one quiet victory after another, often well before the civil rights movement got into full swing.

The history of this neighborhood, and a good deal more besides, is set down in a strange and marvelous volume called *This Is Your Heritage, a Newspaperman's Research, Sketches, Views & Comment/ United States, Hometown, and World History,* by Mabe "Doc" Kountze. In seven hundred or so pages, Doc Kountze, who seems to have been black West Medford's griot, its resident poet and wise man, narrates the history of nearly every family in the neighborhood, from slavery to the present. Prefacing this ungainly, slightly disordered, generous, and often moving story, there is what amounts to a history of black contributions to American and world history—a section that takes a wide sweep, at top velocity, as though one were being blown over the major events of Afrocentric history in a shakily designed balloon. The idea, from Doc Kountze's point of view, seems to have been to connect the young people of black West Medford circa 1970 to their own parents, grandparents, and great-grandparents, as well as with early black notables—Cleopatra, Aesop, and (maybe) Jesus of Nazareth.

The black section of Medford was a reasonably prosperous working-class neighborhood, in many ways not unlike mine. But by 1969 the reigning style, at least among the boys and young men who lived on Jerome Street and Sharon Street and hung at Dugger Park, a strip of grass that bordered the Mystic River, was more than a little disconcerting to the elders at the Shiloh Baptist Church and, I assume, to Doc Kountze. (His general concern about the rising generation was, it's pretty clear, one motive for his writing the book.) It was a style by and large imported from Roxbury, the black ghetto in Boston. The boys and young men wore their hair conked, in do-rags on Friday and Saturday afternoons and at night in gorgeous, often hennaed rolls. They affected tight pants in luxurious colors, the whole Life Saver pack, high-heeled shoes, and silky shirts with flowerlike ruffles on the front, the kind of thing an eighteenth-century French nobleman, a dandy out of *Les Liaisons Dangereuses*, might have put his tailor to work on. They walked with a cocky, bantam-rooster stride. It was the pimp aesthetic in high vogue.

The black girls were very much a society unto themselves. They laughed together uproariously on the bus, goofing on one thing or another. They wore tight skirts and danced, occasionally, in the aisles. They virtually never looked at or talked to a white boy. They referred to us as honkies and ofays, in a high-hearted, rambunctious way, talking loudly and simultaneously among themselves so that we could hear the insult, though never quite be sure who had uttered it.

Johnny Pearl, an enormous black kid with a gimpy leg, once dropped his lit cigarette butt on a bus seat as Dubby was sitting down. Predictable results. I wound up to swat Johnny—friend defense being all in Medford—but pulled back at the last minute. There was probably enough weaponry on the bus to have ended me that morning.

On the day after Martin Luther King's assassination, a day when the elders of West Medford's black neighborhood were in church, many in tears, lamenting the death of the greatest man of their lifetimes, the black kids at Medford High took a different tack. I was walking down the New Corridor with Dubby when a phalanx of tough black kids, maybe fifteen of them, came roaring through the other way. When they saw someone white, large or small, bad or not, they simply grabbed him and tossed him against the wall. No fists, no blades, just a ferocious grab-and-heave, done with furious, adrenaline-pumped strength, so relatively diminutive blacks were tossing big white kids with ease. I saw it coming, forced my back against the shiny pine boards, and stood at terrified attention.

Dubby got the toss. Ronny Jensen, who told all and sundry that he was going to become a pimp of some standing in not too long, an estimable figure in Boston's "Combat Zone," sent Dubby flying. Dubby caromed, then got tossed by another kid, rebounded, and got flipped by yet another.

When it was over, the cyclone passed, Dubby looked at me and, never at a loss, said, "What are they so pissed off at us for? We didn't kill him." This observation, which I found penetrating in the extreme, was about representative of our thinking on racial matters.

There were two worlds at Medford High, black and white, and they lived, on the most immediate level, in tension and remove from each other. It was a kind of small-city adolescent apartheid. But that's only the superficial side of the story. There was also a fair amount of commerce. The phrase that William had accosted me with, "Hey, boy," was a common mode of salutation between whites. It was often followed by the return remark "Who you callin' boy?" which is what a black guy would be likely to say if so addressed. And some white kids did—I did on occasion—provided that the black guy was a friend. But even then, you were playing with fire and knew it. Bad black kids almost always called the whites "boy," sometimes with affectionate intonation, sometimes not. Then, occasionally, they got it back in return. What happened next was unpredictable.

Many white kids took style cues from the blacks (though none of them would have put William's bows on their shoes), affected the pimp roll, and listened, as I did, for a while almost exclusively, to music from Motown. For three or so months, I abandoned Arnie "the Woo" Ginsberg and his Night Train Show, where he spun hits by Jan and Dean and the Beach Boys and Herman's Hermits, and listened strictly to WILD, to catch the Temptations and the Four Tops. What many of us white kids knew about love and loss, albeit at second hand, was in the idiom of blacks. We sang Temps songs to ourselves as we walked down the halls. I never heard a black kid whistling anything by Lennon and McCartney.

The Elvis phenomenon was everywhere. The King had, without ever saying as much, probably without knowing as much, repackaged himself as a black man, or, as some would say, a White Negro. And a considerable proportion of the white guys at Medford High were involved in a similar reprocessing job, talking black talk, walking the walk, wearing some of the clothes, laughing the boisterous seen-the-world, done-the-world Afro-Am laugh, sometimes with a sense of self-parody, most often not. At the same time, of course, they sustained themselves as dutiful Irish or Italian racists, who would no more use the word *Negro* than the word *phenomenology.*

Some days, when the atmosphere on the bus was low-static, I'd plunk myself down beside Jackie Lane or one of the Bronson twins and yack about one thing and another. Jackie was a cornerback on the football team, a barracuda-style hitter. But he had a beatific smile and was easy and blithe about all things under the sun. Sometimes we sat on the bus and talked about the sorrows of wind sprints and of Alabama Quick-Cals, those exercises that our semi-cracked backfield coach enforced on us, where we made synchronized robotic motions and chanted little war chants about ruining the opposition. Often we sat in the middle of the black section—the back—and I felt like a cool enough white guy indeed. But at other times the smog was too heavy, and Jackie would indicate that this simply wasn't a good time for me to sit myself down in the midst of what could erupt into mild to moderate ugliness.

Why did the Medford racial weather shift so mysteriously? Like the questions about why William went around with a German shepherd or why, as the white kids often averred, "When you fight one of 'em, you fight 'em all," any white guy could have answered in a trice: because the blacks were touchy and oversensitive and flew off over nothing. It never occurred to us that the only way they could survive was by getting collectively pissed when the South Medford Bears stomped one of them. Or that being hard-assed was the only way they could sustain their dignity when they looked at TV and saw white people throwing rocks at tiny black kids as they made their way into school in Alabama or Arkansas, or when they saw that the guys doing the fighting in Vietnam and coming home dead were disproportionately black. Nah—they were just touchy, those people.

Across from me in history class sat a black girl named Karen Davis. Karen was fine-featured, pretty, a terrific student, dutiful, scrupulously turned out, a little prim. But she also had a fine, raunchy sense of humor and smiled in a telling way when Mr. Johnson made one of his speeches about truth or facts or about why you need to know history (because, of course, those who do not remember the past are doomed to repeat it). She was, for reasons best known to the gods, extremely fond of me, and we yammered away companionably at any chance we got. Karen was deeply respected by the other black girls, and even on the bus could break off a conversation with her friends, stroll over, and talk a little with me about the history homework or some other such thing. No other black girl could leave the group and approach a white guy in this way. But the idea that a friendship with Karen would develop in any form outside of class or off the bus was simply one I was not in a position to have. It would have been like a cave dweller making a breakthrough in quantum physics.

SO THE interchange between the groups, even before the year I'm describing, 1969–1970, was far from simple. And in that year, when things were bursting open all over the place in America, the racial scene changed in Medford, for both better and worse— mostly for better, I think. The change for me began in Frank Lears' class.

After the snowball fight, things had begun to go pretty well. No miracle took place—I don't want to idealize the process. Still, virtually no one but Sandra would read a book at home. We simply sat in a circle and read the pages aloud in turn. Periodically, Lears would ask a question and sometimes, even then, in February or thereabouts, he would offer a teasing, partial answer to it or stay silent until it was clear that nothing was going to come, and then he would move on to the next query. But sometimes we'd get an actual discussion moving, too. There'd be all-ins about politics, beauty, truth, the good—in short, about all the things Lears probably imagined we'd be talking about on the day he first walked up the sad front steps of Medford High. Even a few mean frog-blurps from Buller couldn't stop the flow.

By then Lears had begun to cast his spell on us; he was starting to bewitch us the way Socrates did beautiful Alcibiades, who compared the great teacher's painful, galvanizing effects on him to the bite of a serpent. Outside of class, we speculated about Lears constantly. What kind of family did he come from? Was he rich? Did Mom and Dad have bundles of dough? (Not if Lears' wardrobe and car were any indication.) Was he in SDS? Did he smoke weed? What kind of music did he really like? Did he have a girlfriend? Was Sandra in love with him? Did he, maybe, reciprocate? And whatever in the hell did he wear that paper clip in his lapel for?

These questions were unanswerable. For, without being at all cold, Lears was somehow opaque. With the exception of Buller, whom he clearly disliked, he seemed about equally affectionate to us all. His look was always kind. By now there was only a tinge of irony in his tone, just enough so that if Henry James were to walk in, Lears wouldn't have to apologize for being a complete flat-brained I-see-the-world-as-it-truly-is-and-must-be American.

And if anything, Lears had become a yet better listener. When he listened to you, the quality of his attention was so easygoing and tolerant, yet so intense, that you felt like no one had ever really paid attention to you before.

But as open as he was and seemed to be—for in his manner he was lighter and more approachable than any other teacher—there was still something impersonal and removed about the man. His pedagogy wasn't about himself and his ideas per se. He didn't, I believe, want you to think the way he did, to love Thoreau, say, as he loved him. (We gleaned this love from a hint here and there.) He wanted you simply to be able to ask yourself the kinds of questions about what you believed, and why, that he himself might ask. He was like a mirror who gave you back to yourself. When we asked and answered questions about Lears' origins, preferences, and desires, we were revealing much more about ourselves than we possibly could about him.

We wanted to find a psychology for Lears, a set of discernible, private motives for what he did. But once you find someone's psychology—once you're able to say that for such and such a one, it all owes to a will to power or an Oedipal fixation or compensatory guilt or what have you—then you can write off their effect. You're superior then to the teacher; you know him better than he knows himself. Lears had a pedagogy, a way of teaching, but he wouldn't undermine himself by letting a clear psychology show through.

And he spared no one (except Buller) his hard-edged questions. Most teachers would early on have seen Sandra as an ally amidst the barbarian hordes, a potential teacher's pet, someone to look to and share some eye-rolling with when Buller said something prizewinningly stupid, when he brought off a sledgehammer blow that sent the little weight flying up the test-your-strength scale to ring the idiot bell. But no, Sandra got the same sort of interrogation we all did.

Sandra, for instance, couldn't connect with Camus' *The Stranger*, the story of the man who feels nothing at his mother's funeral, who conducts an empty, loveless affair with a woman named Marie, and who finally murders an Arab, for no apparent reason. Sandra thought the book irrelevant. Off-the-wall. People weren't like that—that is, they didn't contain, just beneath the deadened skin, the potential for horrid violence. Sandra was, it seems, a Rousseauian, and generally felt that all evil comes from corrupt society. And she could be astute and articulate in defense of the doctrine.

And maybe Lears concurred; he was certainly the gentlest man I had ever met. He touched everything—a pen, the desk, your back when he needed to tap your shoulder—as if it were made of the most precious china. But he wouldn't let Sandra off the hook with her innate-goodness theories. She had a lot of bloody history to account for. What about the wars and pogroms, the massacres, the gleeful bloodlust that simply *was* a major quotient of the human chronicle? And what about Darwin and his theory of the survival of the fittest? Were we humans *total* exceptions to the Darwinian laws, which he sketched in for us (though at Medford High, where the big fish habitually gorged on the small, the theory didn't take much explaining) with a seeming conviction? If so, what accounted for that difference? Did we have immortal souls, disposed to good and bequeathed to us by some god? If so, what god? What particular evidence was there for the innate-goodness doctrine?

There was not a hint of meanness or aggression in any of this. Clearly, he respected Sandra a great deal. And as I say, Lears may have agreed with her. Still, he would not let her, or himself, off the hook.

A few days later, when we were still on *The Stranger*, Lears asked us about solitude. What does it mean to be alone? Is it possible?

What would it mean to be genuinely by oneself? Sandra raised her hand, perhaps ready to treat us to a description of Zen meditation and its capacity to melt the ego beyond solitude into pure nothingness. But Lears must have seen something ripple across Nora Balakian's usually serene face. He gestured in her direction, though she hadn't volunteered.

Nora was a high school princess, a sorority girl. Her autobiography, I'd have guessed, could have been translated into a graph peaking from prom to prom—she was probably invited to them all over the Greater Boston area—with soft valleys of preparation in between. She sometimes affected a teasing nasal voice acquired from Kelly Hunt, vitally alive in my memory for having given a thirty-minute talk on the subject of the pencil in the English class of Miss Cullen—she of the supply-closet imprisonment, etc.

What Nora did was to run through a litany of defenses against being alone. She mentioned listening to the radio and talking on the phone, then playing the songs and the conversations over in her mind. She cited a span of other strategies, ending, perceptively enough, with expectation, our habit of blocking out the present by waiting for things to happen in the future. "Waiting," she said. "Waiting for things to happen to you is a way of not being alone."

"Not half-bad," Lears said.

But Nora did not express herself with detachment. She said I— "This is how I keep from being alone."

"And why," asked Lears, "is it hard to be alone?"

"Because," Nora answered, "I might start to think about things. I might start to think about my life."

Nora had been, up to this point, one of the Elect (as Blake liked to call them, satirizing Calvinist ideas about predestination), meant for all happiness. Suddenly she had gone over to the side of the terminally Lost. One of the great sources of grief for those who suffer inwardly is their conviction that others exist who are always happy. From the ranks of the local happy few, Nora had just checked out, leaving some hints about those she'd left behind.

But she'd done more than that. She'd been honest. She'd told us unapologetically how it was with her. And who had more to lose by such a revelation than Nora, who—beautiful, poised, intelligent—really did seem to embody perfection? If she could do such a thing—talk candidly, self-critically, without pretense—perhaps the rest of us could too.

It was one of those February days when the class was on something of a roll that a group of black guys came banging into the room. This was not standard operating procedure at Medford High. Periodically one, or sometimes two or three students, would stand and bolt for the door, fed up, probably, by what was going on in class. But the idea of an invasion, a sudden influx *into* a classroom, that was something going on in universities at the time, where students were forever disrupting classes to protest the war, but not at MHS.

At the head of the group was a kid named Thurston White, with whom—no surprise—I had some bad history. He was a big, heavy-set guy, with regular features and an appealing baby-face. On his head today he had an African pillbox cap, small and red, with tiny mirrors decorating it. With it he wore a dashiki, mismatched, most anyone then would say, with the hat. There were maybe six or seven guys in the posse, but Thurston was clearly in charge.

"Do you know what today is?" he bellowed at us.

I looked over at Lears immediately, to see how he was taking it. Did I expect that he'd become fatally upset, hop and holler at the interlopers to get themselves out of his classroom? To him, this had to be a strange reversal. He was part of the generation that had burst into offices and classrooms and stopped business as usual at Harvard and Columbia and the rest. His contemporaries had taken over deans' offices, shredded their records in the paper shredder, kicked back in their plush leather armchairs, and puffed their cigars. Now suddenly the tables were turned. Lears was, give or take, the establishment. What would he do with that? Would he fall apart and sputter and rage? Do a Leo Repucci routine?

Lears simply looked a little more melancholy and a little more bemused than usual and replied, "Why don't you tell us."

"Today," Thurston roared, "is the anniversary of the death of Malcolm X."

"Yes," Lears replied, "that's right. And when was he born, Malcolm Little?" Was he using Malcolm's given name—what Malcolm X would call his slave name—to diminish the man? Or simply to show Thurston that he was on top of the game, that he knew something about Malcolm too?

I suspect it was just Lears doing what he almost inevitably did as a teacher, feeding your own emotion back to you in a slightly understated way, so that you'd be aware of the feeling you were putting out. Gently, surely, he was always holding up the mirror, and if you were interested in having a look, well then, go ahead. If not, fine. Maybe later on.

Thurston gave a date; perhaps it was even the right one. But now his tone was subdued, a tinge respectful. I was pleased to see him even slightly diminished. We were anything but friends.

In the ninth grade he and I had gone out for football together. He was a big, soft kid. It was pretty clear that his wish to be there was minimal. I was a kid from another city, unprepossessing in appearance (let us say, generously), with thick goggles and the wrong way of approaching everything. When Thurston and I squared off on the football field, the whole team, along with a number of his friends from Dugger Park, was watching. He was easy to beat up on. Timid. No sweat to humiliate.

And I, to be candid, was simply thrilled. I couldn't have liked it better. Blacks were supposed to be invincible athletes and here was one, quick and strong and with some good skills, that I could toss around like a big stuffed toy. I rubbed it in, pushed him where I wanted him to be and laughed at him a little. Very satisfying. Thurston quit the team two days later and thereafter hated me vividly. And now here he was, a paragon of political dissent, busting into our discussion of *The Stranger* to lay down the word.

But Lears, for his part, would make use of whatever came his way. To him, teaching could turn into a sort of performance art. If a truck went blasting down High Street and blew its whistle on the road, loud and whining, he was capable of breaking into a new riff to tell us, say, how Seneca had believed that the degree to which some grating noise bothered us was a reflection of how much we were full of irritation at the world for not conforming to our wishes, not being perfect and perfectly under our control. Noise sensitivity was an index of egotism. What did people think?

Schopenhauer, on the other hand, thought that noise sensitivity demonstrated intelligence. The ability to be annoyed showed that you were aware, alert, not living the humdrum, tedious way that most people did. Seneca? Schopenhauer? Did either of them seem right to us? Lears was continually giving us means to measure who we were, ways that let us sneak up on our habitual selves from a new angle and see what we could see. For this task, he would use anything that came to hand.

Say that it's Valentine's Day and there are chocolates in class. Some of the girls are mooning at cards they've gotten their boyfriends to send. Well, let's use it. What do you think love is? Is it the soul's longing for the beautiful, as Plato said? Is it a search for the soul's lost mate, as Aristophanes claims in *The Symposium*? Is it a quest for the parent of the opposite sex, as Freud said? (Gross!) Is it the urge to create the best possible members of the next generation without regard to one's own future happiness, thus the proliferation of unhappy marriages (Schopenhauer again)? Ideas? Guesses? Hopes? Lears was infinitely sensitive to our responses, even when they were dim, and he would never rub it in, except of course in the case of Buller, who had decided to go the idiot route regardless of rain or snow or miracle from on high.

Lears now took in Thurston's change of tone and immediately shifted his own gears. He became welcoming, warm, though in his own quirky way.

"Sit down, sit anywhere you like. Perhaps we can talk about Malcolm some."

And the group did, and suddenly they were no longer a gang but part of a seminar. They were here with something to teach. "Now tell us," Lears said softly, "what we need to know about Malcolm X. He lived here in Boston for a while, didn't he? He worked at a dance hall in Roxbury. He went to jail in Massachusetts."

I never had heard of Malcolm X, and I listened as Thurston, with occasional help from his friends, began the story of Malcolm X's life. He told how Malcolm—Malcolm Little—had been born in Omaha, Nebraska, and how Malcolm's father had been killed by white men for being proud and standing up for himself. Then he talked about Malcolm's living in New York and Boston, where he'd been a drug dealer and a thief. Malcolm had gone to jail, as Lears said, in Massachusetts, and in jail he'd made his first contact with the teachings of Elijah Muhammad and the Black Muslims.

What was the teaching about? Thurston and company were a little vague on the question, but it had a lot to do with the fact that white people were devils, who had enslaved the highly civilized black people of the world. Malcolm had preached this gospel and become famous among blacks across America. Then he had broken with Elijah Muhammad because of something Malcolm had said after Kennedy's assassination.

I found myself, as I rarely did, with my hand in the air. What, exactly, had he said? Thurston scowled, but there was nothing especially vituperative in his answer. "He said that it was a matter of chickens coming home to roost." What that meant, Thurston went on to explain, was that white people had lived by violence—especially violence against black people—and now it was coming back home to them.

"And then?" Lears asked.

Thurston had nothing to say. He was finished with his story.

So Lears continued it for him. Malcolm had broken with Elijah Muhammad and started his own church. He had made a pilgrimage, a hegira, to Mecca, and he had come back preaching brotherhood between white people and black.

Lears didn't say these things superciliously so as to trump Thurston and his crew, but to add to the story. When Lears was finished, he made it clear that to think about Malcolm X, you couldn't simply assume that his last theory about race was his best one. You had to listen to the stories Malcolm had acquired from Elijah Muhammad, too, and see if you thought they provided a good metaphor—in the way that, say, parts of the Bible you couldn't take literally provided some good metaphors to some people—about the way it was in the world.

When Lears was done, Thurston added a few words about Malcolm's greatness and, as the clock hopped its last significant hop of the day and the bell rang, rose, thanked Lears and the class for listening, and walked out. He seemed to be blown away—proud and astonished at once—that white people (and the class was all white) would take something like this so seriously. But of course *we* probably wouldn't have, at least on our own. Lears had shown us what it was to disarm someone's aggression and then, rather than gloating at your little rhetorical win, listen—genuinely listen—to what he had to say.

But there was a more striking aspect of the way that Lears had behaved. It was not only his receptivity; nor was it what he had said per se, though his knowledge about Malcolm X was impressive. It was something about his overall demeanor. He acted—there is no better way to put this—like himself. When he talked, he stroked his little mustache and consulted the gunboats and swung his wrist in the baseball card–tossing way. His voice was mellifluous, a tinge ironic, and highly, highly cultivated.

He didn't, in other words, do what every other white guy that I knew generally did when he was in the presence of blacks. He didn't retool himself, get louder or more macho, or try to find a black timbre for his voice. He wasn't on the verge of offering to slap five; he wasn't bobbing his head in a Motown rhythm. He simply acted like what he was: a singular, complex, unapologetically intellectual, non- and anti-macho man with a Harvard degree. This blacking up in the presence of actual blacks is a phenomenon one sees to this day as white guys vie with each other to act as black, to talk and move as black, as the blacks around them.

The moment in Lears' class might even have had some broadly cultural resonance, I suppose. Because when a lot of the Ivy League–educated left-wing guys had their first up-close meetings with the Black Panthers and their ilk, what the Ivy League guys did was to swoon. They fell in love. They were mesmerized by the leather jackets, by the rifles, by the parade-ground drills, by the salutes, and by the rhetoric that took no prisoners. And these intelligent, often brave war resisters began wanting one thing above all else: to be accepted by the black men as true, hard-core fellow revolutionaries. They wanted to be tough, uncompromising dudes. Real men, not pussies.

And weren't the Panthers, with their close-order drills and their uniforms and their discipline and their group solidarity, just a little

bit like the football teams that the swooning SDSers had so despised in high school? I don't know, but I'd be willing to bet a little
that our friend the Peace Hawk, who so hated militarism in its
every form, could go a little gaga in the face of hard-ass black
machismo.

But the Panthers weren't to be swooned over; they were to be
engaged and talked to, one person to another, as Lears did with
Thurston and would do with anyone who came along whose mind
wasn't completely under lock and key. Surely there was no part of
Lears, no matter how sequestered or far-flung, that desired to wear
a uniform, join a club, or perform the equivalent, physical or mental, of an Alabama Quick-Cal or two.

As I left class that day, I was curious—a feeling that at the time
I had little experience with. What did this Malcolm character
mean by saying that whites were devils and that blacks ought to
form their own nation, get rid of us once and for all? I was annoyed
by it, by the general denunciation. But the outrageousness of the
whole thing made me sit up and take notice.

On the way out the door, Lears stopped me. "You know," he said,
"I think you might want to look at Malcolm X's autobiography. I
think that you would get a lot out of that book."

This took me by surprise, this business about myself. Because
though Lears was consistently benevolent, there was a kind of gently programmatic quality to his attitude. For quite some time it
wasn't clear that he really went a long way in distinguishing us one
from another. Who we were and who we might become was our
business. He'd give us the necessary goad, send us flying, or dragging, out of the gate, but where we headed was our own concern.
But clearly he had some notion of who I was and what I might
need. And it touched me greatly, this observation. It reminded me
of my father saying that there was something coming up on Carson
that I was bound to like. That someone viewed me as more than a

shirt and shoes, a walking destination for TV shows and Wonder Bread—this was a singular thing.

But, really, I didn't read books (though by this time I didn't mind hearing them read aloud and discussed in class). And although I had been curious for an instant about Malcolm—he seemed like a badass character from a movie, and something more than that, too—it was all quickly tamped down beneath thoughts of the pool hall and track practice and listening to the pop Top Twenty on WMEX. Race and books and politics and Thurston White: What did all this have to do with me?

MORE THAN a little, it would turn out. For as to politics, well, a sentiment of Saul Bellow's Charlie Citrine applied well enough then to me: I never know what I think until I hear what I say. About a week after Thurston's visit—and maybe in some oblique way because of it, and because of the visit of the Peace Hawk and because of Lears and all that was stirring in me there in that class without my fully knowing it—I heard what I said, and found out what I thought about the war in Asia.

My father and I were alone, watching television, the eleven o'clock news, prelude to Johnny's monologue. War and war protests were on the box. We were silent through the combat footage, where kids in black-rimmed glasses not unlike my father's and carrying weapons often nearly as heavy as they were returned fire from a ditch. Then came the other kids. The Harvard types made their way onto the shadowy screen, black and white and grainy, with their posters and NVA flags and their chants ("Ho! Ho! Ho Chi Minh! NLF is gonna win!") and their headbands and their camp followers, with peasant dresses and lolling, liberated breasts.

My father went apoplectic. He fell into a fury. His face turned bloodred. He snorted from out of the great misshapen nose. They were spoiled brats. Lazy! Morons! He cried out: "Get back home. Get home and do what you're told." Then a blast that might have sent 58 Clewley Road up and into orbit, and that got the landlords discharging the small-scale cannonade on their ceiling. "Do what YOU ARE TOLD!"

That last, *Do what you are told,* was a standing disciplinary slogan in our house. We heard it often. It was a mainstay, along with "Snap It Up!", "Chuck It In!", "Get a Move On!" (And, of course, "Relax!") What it meant was that the house in which we lived was not a democracy, nothing close. It was a monarchy, with one king, who would rule forever, who was never wrong and never to be gainsaid. It was as though, suddenly, he was talking to the protesters and to me at once (and maybe to Frank Lears, too, about whose subversive ways he had now heard enough, thank you). Do what you are told!

Do what you're told! Even now, rarely, rarely, I say it to my own children, and when I do, I feel a shiver through my body, as though I'm momentarily possessed, as though I've been grabbed by a demon that was not my father per se but a devilish rage for order that possessed him also, though given my advantages, given what has so far been an absurdly lucky life, its visitations to me are far less frequent. Who dares to say that there are no such things as ghosts?

Suddenly, for no reason that I could understand, my eyes were hot with tears, and I hollered at him, "How would you like it if Philip and I went over there, to Vietnam, and came back dead? Would you like that?"

My father looked at me like someone had hit him across the head with a two-by-four. For a moment he was speechless, the mental screen gone completely blank. Not, for Wright Edmundson, a common event.

I do not believe that he had ever considered this an actual possibility. His kids killed in Vietnam, sent off, as it were, to a far-flung province of TV land and delivered home in a flag-draped box not much bigger than the modest beds in which he every night gave them their good-night kiss but from which they would not be empowered to wake the next morning.

"Don't be ridiculous," he said.

"It could happen!" I screamed. "Why couldn't it happen?"

"Because," he said. "You're being ridiculous, that's all."

But of course it was not ridiculous. I had applied to college, which would at the time have given me a student deferment, but as my guidance counselor had informed me, my prospects for getting into a good school were less than bright, and I had applied only to good schools. What I did not want to think about—nor, by all evidence, did my father—was that in a few months I would be out of high school, eligible for the draft, and would have the chance to put my football prowess to work in a place where the business about being first off the deck and being lean and mean and agile and all the rest was both about the best advice you could have and absurdly, blackly laughable.

My father went silent—my father, who never, prior to this moment, had left an argument with me without being in a position to declare complete and utter victory. Wright, who believed in razing the last residue of the charred defeated ramparts of his opponent and then sowing the ground with salt, walked away from this one. He left it in the air. For once, my father had nothing to say.

Perhaps I am wrong, but I believe that what I had done was to propel my father to an encounter with the underground and buried river of furious, inarticulable love that he possessed for both his sons, a swarming flood of emotion in a far-inward place that he himself could not travel to through his own volition but which was no less real for that. Being entirely unfamiliar with the terrain, with everything looking so strange, he had no choice but to stare in amazement and be silent. And so he was.

A great victory of thought and inspiration on my part? I was against the war because it might kill me and my brother—and for nothing—before I had the chance to start a real life.

I was being small-minded enough, I suppose. But, raised in America, one often acquires the sense that life, at least life at a certain remove—and it can be a very short remove at that—is not entirely real. Life beyond Medford was something that you watched on TV, that you'd never be pulled into until—Jonesy talking here— it came along and bit a full-size chunk from your ass.

Before the chunk, and maybe before it ate me live and whole, I was awake at least to the possibilities. In Medford, you could readily believe in the prospect of one of the South Medford Bears stomping the life out of you—that's right at hand. But the Cong and the NVA, who are even less graciously disposed, well, they come on after *Gunsmoke* and before Johnny.

My cry was small-minded, selfish—say what you will. But without many forces bearing on me, without Lears and all he had brought, I probably would not have mustered the wherewithal to cry out at all. I would have stood straight and walked into the army or marines and done the drill with no thought, with no critical power applied, just as I'd been taught to do things in football, where the head, the helmet, is reduced to a simple weapon, aimed by others, the coaches and the manly code. Being able to scream in horror about my own doom and my brother's was a sloppy, slobbering blow against the code. (Do what you're told!) Later, maybe, I'd be able to slow things down, ask myself a few better, Frank Lears–style questions, think things over on my own.

Chapter Ten

SOCRATES ROCKS

The Doober and I succumbed to the course, succumbed to
Frank Lears, at about the same time. Though I have to admit,
Dubby's secular salvation was a shade more flamboyant than mine.
I think I saw the stirrings in the Doober well before anyone else
did, maybe before he himself knew what was going on.

It started one day—it was probably in late March, spring coming
on—when Frank Lears turned up in class with a record. This had
become fairly common practice. He'd gotten hold of a beaten up
old phonograph and installed it in the back of the room, and every
Friday, and any other day when Lears was inclined, we got some
music. I remember hearing Billie Holiday, Mozart, the Incredible
String Band, the Velvet Underground. He also showed us art
books, and read us a poem from time to time. Usually, the music
was something I—and probably most everyone but Rick—hadn't
heard before. But today he had the Rolling Stones (we all knew the
Stones), and he was playing a song called "Connection," in which
Mick—no surprise—laments his inability to make one. "Connec-

tion, I just can't make no connection. / But all I want to do is get back to you."

Lears played it once, then he played it again. He cranked the thing up and let us get a full blast of the messy, hardscrabble sound. We all held our breath for him. We half expected a gang of submasters and sports coach–types to come bursting in, axes flourished, like Eliot Ness's men in *The Untouchables*, ready to send their thick blades through the contraband, which in this case wasn't hard liquor but American blues, as created by the likes of Robert Johnson, Satan's star guitar pupil, it was said, then remade in grimy, fish-'n'-chips-and-urine-stinking London, and sent back to us, here on the well-lit top floor of the Medford High School building.

When Mick and the boys started laying down their high-hearted, piss-anywhere noise, Dubby suspended his major self-appointed task, the coloring in of the o's in Freud's *Group Psychology*. (The Doober was by now a couple of books behind in the coloring project, the creation of a pointless connect-the-dots puzzle on each page of his book, and fretted no end about his inability to keep up, to meet his responsibilities, to pass the highly fraught subject of o-coloring.) But the music got him. He looked like a scholarly monastic who's been sitting at his high-backed chair illuminating one of the lives of the saints when suddenly he hears the sound of a lute, perhaps (he thinks) a lute with a perfumed damsel bending o'er, pouring through his open casement.

When the song was over, Lears began asking questions. He asked us what connection we thought the Stones had in mind. Why Lears was asking questions about rock music, we had no clue. But we liked him now. He was our man. So we did our best to answer.

Was it about wanting to connect with someone you loved, hoped would love you, etc., etc.? (Carolyn)

Was it about feeling connected to the world? A part of all that is, ever was, and shall be? (Sandra)

But then the Doober raises his hand. Raises his hand! This is about the fourth time all year that he has done so, the other incidents being associated with bathroom trips and wisecracks that, for the purposes of contrast, seemed best prefaced with a piece of official protocol. (Lears, on reading a passage of poetry: "Some people have described these lines as breathtaking." The Doober, face fire-engine red, cheeks popping, eyes rolled back, rigor mortis attacking his legs, sends a diffident hand into the air. Recognition from Lears. "Can I, can, can I, can I breathe now?" "Yes, Donald, breathe away." A bellowslike suspiration, followed by mock post-coital collapse. "Thank you, Mr. Lears. Sir.")

This time the Doober wonders aloud if maybe Mick isn't trying to make a telephone connection, maybe to someone he's left behind while he's on tour.

Lears, obviously, is not pleased. So far there's been lots of half smiling on Lears' part, getting progressively less amiable, as though we were kids who, given a fascinating new toy, at first couldn't figure out how to play with it and then, frustrated, began working to dismantle the thing. Now all he can spare for the Doober is a very light frown.

But Lears has it all wrong. This is a breakthrough. The Doober, the doughnut repository, the human beer-recycling op, the near–bridge jumper, the math dope, the self-professed failure in this life and beyond, has anted up and tried to answer a question. His answer is nowhere, at least as far as Lears is concerned. But the Doober has tried, by his lights, to answer seriously a question posed in a class. Lears, who should, in the provinces of his own mind if nowhere else, be walking up a dense roll of carpet, gunboats sinking deep into the crimson plush, to get the teacher-of-the-century award on the basis of this moment alone, or at the very least commending the D with a "Not half-bad," doesn't appear to notice.

Instead, he keeps after us. He won't let it drop. "What kind of connection?" "What's going on here?" "What do people think?" Finally, in a voice that actually displays a hint of petulance rather than the varying and not easily parsed blend of affection and irony that's standard with him, he says, "Did any of you ever think of a drug connection? He's interested in scoring some drugs, isn't he?" We all nod our heads in brief homage to the more highly developed hipness of our teacher. Dubby grins like a junior-level fiend who's quickly climbing the career ladder. He's recently discovered pot.

But why was Lears badgering us on this, of all things? Lears, as I say, brought in music, and as time went by, he began to bring in more and more rock and roll, including some stuff we all *had* heard. And he questioned us pretty hard about it. What do you suppose this Pepperland is about? Why can't Mick get satisfied? What is the Jefferson Airplane keening about? Why are the Grateful Dead so blissed-out?

He must have been trying to get us to listen to and think about the music we only heard. For me, rock was background music, aural ambience that I surrounded myself with as I sat in my room avoiding my homework, and dreaming. I used it the way the eighteenth century used Bach, as aural tapestry, though my tapestry was loud tie-dyed, not velvet brocade, intricately patterned.

But in fact, once Lears began asking questions, I could see that rock, or at least some of it, unfolded a vision. The vision was often foul (the Stones specialized in this one), but sometimes it bodied forth a world that conformed to the best human wishes (or to the entirely self-vaunting wish of the guy with the long, strong guitar in his hands). When I was sitting in my room stumbling through my favorite tunes, I was singing songs of innocence and of experience, regaling myself—and any unfortunate who happened to pass—with tales about utopia and disaster, and much else as well: I simply didn't know it, had no clue. I was a little like Molière's Bourgeois Gentilhomme, the character who speaks prose all the time, without knowing as much.

In a way Lears eventually helped me see, I wasn't quite the uncultivated, unwashed alien I imagined myself to be: For a few hours a week, listening to the radio, putting on records, I was a member of a ragtag tribe initiating its mythology. I wasn't seeing the deities being born, exactly, but I was present while the demigods—Mick's devil, John and Paul's Walrus, the Beach Boys' surfer girl; there was no end to them—were being set loose to stumble or fly in the world, to be worshiped in good, vulgar fashion as newborn glowing deities, archetypes to be adored and (maybe) emulated, or cast aside as too campy, inspired by dreams far too vapid for the times or just flat-out dumb. (Little surfer girl! Jayzus!)

These musicians, Lears might have told me if he were the sort who'd assert much of anything, were trying (and often enough failing) to be the Shelleys and Byrons of the moment, similar in their aspirations for shifting their audience's inner weather and just as readily detested by all the paragons of tired virtue. ("Shelley the atheist is dead," a British paper cried after he drowned. "Now he knows whether there is a hell or not.") For were the rockers not here to do something on the order of what the Romantics had tried to do: to re-create consciousness—sometimes with an assist from a mind-blasting substance, sometimes not—and in so doing renew a portion of the world?

The reason Lears got ticked off when we didn't come up with the drug-connection answer wasn't that we were all being so dim. We'd behaved in much dumber ways without provoking his mild ire. The reason was, I think, that all of us, or a good many, *knew* the answer—I did—and wouldn't break the taboo against talking about something like drugs in school. We were keeping the conversation timid and artificial when, as Nora had showed us, and Socrates had long ago averred, it ought to be conducted full-out: "This discussion is not about any chance question," the philosopher says, "but about the way one should live."

Dubby was trying to answer. He was offering the best he could. And, to his credit, he hung in, undaunted by Lears' dismissal. He kept listening, tossed in a word or two. Once he was on the road, even his guide and mentor wasn't going to boot him off.

Why did *I* listen to this stuff? Why was I, by this time, something like a rock addict? Prodded by Lears, I groped around for some answers. The Stones were here to unfold a jump-back-rat's vision of the world—crumbling, smoke-blackened, teeming and fetid, with, here and there, behind polished, bolted-oak doors, a pocket of pleasure for the lucky and bold. The only way to counter this world, they knew, was to follow their lead and live without illusions, to be a grinning predator rather than squealing prey. The Stones hated the world as it was, or affected to, and stored some contempt for the worldliness they had to develop in order to get along, and more than along. In a way, they were chanting the secret history of Medford life: Never kept a dollar past sunset; never want to be like Papa, workin' for the boss every night and day. Just gimme some love, fast and loose, to keep my grin up, keep me happy.

With the Beatles, you dreamed and then awoke to live inside the dream and never leave. In their most memorable songs, memorable at least to me—"Strawberry Fields," "Here Comes the Sun," "Lucy in the Sky with Diamonds"—and dozens more, the iron law of compensation was off. You simply didn't have to pay for your pleasures. The colors were soft and pure, all gentle sunset wash, and the world was an opium vision that never faded. You floated across cloud fields, free for once, and never had to come down. The Beatles looked out on Medford High life and said, "No, thanks"; rather than diving deeper and deeper into the wreckage, like the Stones, they set sail, on perfumed breezes (and a little of whatever the dealer had today), for another world. Tangerine trees and marmalade skies.

Perhaps I never quite had these thoughts—not full-out, anyway. But I began to feel intimations of them, began to feel that I lived in a certain singular time, had a culture, was part of something, and largely because Frank Lears simply asked me to lift up my head, hear what I listened to, and see where the music might lead.

TEACHERS WHO matter sow seeds like this all the time. Some land on the rocks, some in sand, some flow away with the river, as the Bible assures us. But some take root, too, and they produce and yield. The sad part is that often it takes the seeds twenty years or so to break ground and produce green shoots, and because the beneficiary doesn't remember who tossed them from his bag, or because the sower has sped away to some other world, he never knows. He acts simply on faith, knowing that someone did it for him and that, maybe, he can do it for another. Lears, with an assist from a thug genius, the sort of guy he probably couldn't have spent a comfortable ten minutes with, did that much for Dubby—and for me, too.

It wasn't *The Stranger*, the book that touched Nora as it had, that got to me and the Doob. No, the book that conquered us was Ken Kesey's *One Flew Over the Cuckoo's Nest*.

Cuckoo's Nest is now something like an American myth: You know all about it; you've read it even if you haven't turned a page.

It's a little like the Frankenstein story: You seem to get the basics simply by virtue of living for a decade or so.

So everyone knows the story of how Randall Patrick McMurphy—initials RPM to denote force, dynamism, unruly power—turns up in a mental hospital dominated by the Big Nurse. Big Nurse is the queen of the Combine, the system that keeps the patients (that keeps us all?) docile and cowed. She uses fancy psychiatric diagnoses, subtle humiliation, head-on ridicule, and, when need be, electric shock to hold the patients in line. Big Nurse and McMurphy recognize each other as blood enemies from the start. The opposition is nearly Manichaean, as though a couple of comic-strip antagonists, or maybe a pair of warring deities, are facing off. Big Nurse is all for order, routine, submission, the dream of all-conquering Apollonian perfection. McMurphy is a throwback to an earlier, rowdier, more righteous time. He's grit and self-reliance, a two-fisted Emerson, scarred, sexy, always ready for a brawl, made to rumble. He's a high Romantic avatar, who wants to be all in all in himself.

It was on about the fifth day of reading Kesey aloud in class and discussing him (I and most of the rest of the group would still read nothing at home) that a chance remark that Lears made caught my attention. He said that prisons, hospitals, and schools were on a continuum and that Kesey, with his bitter portrait of the mental hospital, might be seen as commenting on all these places at once.

The idea, elementary as it was, smacked me like revelation. Here was a writer who was not on the side of the teachers, who in fact despised them and their whole angelic apparatus. Here was someone who found words—gorgeous, graffiti-styled, and apocalyptic—for what in me had been mere inchoate impulses, unheard groans of the spirit laboring away in its own darkness.

I can hardly express how I savored that novel. When McMurphy and his crew of sickos broke free and went fishing and partied and got drunk and thumbed their noses at Big Nurse and the pip-squeak shrinks she controlled, I had to throw the book up in the air and holler. They were rebelling against Medford High as well as against that hospital. And when they put McMurphy on the gurney and wheeled him back to the ward after his lobotomy, I was stunned with grief. This is what *they* would do—the omnipresent *they*—if you stood too squarely in the way of their machine, the ever-threshing Combine. When the Chief smothers the "fake" Mc-Murphy and sends the humongous tub through the window, breaks out of the institution, and goes sane, I myself jumped up and danced around the periphery of my room at 58 Clewley, glee-ful that for once, if only in someone's roaring imagination, the Combine had lost.

I had no idea such books existed. I thought that all the vol-umes on the library shelf had been written by the MHS teachers or their surrogates. They were put there to enforce good manners and proper deportment, or simply to bore us to death. But here was someone who was clearly on my side. And perhaps there were more like him.

I asked Lears about it one day. "Are there other books like this?" For I feared, truly, that *Cuckoo's Nest* might be the only one of its sort and that I would have to read it over and over again for the rest of my life. Lears caught what I meant immediately. "Sure, sure. Try Allen Ginsberg, try Jack Kerouac. You might even like William Bur-roughs."

What he didn't say was nearly as important as what he did: He gave me a few more addresses where similar enlighteners might be found. But he didn't start talking about a group called the Beats, whom we all already know and understand and can discuss in dis-passionate prose. No, these were, potentially, liberating gods, however flawed he himself might take them to be (and from some later hints I suspect that he took them to be more than a little), and he wasn't going to try to dispel their powers. He wanted us to be influenced by books—to face them as nakedly as we could and to see what would happen. The results might be dangerous; they might send us down the wrong road as well as the right. Good, then: Human beings are meant for danger, and for failure, sometimes, too.

I've often thought since then that much of what passes for literary criticism and the teaching of literature has an effect just the opposite of the one Frank Lears tried to create. The unspoken—and, to be fair, often unintended—objective is to inoculate students against great writing. By setting the work in context, placing it in history, assigning analytical essays of whatever level of sophistication, the teacher is actually demanding distance, detachment: Don't, whatever you do, be influenced by this. Don't adapt it to your own situation, use it as a map of your world, then go somewhere with it.

Lears simply helped unfold the visions of these writers, and he trusted us to make what use of them we might. If you want to go the Buddha's path—we read *Siddhartha*, after all—then by all means try it. Sure we'd ask a question or two before taking a step. But the questions always bore on life. What would it be like to believe this book? What would happen if you used it as your secular Bible? Could you live it?

In general, teachers do not ask these questions, in part because they are afraid of what will happen if they do. They do not want to be "responsible" for students' screwing up their lives because they give themselves over uninhibitedly to Whitman and try to live as the old queer anarch would, or to Dickinson, who created her own God and her own cosmology and lived with them. Many teachers,

I suspect, don't trust kids to sift these matters for themselves. Nor do they even really trust other adults to do it. The idea of a society full of people running amok, using the poets and artists to remake their own minds, individually and with only their own judgments and disasters and disappointments as inhibiting walls, can make teachers crazy.

Lears, aloof and benignly superior person that he could be, was much more democratic. He obviously believed, on some level that never needed articulation, that if you impelled people to imagine boldly and judge with some rigor, they could recast their lives a little, maybe more than that, and that the collective result, despite plenty of disasters along the way, would be to the good.

If he did not develop this sort of trust, he would have flopped utterly as a teacher of working-class kids. We would have seen that, really, despite all appearances, he was an ambassador from his class and his university, neither of which have ever given much of a damn for the people who clean the streets and the dorm rooms. Lears was willing to unfold visions, to kick back and see what would happen. When an elitist meets up with this kind of openness, he says it is a recipe for chaos. Lears seemed to feel that his approach was a recipe for change, growth, wonderful mutations, quirky shifts and slides.

He clearly didn't want to turn us into little Thoreauvians, or make us love SDS or the splinter wing of the Democratic party. Though he might have vaguely approved if these things had happened, he would have recognized that approval as the trivial thing it was. Really, all he seemed to want was to make us look at ourselves from new angles, become judgmental aliens in our own lives, and then to show us a few alternative roads. If we took them, all to the good. If not, who knows?—maybe something else would turn up for us later. Of all the teachers I have had—some of the world's best-known, in fact—Lears was the purest in his evident wish to make his students freer. He would be sorry about the costs, for relative autonomy can have many, but nothing would deter him.

And it is Lears' sense of what books can be that I took from him at midlife, in the midst of my own teaching crisis. I had, as I say, become an infinitely diverting guide to the intellectual territories— a "superb lecturer," as my students liked to call me—who could describe, analyze, interpret literature with no little flair. But none of my students seemed changed by all that pyrotechnic interpretation. On the contrary, it seemed to make them (and me) more complacent than before.

What I was failing to do was to take Lears' second step. All well and good to ask What does this book mean? But one also needs follow-up questions: Is it true? Can it be the basis for a life? Does Proust know something about jealousy and eros that should change us? Does Wordsworth's sense of the origins and the cures for depression, or melancholia, as he develops it in "Tintern Abbey," have any value, any use, in this, a moment where brutal despondency, most often administered to by drugs, has become unbearably common?

It's a technique for causing trouble, this kind of questioning, now just as much as it was when Frank Lears used it on us in his subdued way. But I'm convinced—and experience has borne me out—that if the reading of secular books is going to matter, we need to look at them as Lears did: not just as occasions for interpretive ingenuity, for showing how smart we might be, but as guides to future life, as occasions, sometimes, for human transformation.

*   *   *

DUBBY, TOO, fell in love with the Kesey book. He began, as temperament and his seeming destiny and the need to be a small-time Samuel Beckett character required him to do, in his project of coloring the *o*'s (he skipped ahead to get to the Kesey, leaving the Freud book behind, after a lot of agonizing), but he didn't get beyond the first couple of pages. Somehow he screwed up and began reading the thing. Dubby read the book faster than I did, and more times. He read it, as I recall, until he simply used it up. It fell apart in his hands, it was so worn. It disappeared. Into him.

Dubby, you'll recall, was an actor, and long before Jack Nicholson and Milos Forman diminished McMurphy by depicting him as an individual in a bad situation, not a grand, sloppy metaphor for the way it is, or might be, with us all, the Doober took on the role.

Dubby went after the stride and the grin and the swagger first. He played McMurphy like the archetypal American just arriving in some new place: out of his element, secretly unsure, worried about his lack of education or name, but determined to comport himself as though he might want to purchase the entire operation. Dubby-McMurphy at times put on a pair of invisible suspenders and did some work with them. He stretched the suspenders (red, I imagined) out and let them snap back with a satisfying, silent *thwack*. He also got the laugh down, big and booming, as Chief Broom described it. All this was done with a nice if mild dash of self-parody. You never forgot that Dubby was a poor beta playing a muscle-bound brawler (but maybe that's what McMurphy was on certain days). And there was a lot of loud-mouthing and delivering of frivolous threats and expostulations about girls lining up on the left and on the right and waiting patiently for their turn.

But what you couldn't miss was that Dubby wasn't so shabby in the role. He *was* big, though I'd never really noticed it—about six-feet-two, and he had filled out considerably; when he walked the

McMurphy walk, you could see that he wasn't necessarily the chicken-chested crouchling he had so often seemed in the past. He was a big, formidable kid, funny and handsome and, when he was doing the McMurphy, seemingly happy.

Maybe it really all owes to some unnamed hormone that suddenly squeezed itself loose from a still misunderstood gland and began coursing its way through Dubby's system. Maybe it had nothing to do with Ken Kesey or Frank Lears or anything in the outer world, but suddenly things started looking up for the Doober.

There was, first of all, the breakthrough in geometry. He had, he told me in astonishment one day, been in the service of a strange delusion. For quite a while he thought that Mr. Repucci wanted him to do well in math. He believed that Leo—like Mrs. O'Day and like the members of the O'Day family's equestrian branch, Sweetie and Jack, his fellow riders of the invisible escape ponies—hoped for his eventual success. Leo was, after all, constantly inviting Dubby in for extra help, offering to share an after-school afternoon with Donald, where he could sit and grind over math problems for hours in the thinning light. So Dubby had figured that by not turning up for these sessions, by not doing the homework, by flunking and fucking around, he was sticking it to Leo in admirable style. He figured it must have been pure torture to Repucci to have to hand back another test with the score of 16 out of a possible 100, sad testimony to a dedicated teacher's failure.

But it struck the Doober suddenly—high school breakthroughs are splendid indeed—that Mr. Repucci really couldn't care less if Dubby did nothing in class. In fact, Mr. R preferred it that way. It was fun to flunk the Doob. Mr. Repucci was having about as good a time with Dubby as Nurse Ratched generally had with shaking quaking Billy Bibbit, whose life she controlled as if she'd equipped him early on with electronic implants.

So Dubby resolved to continue tormenting Mr. Repucci at every chance he got—he made up a limerick of almost astounding cruelty about recent deaths in Leo's family—but to pass geometry on this, the third, try. After all, Dubby averred, I know it better than anyone by now, Leo included.

Dubby also went out for the baseball team. I came along to watch him and lend a little moral support. The Dub was terrified. The baseball coaches were crotchety old men, human hemorrhoids, the Doober called them, and brutal in their assaults on all ineptitude. They stood around in windbreakers, spitting on the ground and rubbing their yellowed hands together, grumbling like ancient buffalo. Dubby turned up not in a baseball cap but in a baby blue beach hat tilted low to one side. He did this because Artie Mondello and I had given him a money-saving haircut. There was now a broad, empty track leading from his left ear halfway to the top of his cranium. Without the beach hat, he looked like a particularly friendly alien. Not too long after the immortal haircut, Dubby showed me and Artie a photograph, gleaned from *The National Enquirer* or a comparable publication. It showed a man beaten and in flames, kneeling in the middle of a highway. Headline: HIS FRIENDS DID THIS TO HIM.

Dubby had a lovely swing, Stan Musial reborn, and his eye was sharp from all that time in the poolroom hustling younger kids and splitting the money with me. (One day when we were driving along in Dubby's beat-up convertible, I saw a piece of paper flash, pass like a fast-blown leaf, in front of the windshield. "Haaah!" said Dubby. "That's ten bucks each." He'd not only identified it as legal tender; he'd made out the denomination.) I can still see him smashing one liner after another into right field. With every hit, he stood bigger and bigger at the plate, until he looked like Chief Bromden about to stride out of the ward. The coaches, however, didn't bother to watch. The team was picked from the beginning. They had their guys. So they stood in their tired circle and barely gave Doober a look.

I heard that when they cut Dubby, he went up to them, the old tobacco-squeezing gang, and told them that they'd made a stupid mistake and then invited them to enjoy what would probably have been their first erotic consummation in years, albeit in private. He took off then; he hopped the fence in a big bound. No one was willing to tell the coaches what his name was.

He also got himself a date. With Margaret Kellerman, a red-haired girl, whose bra strap Hicky Daniels traced in English class while Miss Cullen suffered her persecutions. "I liked her," said Dubby. "You could talk to her. It was like she was a guy." No higher praise than this. But she already had a boyfriend, from whom she was taking a brief sabbatical. Dubby went back to hanging with me and John Vincents, the Navajo. We played games of floor hockey in the D's room, where Dubby was goalie, using a ruler to defend the net (the space between his dresser and bed) against the flight of a balled-up sweat sock.

At the time, Dubby could not skate. But two years later Dubby was the star goalie for Graham Junior College. He was, I understand, the best baseball player the place had seen in a while, too.

So, he read a book and he went out and got a date and swung at a baseball and passed geometry. My, my. Then he went to junior college and put his floor-hockey game to work. Thank you, Mr. Lears. Thank you, Ken Kesey.

But it's more than that. Things that would have floored Dubby before became material for a brisk routine, a self-deflating, self-congratulatory tale. When he drank beer, he stopped breaking into sudden tears and repeating the words "My poor mother, my poor, poor mother." Poor, because he had disgraced and disappointed her so. Now, he'd drink two or three, stop, and insist that we go to the dance at Arlington Catholic Girls High School, boasting that Catholic-school girls found large-scale maniacs like himself just the thing to lead them into temptation. In fact, such girls were remarkably fond of Dubby and even of me, we being among the forty or so boys in a room three hundred strong with the flower of Catholic girlhood.

The person who became a junior-college hockey goalkeeper could easily have become somebody who graduated from high school (barely), lived with his parents, took a crummy day job, with drinks every Friday at the Shamrock Grill, beer twenty-five cents a pop, accompanying shot for a dollar, ranting about Jews and blacks thrown in gratis. But he didn't go that way. I can't tell you what happened to Dubby, not in the long run. But the last time I saw him, skating away from the goal after winning (about 8 to 6, I think) a hockey game played on an actual noncarpeted surface, with no balled-up sweat sock in evidence, there wasn't a place in him for that kind of life. Dubby, at least for the foreseeable future, was going to enjoy his being rightly in the world. May he never have ceased doing exactly that.

SPRING CAME on, and as the weather warmed up, the class occasionally went outside to sit on the grass and hold our discussions. We usually repaired to the site of our all-in snowball battle, the place where, in a certain sense, a sense maybe unknown to Lears, the class had been born. There, it was hard to see us from inside the school building. Going outside sometimes resulted in one or two of us nodding off, but Lears didn't much care; he had most of us most of the time now. He sat cross-legged, medicine man–style, and swung his wrist and laughed, and we answered the questions he asked, because what he thought mattered probably did.

What did we talk about? Anything and everything. The book at hand sometimes, or a fragment from another book that he'd found interesting and had copied up for us. Is it right to let your country, which you love, put you wrongfully to death, even when there is an easy chance to escape? (Socrates thought so, and drank the hemlock.) Should you stay with your family, even when life in it becomes a vivid squalor? (Socrates said that being married to Xanthippe, who yelped at him all the time and brained him with that pot of urine, apparently in full view of his friends, was a good thing, since if he could learn to put up with that, there would be little in day-to-day life that could daunt him.)

We talked about Thoreau and Emerson—a great deal about Thoreau. We talked a lot about civil disobedience and whether or not you should break the laws of your country when you felt it was doing something outrageously wrong. For Thoreau, the issue was American slavery; for us, it was the war in Asia, and a few other matters as well.

Lears gave us background information when we needed it. He told us, for instance, how indebted to Thoreau Martin Luther King and Gandhi had been. King we knew, or presumed we did. But Gandhi we had little idea about. Someone—it might even have been me—said as much, and we were treated to a very good, off-the-cuff account of how Indians had used nonviolence to end the British Raj. Almost always there was a little bibliography. If you're interested in Gandhi, try Erik Erikson's book, then a few words about what people thought to be its advantages and defects. We wrote down the names from these glosses, these pocket histories, and for the most part thought no more about it. But years later, I, and others too, probably, would become curious about Thoreau or Gandhi, the soft bell would ring and a feeling of curiosity, mellowed and aged because of Lears' easy, welcoming style, would well up.

It was a continual invitation to the world that Lears was laying out. Part of his secret was that he did not take it personally, not at all, if you demurred. He was a host who could never be offended. He believed, I think, that the life from which he drew the curtain was a marvel and that we would come around to it sooner or later. And if not, who had we to blame but ourselves? The inner spirit had simply been too weak.

It was during this period that Sandra's status changed completely. For a long time, when Buller inveighed against women's lib, some of the guys in the class would do a merry chimp bounce in their seats and stare disparagingly at Sandra. Sometimes when she talked, fits of coughing and mock sneezes broke out. But all this came to an end. Now people sat beside her, solicited her opinion, walked off with her after class. On some days, you could see Sandra and Cap chatting happily away. I imagine she still thought that a lot of us were playpen escapees, but she never showed it. She was serene and kindly and dignified to the end.

IT WAS a first, this outdoors business: No one at Medford High would have imagined doing it. One day, outside, just as we were wrapping up a discussion of Thoreau—who of course was Lears' intellectual idol, but to endorse whom he would never have said an overt word—Lears gave us a solemn, mischievous look, the sort of expression that shrewd old rabbis are supposed to be expert in delivering. "There's been some doubt expressed about our going outside."

Then he told a story. In the faculty cafeteria, with plenty of the other teachers milling around, Lears had been approached by Jingles McDermott, the submaster, the disciplinarian. Jingles, the coin and key jangler, had the sly, bullying style of a hard Irish cop. He had a barroom face, red nose, watery eyes, the hands of someone who labored for a living. He was stepping up to put Lears in his place.

Jingles got rapidly to the point. What would happen, he'd asked Lears, if everyone held class outside? This was familiar stuff to us all. McDermott's question came out of that grand conceptual bag that also contained lines like "Did you bring gum for everyone?" and "Would you like to share that note with the whole class?" Jingles was trying to treat Lears like a student, like one of us—and in front of their colleagues. At Medford High there were two tribes, us and them. Lears had defied the authorities; clearly he had become one of them, a student, of no use or interest whatever. But in fact Lears was of no particular clan but his own, the tribe of rootless, free-speculating readers and talkers and writers, who owe allegiance first to a pile of books that they've loved and then, only secondly, to other things.

McDermott did not know this. Nor did he know that Lears, however diminutive, mild, and mandarinly self-effacing, pretty clearly thought well of himself. So McDermott would not have been prepared when Lears drew an easy breath and did what every high school kid would like to do when confronted with this sort of bullying. He didn't fight it, didn't stand on his dignity. He simply ran with it. What if everyone held class outside on sunny days? Suppose that happened? And from there, Lears went on to draw a picture of life at Medford High School—a picture that had people outside on the vast lawn talking away about books and ideas and one thing and another, hanging out, being lazy and getting absorbed, thinking hard from time to time, and reveling in the spring.

It was Woodstock and Socrates' agora fused, and Lears spun it out for us, just as he had for McDermott. What if that happened, he asked us (and the submaster)? How tragic would it be?

This vision of the renovated school took a long time to unfold and it had something like a musical form, ebbing and fading, threading back through major themes and secondary motifs. And in my mind's eye I could see McDermott wilting, growing too small for his wrinkled, sad clothes; I could hear his nickel-dime pocket symphony getting softer and softer. He would soon have known, as we did, that Lears could produce plenty more of this (he was the most eloquent man I'd met) and that it was time to cut and run. What struck me about the performance—and I believed Lears' rendition of it, word for word: He was unfailingly, often unflatteringly honest—was how serene and artful it was, as though Jingles had commissioned him to create a small piece of on-site spontaneous art, to paint a picture, which, in effect, Lears had.

Am I wrong to think that Lears was bragging a little as he unfolded his vision of a renewed school? Because, really, what he was describing to Jingles McDermott was the class he had created with us. This was a class that people looked forward to going to, that we talked about all the time, nights and weekends; a place where you could speak freely, from mind and heart, and never be laughed at, in fact be heard by a group as you might never have been heard before, for Lears had by then taught us some of his art of listening. Here we forgot that we were something called "students" and were subordinate to a "teacher," who flourished a grade book. Lears simply let us grade ourselves. As I recall, there were very few A's.

We went outside whenever we chose after that. It was very odd: I had been at Medford High for four years, and I had never seen McDermott's side lose a bout. I'd seen a kid from the South Medford Bears spit in a teacher's face, but soon enough the police wagon was there and the big boy was trussed and bawling and on the way to jail. After class was over on the day that Lears told us the McDermott story, Cap pulled me aside and said, "You know, Lears can really be an asshole when he wants to be." In Medford, there were fifty intonations that you could apply to the word *asshole*. Spun right, the word constituted a high form of praise.

Of course, McDermott was a broad target. America was in crisis and people were assuming—or being cast into—intense, allegorical identities: pig, peacenik, hawk, dove. McDermott had turned into an ugly monolith, at least in our eyes. In Asia, the Viet Cong were making fools of his spiritual brethren: Nixon, Westmoreland, McNamara, and the rest. His sort were on the run. In the next few years it would get worse for them. But Lears, for his part, hadn't treated Jingles as among the lost, even though he probably had it coming. Instead, he'd invited him to a party, an outdoor extravaganza. At the time, McDermott surely couldn't discern the invitation in Lears' extended aria, but who knows what he might have seen later on as he turned it all over in his mind?

The next day, when I bumped into him at his locker, Dubby was ecstatic. He went word for word over what Lears had said to Jingles, a particular persecutor of the Dub's. "He was just like R. P. McMurphy," Dubby averred, "the way he stuck it to Jingles." I agreed and joined in the celebration.

But later it occurred to me that this was not entirely true. Lears was like McMurphy in that he obviously hated needless limitation, arbitrary authority. But Lears' response was not to throw punches, as McMurphy was prone to do. No, it was words instead of body blows that Lears traded in. The power that Lears had by virtue of knowing how to talk and write, commanding irony when he needed it, being able, when pushed, to impale an adversary on the point of a phrase—this power became manifest to me. And I thought back through some of the worst moments of my life, and I began to see how differently a few of them might have turned out if I could only have spoken half well rather than pitched a fit or thrown punches. Even in the face of violence, a sure mind, I began to believe, might bring you through. I, at six feet and two hundred well-muscled pounds, was afraid of Jingles McDermott. Lears, diminutive and rather anxious, was not. In fact, Lears may have feared almost no one at all. For such power and such freedom from being afraid, I longed, and I began to think about how I might go about getting them for myself.

One Flew Over the Cuckoo's Nest, the book that sent Dubby into that beautiful spin, sent me off to the library.

I can picture myself there on a Monday morning in early spring, skipping school (or my first five periods; I'll be back in time for Frank Lears' class), reading as if my life depended on it, as if the books were repositories of a rich oxygen that I needed to consume. I have become, overnight, an obsessed reader, a library cormorant, as Coleridge liked to call himself.

There I sit at the table by the periodicals section in my blue-and-white leather-trimmed football jacket, a small white Mustang embroidered on the front, with my number, 66, on the horse's midriff. I'm wearing thick glasses, gold-rimmed, semi-hippie–style now, track shoes, and yellow and black love beads, and I'm reading ferociously—reading, if this is possible, with the same slightly cracked ardor that I used to bring to football.

I read in a rage that so much that was palpably my business had been kept from me. It's like finding that the post office has for years been syphoning away packet after packet of the most engrossing letters—some of them approaching love letters, no less—

addressed personally to me. And who has been guilty of this malfeasance? Who are the corrupt officials? The faculty of Medford High are the main conspirators. They are the ones who had come on with *Silas Marner* and *Ivanhoe* and *The Good Earth* and implied that all of literature was simply more of the same. A line by the poet Richard Brautigan summed it all up: My teachers could have ridden with Jesse James for all the time they stole from me. I read it and wept, angry tears sliding over my face and down onto the bucking mustang.

I was probably an absurd sight in that library, with my jock-freak garb and my piles of books on either side. Sometimes I would get so enraged at all I had missed that I would open two books simultaneously and, jerking my head from one to the other, try to read them both at once.

But I could not have cared how absurd I looked. In paradise, and that's where I was, no one is bothered overmuch by self-consciousness. I read Hemingway and Steinbeck; Burroughs and Kerouac and more Kesey (as Lears advised); I read Whitman, tried to parse Dickinson, puzzled over Faulkner, looked into Salinger, scratched my head over Susan Sontag, mused over Brautigan, finding *Trout Fishing in America* the ultimate in rueful charm. I read Hunter Thompson in *Esquire*, a magazine that shocked me by suggesting, with the subtlest piece of innuendo, that *Playboy* was a magazine for rubes. Up until then, I had thought that to have a key to the Playboy Club in Boston was to be atop the world. *Esquire* compared it to wearing galoshes and to covering one's fedora with a plastic protector. I read Abbie Hoffman and James Simon Kunin's *Strawberry Statement,* about the takeover at Columbia University. I read Ginsberg's "Howl" and memorized a chunk of it, imagining it the greatest prophecy yet to issue on earth. I was having a blast.

For the first time I could remember, I was no longer lonely, for I had found many, many compeers in relative weirdness. A line from Dylan could have been my slogan up until then (had I gone out early, it could have been my epitaph): "If my thought dreams could be seen / They'd probably place my head in a guillotine." But I got to look in on the thought-dreams of others, and they—the articulate, the celebrated, the published, recognized, and renowned— were often exponentially weirder than I was. Ginsberg? Compared to Ginsberg, running around his house "a sex pest," as he later called himself, with his prolific boners and kooky homo visions, what were my own extravangances? But Ginsberg and Whitman, who was ready to make love to all creation, bonk everyone and -thing on sight, were willing to flourish all their temperamental weirdness and call it bliss: "The flag of my disposition," as Whitman had it, "out of hopeful green stuff woven."

I could no longer take myself to be quite so strange a number, so irreducibly radical an integer, as I'd thought. More than that, I now had ears into which I might confide my own views about things. For in my mind, I carried on expansive conversations with these writers. Authors live in their ideal form for the young in the way that they cannot for the purportedly better experienced, who have met a few and have had to concede that the generous spirits on display in books rarely flourish moment to moment, in actual time, and often have been created through the most arduous processes of revision and, alas too, of suppression. But they were real to me—the Whitman, for instance, who pledged that he would be up ahead waiting for me when I was able to "shoulder my duds" and take to the open road—and so they assumed a more pressing reality than many of the actual beings whose flesh and blood selves I came in contact with every day. My authors were alive, and they spoke to me. When Nietzsche was in the army and suffering badly—though he affected a military mustache, he was never much of a soldier—he would sometimes call out to his favorite writer, the one who had set *him* free: "Schopenhauer," he'd intone. "Help me!" From time to time, I suspect, Schopenhauer probably did.

I was never for a moment cowed by these books, by their grandeur or sophistication. I didn't need—and wouldn't, until I went to graduate school—to hear Emerson's lines about young scholars reading Bacon and Locke in libraries and sitting in awe, frozen, afraid that they would never amount to anything by comparison, forgetful that once Bacon and Locke were merely young scholars sitting in libraries. No, the line that would have done duty for me, had I known it, was Keats's about connecting with the "immortal freemasonry of intellect." Emphasis on *free*. As soon as I walked into the library during schooltime, taking my chances with the authorities, I was in—part of the crew. All the books had been written and placed there for me. I was grateful, but I also knew that without me, and others like me, poor scholars as Thoreau calls us, needful but not ready to prostrate ourselves in thanks, the books would molder and turn gray; they'd become substantially less.

I also read to learn a language. My own, English. Because the truth is that I could not use it until then. I wanted to be able to talk somewhat the way Lears did when he was on a roll—though I wasn't ready to go all the way with him; I wasn't quite set to become someone who would plunk words like *ersatz, propinquitous,* and *mendacious* into conversation. But I did want to command words, and I wanted to infuse them with my own inflections, to speak my piece as my grandmother was fond of saying, and doing. I liked what Lears had done to Jingles, and I resolved to stop smacking people in the head (and getting smacked back by them) and to use words to put myself across. But do not think me too virtuous—I had seen how much longer words can hurt than the best-thrown punch.

I had not become a pacifist, by any means. I would still be happy to fight to defend myself; I would fight to defend my country, though I resolved that defending my country couldn't entail traveling halfway around the world to have it out with Asian kids. I was by then very fond of Muhammad Ali's line, issued when the government was preparing to pounce on him and order him into the army in his country's supposed defense: "Man, I ain't got no quarrel with them Viet Cong." If the summons came, and it might, there was no way I was going. Let Jonesy and the rest of the defensive line say what they would: This was not my fight.

The Buddhists believe that when you are reincarnated, you forget all of your past lives. But when you are young, every book you truly fall in love with is a life of yours, one that you have, as it were, lived in the past and now can remember in full. It is a blessing of remarkable proportion, for through books one is incarnated many times—not only, say, as a questing sailor aboard a whaling ship, a mortally ill heiress, a woman taken in adultery, but also as the mind who conceives and renders these things and experiences the world in a certain manner. Those aghast at having only one life on earth are drawn inexorably to books, and in them find the deep and true illusion of living not just their own too short life but of inhabiting many existences, many modes of being, and so of cheating fate a little.

Mostly what I read for, I have to admit, was to find out who I myself might be. I was perpetually in hope of hearing my own inarticulate thoughts and feelings put into words by someone who had gone deeper into life, and into language, than I had done. Many years later, I would read words from an author who felt that he was trying to do precisely this for his readers, and I would feel that, from what I supposed to be the other side of the mirror, he had crystallized the terms of my early quest almost perfectly. "It seemed to me," he observes, that readers "would not be 'my' readers but readers of their own selves, my book being merely a sort of magnifying glass like those which the optician at Combray used to offer his customers—it would be my book but with it I would furnish them with the means of reading what lay inside themselves. So that I should not ask them to praise me or censure me, but simply to tell me whether 'it really is like that,' I should ask them whether the words that they read within themselves are the same as those which I have written."

What I did not know is that, in all probability, one can acquire one's own voice—which is to say the evidence of one's own freely formed character—from no other individual. It is only the incessant labor of combining your own experience, taken in and metabolized by intense feeling and thought, with what you have acquired in books that actually creates and re-creates a free-flowing identity. At seventeen, I was looking for an easy way—a voice to adopt, a self to put on, as though it were a tailor-made suit of clothes commissioned especially for me. We think that an author can provide answers, when all that he or she can actually do is provide incitements, inspirations, goads. "Reading," Proust says in a more circumspect mood, "is the threshold to the spiritual life; it can introduce us to it; it does not constitute it."

The book I am reading on this slightly chilly spring morning is none other than *The Autobiography of Malcolm X*. Lears was right about it. (Thurston White, though it hurt to admit it, was, too.) It is some piece of work. Already, it has gotten me into trouble.

*   *   *

I HAD begun the book on Saturday night, while waiting for a couple of friends to pick me up for an evening of beer and light conversation. They are, predictably, late. And by the time they arrive, eight-thirty or so, I am far gone in the pages.

The car horn honks outside. My father, who is for some reason known best to the gods actually at home on a Saturday night, hollers out immediately, "I'll be right out!" He says this whenever friends of mine honk outside, just as, whenever the garbage truck pulls up, he hollers, "Thanks. We don't need any more." But in the former phrase—the "I'll be right out"—there's more than a little longing.

Soon I am lying down in the backseat of the car, a Chevy Nova, property of my friend's mother, who, if she knew the use to which it was now being put, would need to repair to the nearest sanatorium that would allow her to continue making her own marinara sauce, since she can bear no other. I'm swigging merrily from a quart bottle of Schlitz Malt Liquor, the bull rampant on the label, totem animal for the night, and reading on in the volume that my friends in the front seat refer to as "the coon book." Whenever they pop this phrase, I say something fetching about their sisters or mothers, or both. Mostly, they're annoyed because I'm completely absorbed and not joining in the cruise-and-booze festivities, which include, but aren't limited to, shrieking out the window, flipping cans at pedestrians, urinating gleefully in each other's direction during pit stops, and slamming the roof with a flat palm when a pretty girl materializes (when *any* girl materializes) on the sidewalk or in a passing car. I have also demanded that the interior light stay on so that I can read. This annoys the driver to no end.

The Malcolm X book was, I believe, the first one that I had ever bought freely with my own money. I actually went to a bookstore, a sort of establishment I had never entered, in order to make the purchase. It was probably BDI money, come to think of it. Having done what he could for my erotic enlightenment, the Walrus, of whose stories I was now so dead weary that I wouldn't even turn up for work ("C'mon, Mark, five balloons an hour for Chrissake"), was now sponsoring my literary education.

I tried to get my friends interested in Malcolm by talking about his criminal past and what a hard guy he used to be. I told them what I took to be an amusing story from the book. When they were being sentenced for a sequence of crimes they'd committed around Boston, Malcolm, then still Malcolm Little, and his partner, Shorty, heard the judge pronounce a string of sentences: five years for this, three for that, six for something else. Then the judge added that they'd be served concurrently. Shorty, who had no idea what *concurrently* meant, thought that a few petty crimes were adding up to life in prison. The anecdote fell flat, probably because my pals didn't know what *concurrently* meant, either.

But really, I myself wasn't all that intrigued by Malcolm's criminal past; I'd heard that kind of story before, about a dozen small-time Medford hoods. No, what I, who, living as I did in West Medford, had an almost visceral fear of blacks, learned from Malcolm X first of all was that he went through half of *his* life terrified—terrified of white people. And why not? By his account, whites did outrageous things to him and other blacks on a devoted, ongoing basis. It was our racial sport and pastime. In an autobiographical sketch by James Baldwin, whom I'd been reading the week before at the library, while down on High Street my Latin class groaned on without me, I'd learned about how, when he was about ten years old, a couple of white cops pulled him into an alley and began beating him up, whaling the shit out of him, as we'd say in Medford, and calling him a little nigger and all the rest. For what? For nothing. Just to put the fear of God, that is to say the fear of white people, in him. It was also the cops' idea of a good time, something diverting to fill the afternoon. Had I read a newspaper with any intensity or looked hard at the TV news, I could have sensed that as much was going on every day in America still. But this I had not the imagination to do.

William Billings, as a side note, looked a little different now, too. That whole bit with the dog was about nothing so much as protection—protection from me and the likes of me, really. He was scared, too; it's simply that if he showed it, he'd be making himself yet more vulnerable.

I couldn't believe, along with Malcolm and Elijah Muhammad, that whites were devils, but when I got to the point where the Muslims unfolded their doctrine, I could see why a half-reasonable black person could easily think so. If you looked through the history of rapes and lynchings and slavery and general abuse, it seemed at least a viable explanation.

The people who said, like the SDS Hawk, that we were a war-crazed nation because of what we were doing in Asia weren't easy to take in stride. But when I heard what I did from Malcolm X about the way black people generally were treated, I saw why some of them were as enraged as they were. (And it blew me away that any of them could take the nonviolent route.) I also had to begin forging a new take on America, the place I'd been an unthinking booster of since about inception, a bespectacled classroom Cold Warrior. It was clear to me that you couldn't really say you knew much about the country until you'd at least made an effort to see it from the point of view of blacks.

It would be foolish for me to take credit for a moral breakthrough that I ought never to have needed to make in the first place. But all over America such things were happening. Spurred on by Malcolm X and James Baldwin—and people like Frank

Lears, who asked you to take these matters seriously—white people were starting to try to see the world through the eyes of the slaves' grandchildren.

What mattered to me personally about Malcolm was that he was a reader and that he had an absolute conviction that knowledge could get you a better life and let you help the people who were around you. There are rhapsodic passages in the book about the reading he did in jail and the way he worked to write legibly. He saw that by doing this, he was getting back at white people. I myself had been of the school of Dubby. I believed that I was showing the authorities at Medford High what a true rebel I was by never doing my homework and staying disaffected. In fact, that was just what Medford High expected and wanted of me: I should stay ignorant, the better to become a good factory hand, a stand-up guy on the city crew, a sterling clerk-typist with an honorable discharge. What Malcolm showed me was that you could shift your destiny by acquiring knowledge, by reading, learning things. I had never heard anyone describe the process in such stirring terms before. But I knew better than to get too loud and moist on such matters when I was driving around sloshing Schlitz Malt Liquor with the duo up front, so I shut up and read.

You can't lie down in the backseat of the car and have much control over the navigation, or much awareness about it either. And it wasn't long before my friends had brought me under the awning of a very familiar oak tree, just beginning now to bud. There they stopped. I looked up at the tree in sweet, drunken puzzlement— Malcolm was going on about the joy of reading and we were, momentarily, one—from where I lay in the Nova's backseat.

"Last fuckin' stop, Mark [Mahhhk]. You gotta go."

"Yup, time for you to get outta here."

The budding oak tree was the tree that brushed against my bedroom window at 58 Clewley Road, the sound taking my dreams down various strange paths. My friends, tired of my nonsense, had brought me back home and dumped me. It couldn't have been later than ten-thirty—way too early for a Saturday night. Still, time for me to get outta here.

I heaved myself up, said good-bye without protest, and took leave of the Nova. It wasn't until I was halfway up our hall stairs that I realized I still had the quart of Schlitz Malt in one hand; in the other hand, my right, the one I was attending to, was Malcolm X's book. I hustled downstairs to the street, took a long, slow chug, and tossed the half-empty bottle, rampant bull and all, into our trash bin.

HAPPINESS, SOMEONE said, is complete absorption. If so, that morning, reading *The Autobiography of Malcolm X* in the Medford Library, I must have been in bliss. The whole world simply disappeared, as though the genie who had let reality pour forth out of a cracked magic lamp had called it all back in, leaving just me and that book alone. When I looked up at the normal, non–frog hopping clock that presided in the library, I saw that if I was going to get to Lears' class on time, I would have to hustle. It was hot outside by now, so I left my football jacket—who really wants to swipe someone else's football coat, embossed with another's number, in my case 66, two-thirds of the number of the beast in Revelation?—there on my seat and began to sprint for the school building, about half a mile away.

I was wearing track shoes, not the ones with the metal bottoms, fortunately; I was in fine shape from beer drinking and weight lifting and putting the shot (or throwing the shot, as the coach said) and occasionally even running the quarter-mile with the track team, and I could fly. I tore down into Medford Square, past Brigham's, where the Medford High boys and girls came together, site, for me, of multiple social snafus and idiocies, then down past the entrance to Stag's poolroom. The cave was just opening up for the day; a few of the customary dwellers—the local hustlers, Hank the Hat and Paulie, who spun the Blind Girl—were grumbling down the stairs; they seemed disconsolate, as though they were on a payroll and headed for mandatory labor in the mines. As I cut the corner onto High Street, I glanced toward Papa Gino's, forbidden territory for me, the place where the South Medford Bears gathered in their gang jackets, surrounded by their girlfriends and female admirers, all in leather, luring and dangerous, like gorgeous black spiders.

Then into the side door of the school, up one flight of stairs, and then turning to another, where, still on the fly, I encounter the form of Mace Johnson, former coach of the Medford Mustangs and still, nominally, my teacher of American history. In the mirror today, before taking off for school, he must have looked particularly formidable to himself. He was spiffed up, wearing a blue suit and a gregarious yellow tie.

Mace Johnson, I could tell, wanted me to stop, wanted me to explain myself and my absences from class and my flying hair and crazed shirttails, but some kind of momentum seemed to be on my side.

"Hello, Mark," he says in the basso profundo, stop-'em-where-they-are voice. I'm sure that in the back of Johnson's mind, pushing relentlessly forward, is the view that there are three things he hates: small dogs, women who smoke in public, and half-promising former linebackers who let their hair grow wild (or, as wild as the Beatles had it in, say, *A Hard Day's Night*—not very) and read all the time and never come to class, and, and, and . . .

But I haven't got time for the homily. I'm hardly touching the stairs. I'm on my way.

"Hello, Coach," I pant. (I still gave him that, the title—would give him that today, if I saw him.) Then I was gone.

I am faster than I imagined—or maybe the clock at the library is a little aggressive, a bit brisk—for a librarian's idea of paradise, I sometimes think, is everyone out of the library (but himself) and all books restored to their rightful place on the shelves. So when I get to Frank Lears' room, he is sitting there, alone, hunched over the sad gray desk, thumbing through a book, making notes in his insects-on-a-spree script.

And this, reader, ought to be the climax of the book. In a film version of this story or in a novel, this would be the moment when I had my major encounter with Frank Lears. It would be the final dramatic turning point, the end that was, in effect, a beginning. (Raise the music level a little; sail the point home.) In light of my new passion for learning, my unassigned assiduous reading, my subversive class-cutting for higher purposes, and my repeated quotations of Richard Brautigan and Allen Ginsberg, he recognizes me as part of his tribe and we go through a short ceremony of investiture. It would be a little like the day Mace Johnson ushered me into the cult of gridiron manhood for sending poor Tom Sullivan ignominiously to the dust and humiliating Frank Ball. At the end of our discussion, mine and Frank Lears', a hug might even ensue. He would be tentative, unsure, but eventually he'd succumb to my bearish, football McMurphy–style joie de vivre, and neither of us would hold back.

But the real climax to this book, if it is that, comes a little later. The fact is that now we exchange soft greetings and I begin reading my book, the autobiography, just as he's reading his. We're like a couple of monks alone in the chapel making what use we can of the light.

For, of course, there is no club to join; there is no group investiture. What you are when you go Lears' route is someone who, not entirely unbeholden to books and to others, has nevertheless decided to find truths for himself, maybe to find truths that fit only himself. I must create a system of my own, says William Blake, or be enslaved by someone else's. Is it a surprise that in his day-to-day life Blake was one of the loneliest of men?

Soon my fellow students begin jostling and jiving their way in. Lears seemed relieved. He probably felt the pressure for a big encounter, a climax for now and the future, just as I did and was glad to have the thing curtailed. On they came, Dubby and Rick and Cap and Sandra and Nora and Tommy Buller and Carolyn and the rest, all up, in a fine mood, even though they'd been through five periods of dreck, because here, in Frank Lears' class, something good was likely to happen.

It was not until years later, long after the class was over, that I realized that all the books Lears assigned us were on a theme. *The Stranger, One Flew Over the Cuckoo's Nest, Group Psychology*—they all dealt with the oppression of conformity (among other things); the last, *Siddhartha,* was about the Buddha's serene, fierce rebellion against it. We were all weighed down by conformity, Lears could apparently see. And he also knew that we, his philosophers-in-the-making, were oppressors in our own right, passing on the ways of the system, the Combine, as Kesey called it, to the weaker and duller kids.

The books were an insult, an affront. He had diagnosed our worst qualities and had gone at them, though without ever saying as much directly. He was as much our attacker as he was our guide. Teachers, freelance spirit healers that they are, or ought to be, make their diagnoses, then concoct the elixir, which can often burn going down. If at the end of the year, when he had us under his spell, he had come rather to like us—his irony, never on hold, was surely diminishing—I am sure we still never became people he pined to spend free afternoons with. We were supposed to change. Many of us did, and surely he was glad, but it did not make him swoon over us, love us as though we were his own creations.

In America, the story of the great good teacher is told over and over again. It is the story of the man or woman who comes upon a hapless group of kids and helps them remake their lives. In the standard version, in the myth, that teacher is always fired by the highest of motives, chief among which is a love for the students that is unequivocal and that begins the day they walk through his door. The love never falters and never ends. Years later you can go back and visit the great teacher; he will remember everything about you. He will exult in your accomplishments. Your defeats he will put in proper perspective.

This great good teacher of popular legend is full of broad, generous, and generally applicable truths, which he dispenses to all. In these truths there is, of course, nothing shocking. They are things we all know on some level—put your family before your career; try to enjoy the little things—but in our hustle and bustle have forgotten. The great good teacher is happy and one with himself, and he wants us to be the same. He will die with a smile on his face.

Lears, on the contrary, was a great teacher in large measure because, at least at the start, he clearly did not like us much at all, and showed it to anyone who had an eye to see. Essentially, I think, Lears held us in contempt. At the beginning, I believe, he felt about us collectively roughly the way he did about Buller from the first day to the last. He did not love us as individuals or as a group. But I believe he did love freedom—he wanted to live among free people, in part because it made his own life richer. And the prospect of offering us a freedom of our own moved him and made him work hard and take chances and stand up to people like Jingles McDermott, whom he would probably much rather have avoided. In fact, he might have wanted to avoid the whole bunch of us, but once in, he did what he could. What I liked most about Lears, I suppose, was that for all the minor miracle of what he accomplished with us, he was no missionary: He served us but also himself. I think he got what he wanted out of Medford High, which was a chance to affront his spiritual enemies, though with some generosity. His goodness, as Emerson liked to say, always had an edge to it.

As well as some sorrow: Good teachers have many motivations, but I suspect that loneliness is often one of them. You need a small group, a circle, to talk to; unable to find it in the larger world, you try to create it in the smaller sphere of a classroom. Lears, who seemed at times a little lost in his life, a brilliant orphan, did something like that with us. When he saw the material he had to work with on that first day, he must have been on the verge of stepping out the window.

But one distinction is worth insisting on. He clearly wanted people he could talk to, who would consider caring about what he cared for, who would get his jokes. But he just as clearly did not want us to think as he thought. He wanted us to forge ourselves, and if those selves were antithetical to him, entirely un-Lears-like, then so be it. The only crime was standing pat, not thinking, refusing to ask and answer the questions, refusing to put one's own beliefs up on the rack and twist and tear them a little.

The late sixties were a particularly good time for this kind of teaching. There was a feeling abroad that everything was up for grabs, that all consequential things might be remade. People who felt that way, and I came to, did so because they thought there was never a time where there was more room to be an individual, to strike your own path. And yet—here is the important distinction—in doing so you remained part of a large, collective movement, a movement to get rid of the war, to make women and men potential friends, to help black people get a clean shot at the promises that everyone else took for granted. It was like playing in a very good jazz band, being alive then, a band where the wilder and weirder you played your solo—provided it was truly yours—the better it fit in with the whole, the more the performance expanded.

And Lears, who seemed to me the spirit of the sixties (in the best sense) as much as the spirit of Socrates, brought us to the point where we could join that rambunctious collective if we wanted. We knew what it was about. And we could have our particular say in it, too, hear our own voices, make our own notes. Free in himself, he tried as hard as he could to make others free. And that, centrally, made him—I'd like to say again that it made him a great teacher, but Lears himself detested grandiloquent praise. He was a master of understatement, of litotes, in all its forms. To put it in his own subdued idiom, Lears wasn't a bad teacher, not bad at all.

ON WHAT seemed to be a whim—here comes the nonfilmic climax, such as it is—Lears decided that we weren't going to have a discussion that day. Instead, we'd just listen to music. He went to the beaten-up phonograph and put on a group called the Incredible String Band, whose music I immediately disliked. I buried myself in Malcolm X—he was coming back from his pilgrimage to Mecca now, about to declare for the unity of all men and women, regardless of color, and then be murdered by the minions of Elijah Muhammad—and tried to shut out the String Band's racket.

In between passages on brotherhood and an end to violence, I sat and pondered, and thought over the course. I thought about

Dubby whipping his spitballs the first day, and our tormenting
Lears and imitating him and trying to make him crack during the
days when Sandra was the only one who would read or pass a civil
word with him. And I thought about all his efforts to wake us up,
we being devoted to sleep at all times of the day, whether sitting,
walking, or lying prone. I thought about the Milgram experiment
and the game with Rick; I thought about the new books and
the SDSers and the proto-Panthers and about Nora's saying "I"
and the victory over Jingles, and the Doober's coloring the *o*'s and
doing the McMurphy imitation, and about the snowball fight that,
whether Lears knew it or not, was probably the thing that broke
the course open. He had trusted us enough to let us kill or at least
maim him if we liked—but we didn't like. He was our man, with
his gunboats and padre's hat and his refined accent and his inscrutable paper clip. He was the best mapless guide to the future
we'd ever get.

As to me and my future, an acceptance from the University of
Massachusetts at Amherst came one day in the mail. I'd been on
the waiting list, and the word was that no one *ever* got into U Mass
from the waiting list. Art Mondello's father, who was multiply connected, may or may not have had something to do with this. Artie
did once observe that I was the only person he knew whose college
acceptance might have "fallen off the back of a truck."

I loved U Mass, but in some ways it still reminded me of
Medford—being in the state of Massachusetts was probably
enough. So I transferred to Bennington College, a place that,
while I was there, from 1972 to 1974, operated about equally
under the aegis of John Dewey and the god Dionysus. In time, I
became a teacher myself, and did a stint at a marvelous hippie
boarding school that, alas, came flying apart. It did so, most people
would say, because we gave the students too much freedom, but

I'm not sure that was so. From there, I went to graduate school at Yale. The edition of Freud's *Group Psychology* that I used while working on my dissertation, a literary critical reading of Freud that became my first book, was the one that had belonged to Dubby O'Day. The *o*'s were colored in to about page 17. Now I teach at the University of Virginia, Mr. Jefferson's school, though Edgar Allan Poe, its most famous student, lurks around the margins.

I got to study, as I say, with some of America's best minds. But none did for me what Frank Lears did. For he'd set me on my way. Not much, after that, was needed.

Which is not to say that since then all has been sweetness and light. For one pays for the kind of mental exhilaration that Lears began. One pays in self-doubt and isolation, in the suspicion that what seems to be true resistance to the givens is merely perverse and ill-tempered, a facile way of always having something to say. Lears' path, so appealing in its first steps, distanced me from my family, cut me loose from religion and popular faith, sent me adrift beyond the world bordered by TV and piety and common sense. One step down that road followed another, and nearing fifty now, I probably could not turn around if I wished to.

But of course—as it is probably plain enough to see—I never left Medford *entirely* behind. I owe it many things. I owe it an abiding inner quotient of irascibility; I owe it, too, a deep tendency to see much of life in terms of oppositions, thesis against antithesis, me against him, linebacker against the guard—what football calls going one-on-one and what, refined away from its physical bruise and crack, thinkers like to refer to as the dialectic. This way of thinking and feeling is, naturally, a recipe for a life of conflict. But without Medford and football and brawling and all the rest, I wonder if I would have had the wherewithal to hang in and say the unpopular thing, cause salutary trouble, and take the hit quite as much as I have managed to do. I wish, truly, that I had had the stomach to do it a little more.

As to my father and me, things did not go well between us. After that night when I screamed in rage at the chance of me and Philip dying in Vietnam, things changed. One way to describe the transformation would be to say that I was one of the first Americans to hear a version of what would become known as the White House tapes. On the tape recordings released during the Watergate scandal, Nixon revealed himself fully. The tapes were full of rage, rants of the most dismal, bitter sort. My father anticipated many of these for me, going on at great length and with teeming fury about hippies, draft dodgers ("Do what you're told!"), malcontents, the eastern establishment, and, obsessively, the Kennedys. (Though, unlike Nixon, my father was anything but a racist or an anti-Semite.) All of the resentment he had kept under wraps, at great effort and in hopes, I think, of maintaining relations with his son, he now let fly. Things were past hope.

When these barrages came, I just grinned and left the scene: No way I was going to give him the satisfaction of getting to me. He was going to be the raging child now; I, the secure, thoughtful adult.

Of course, when times were propitious, I took my own sort of revenge. I would gas away about this subversive new book or that, Abbie Hoffman's *Revolution for the Hell of It,* maybe, or Kunin's *Strawberry Statement.* Of course now I talked constantly about Lears. Frank Lears said this and Frank Lears said that. I was showing my father that he had been cast aside, disowned as the proper authority. And I suppose he was trying to show me that he did not care much, that he was sticking to his rusted guns.

But, a father myself now, I know that the child can inflict more pain by withdrawing his esteem (his love) and transferring it to another than the parent can ever exact in return. The child has all the world before him, many things to discover and become. The father's horizon is shrinking—he has achieved what he can in life; most of his best moments are behind. The sense that the child is his child—spiritually, in the mind and heart—and will go on and continue his work in the world, with some improvements and maybe a salutary swerve, this hope helps secure a father against the despair of age. But how few fathers can sustain the belief that this will be so?

From a distance, it almost seems the natural order of things that children will leave their families and strive to put themselves under the influence of other guides, different from their own mothers and fathers, more attuned to their rising hopes, often ready to flatter and to idealize them. This is the way of human growth. Plato leaves his own family and goes off to make Socrates his father; then Aristotle leaves his to become Plato's progeny, at least for a while. But how sad the process is for the father left at home. "I'm so proud of all my son has accomplished," says the abandoned one. Yet the prouder he can claim to be, the more completely, in general, he has been left behind, repudiated for another.

After I went away to college, my father and I stayed in touch, casually, emptily. Our last moment of real contact came just a year before he died. He had come to visit me at Yale. I remember him in white after-golf shoes and matching white nylon jacket standing in the midst of the Gothic piles at the old college, themselves a touch absurd. He stood there and stared at the great towers, which, whatever the reality, bespeak learning, leisure, the mind's thriving life. And he said, almost under his breath, "Imagine, spending your life here instead of in some plant." He meant Raytheon, his company, where he had now been for twenty-five years. I had never heard my father express regret about anything. Whatever he had was always good enough—grand, in fact. There was never any problem, and wouldn't be, so long as we'd all just Do What We Were Told (and Relax).

My father had more than enough intellectual talent for Yale, surely as much as I did. He should at least have tasted such a world, which was the best one I myself had known. But at the moment when I could have shared a new life with him, that year in Frank Lears' class, and helped us both grow out of the old skin, I used my new learning, my new mind, as a weapon to sear him. Perhaps I had little choice. The Vietnam War was, in one of its less significant corners, a war between us, my father and me. I suppose our future life together, his better life, was one of its barely acknowledged casualties. My father had already lost a child, his girl Barbara Anne, a grief that was for him too deep for tears. Now a son was gone, too.

In a report that a psychologist did on my father just before he died—seeing a shrink was part of his sentence for a drunk-driving conviction or some such thing—the psychologist remarked on his visiting Yale, being drawn to the place, and having said to himself, "There but for the grace of God go I." But *grace* was not the word my father intended.

THAT YEAR of teaching was the last for Frank Lears. He got married, went to law school, and eventually moved to northern New England, where he could pursue a life a little akin to the one Thoreau, his longtime idol, managed to lead during his stay at Walden. I haven't seen Frank Lears in about three decades. But I do carry around with me the strong sense that the party he invited us to, me and Nora and Dubby and Rick Cirone and Jingles McDermott (but not Buller, no, not everyone, quite), is still a live possibility. Sometimes I even stumble on an installment of it, or help create one.

And often when I do, an image of Frank Lears rises up in my mind, an image from the day when he put on the String Band. (Climax—no cameras on the set; the director has stalked off in frustration—is now.) I dislike the record, and sink further into *The Autobiography of Malcolm X*. Lears cranks up the music a little louder. I keep reading. But then, curious, I raise my head. The racket of the String Band pours in. And there in the back of the room, is Frank Lears, dancing away. He's a maladroit dancer, stiff and arhythmic. Not until I saw Bob Dylan onstage did I ever see someone move so self-consciously. But it struck me that this was probably the first time anyone had ever danced in this building, or at least in this classroom. The air was too heavy with invisible, gray weight: Most bodies, given instructions, probably couldn't have moved.

But here was Lears bringing it off. In the future, years down the line, maybe they'd have everyone at Medford High School up and dancing to the Incredible String Band in geometric unison or in spontaneous disarray. They'd teach mini-courses in the String Band's kind of music, whatever that might be. But not then, and not for some time to come, either. No—here was Lears alone, dancing by himself. He was shakin' it hard; he was letting go; he was workin' it, as they said then, on out. And why not? When you let Socrates out of the box for one more run, he *will* dance. Lears had scored a semi-benevolent victory over the place. You could say he'd beaten us at our own game; but, really, he'd shown us a new one. He had a right to a little celebration.

Acknowledgments

I suppose that if any kind of book should spring fully formed from the mind of its author it would be a memoir. But at least with this memoir, that was not the case. I had considerable help along the way, which it's a pleasure, now that the labors are nearly ended, to acknowledge.

Chris Calhoun's contribution stretched far beyond what anyone would have the right to expect from even the best of literary agents. He was crucial in getting this project up and running, then provided ongoing insight, generous support, and amiable advice.

Alex Star saw the possibilities for this subject well before I did; he published an early essay that was the book's seed, and continued to take an interest in the book long after any professional obligation had lapsed.

Daniel Menaker took the project on at Random House, believed in it before there was much reason to, then, at exactly the right moment, cast his superb editorial eye on the manuscript. I have profited from his help no end.

Katie Hall took the book over and, with dash and generosity of spirit, saw it through its final phases.

Michael Pollan read and reread the book, always improving it with his comments and continually bolstering me with his encouragement. Those who know Michael and his work will understand how fortunate I am to have such a friend.

ACKNOWLEDGMENTS

I am grateful to my colleague Chip Tucker, who brought his considerable learning and acumen to bear on the manuscript and, as he has with all my books, made it palpably better than it would have been without him. My former teacher David R. Lenson read the book and responded with great high spirits and plenty of fine suggestions.

Michael de Leo gave me the benefit of his wit, good humor, and considerable insight. I thank him profusely.

Thanks also to Veronica Windholz for numberless useful interventions, to Megan Marshall and Jason Bell for wise advice, and to Greg Adams for a critical favor at the right moment.

My sons, Willie and Matthew, kept me afloat during the hard times and enhanced the good ones no end. To my wife, Liz, I owe the most of all. She is my first reader, first editor, fervent ally, and sage adviser. All through the writing of this book, I had the blessing of her love, humor, steadfastness, and grace. No expression of thanks could encompass all that she has done for me.

MARK EDMUNDSON is a professor of English at the University of Virginia. A prizewinning scholar, he has published a number of works of literary and cultural criticism, including *Literature Against Philosophy, Plato to Derrida*. He also writes for such publications as *The New Republic, The New York Times Magazine, The Nation,* and *Harper's,* where he is a contributing editor. He lives in Batesville, Virginia, with his two sons and his wife, the writer Elizabeth Denton.

A Note on the Type

This book was set in Fairfield, the first typeface from the hand of the distinguished American artist and engraver Rudolph Ruzicka (1883–1978). In its structure Fairfield displays the sober and sane qualities of the master craftsman whose talent has long been dedicated to clarity. It is this trait that accounts for the trim grace and vigor, the spirited design and sensitive balance, of this original typeface.

Rudolph Ruzicka was born in Bohemia and came to America in 1894. He set up his own shop, devoted to wood engraving and printing, in New York in 1913 after a varied career working as a wood engraver, in photoengraving and banknote printing plants, and as an art director and freelance artist. He designed and illustrated many books, and was the creator of a considerable list of individual prints—wood engravings, line engravings on copper, and aquatints.